Spessart Roots
A History of the People of a German Forest

Mary E. Wuest

Mary E. Wuest —
Spessart Roots: A History of the People of a German Forest
/ MaryWuest.
p.   cm.
Includes index, notes
1. Germany — local history. 2. Spessart Forest [Bavaria]
— regional life, customs. 3. Fix family. 4. Wuest family. 5.
German emigration to the United States.

ISBN 978-0-615-77199-1

Cover: **The courtyard of the old Wüst farmstead in Grosskahl
around 1943, when it was in the name of the Jordan
family.**

For
Andreas and Lena
&
Johann and Anna Maria

Contents

Illustrations and Maps

Introduction

I grew up in Michigan. During summer vacations, we often visited my grandfather and aunts in Cincinnati, Ohio, where we heard stories of my great-grandfather, Andrew Wuest (pronounced "Weest" in the United States). We heard of his founding a mattress company in Cincinnati in 1850, shortly after arriving in America. The company, which remained in the family until 1999, was ever a point of pride among Andrew's descendants.

About the time of founding the business, the price for a mattress was $1.25. Profit margins were slim; as Andrew later claimed, he usually "either made a dime or lost 25 cents." In 1874, the company registered a patent for a type of mattress frame with a hinged head that could be elevated, a predecessor of the modern day hospital bed.[1] By then the firm had become Andrew Wuest and Son. Still later, after Andrew's oldest son, Adam, inherited the company, it became Adam Wuest, Inc. Continually growing, it was relocated in 1946 to a large six-story building on the outskirts of downtown.[2]

My aunts listened every day to the popular Ruth Lyons local radio show which ran advertising for the company. From my childhood visits in the 1940s and '50s, I still remember Ruth Lyons's broadcast of the slogan: "Get lots of *west* with Wuest."

To increase national sales and establish a brand name, Adam Wuest, Inc., joined with several other mattress manufacturers in 1930 to form Serta Associates, Inc., headquartered in Chicago. Thus, in addition to selling locally under its own name, Adam Wuest, Inc., expanded its national market by selling its products to Serta. Nearly every year from 1930 until the Wuest firm sold in 1999, a Wuest family member served on the Serta Associates, Inc., Board of Directors.[3]

The Wuest firm sold almost exactly 150 years after its founding, when Serta International acquired it in 1999. It had prospered through six generations of family ownership and management.

Hearing stories about my great-grandfather and his company aroused my curiosity about his origins and his home in the Old World. Andrew, born Andreas Wüst, emigrated from Grosskahl, Germany, a small village in northwestern Bavaria, in the interior of Spessart Forest. Grosskahl is about 26 miles (42 km) east of Frankfurt.

All four of my paternal great-grandparents hail from a small cluster of villages in Spessart Forest: Grosskahl, Grosslaudenbach, and Edelbach. Driven to know more about the area, I have visited the Spessart several times, meeting and talking with its inhabitants and collecting books and periodicals on its history. I learned of hardships throughout the centuries: times of war, hunger and sickness, and life under serfdom. I became familiar with many tales and legends of the forest. I also began to comprehend the tremendous pressures forcing mass emigrations in the mid-19th century.

With slim expectations, I searched for living relatives, expecting to find no verifiable connections; it had been 150 years since the departure of my great-grandparents. Finding a common ancestor among today's inhabitants meant finding others who knew their own ancestry going back six or more generations. With luck and help, I found not only one set of relatives, but two—families descended from the same ancestors as two of my great-grandparents, Johann K. Fix and Maria Magdalena Gessner.

I was exhilarated and felt an even closer attachment to the Spessart. This feeling deepened when, through the help of a local historian, I located the homes of my two great-grandfathers. Although largely rebuilt on the old foundations, both houses remain.

Shortly before his emigration, Andreas Wüst was one of about eight adults, mostly his siblings, living in a crowded house in Grosskahl. Andreas's oldest brother, Karl, the registered owner of the house, was the only married sibling in the home. As I learned more about marriage restrictions, particularly in that region of Germany, I understood another pressure forcing young people to emigrate: a prospective groom was required to petition a committee made up of local authorities. If the applicant was poor or owned property deemed insufficient to support a family, the committee generally denied the petition.

Following several of his brothers who had preceded him to the United States, Andreas emigrated in 1847. His intended bride, Maria Magdalena "Lena" Gessner, from Grosslaudenbach, just south of Grosskahl, soon followed him. They married shortly after her arrival, before departing for Cincinnati and their new home.

The home of Johann K. Fix, my other paternal great-grandfather, was an inn in Edelbach, a village a short distance east of Grosskahl. Although he was the owner of the inn, Johann was unable to make a go of it, due to the extensive general poverty. Johann and his wife, Anna Maria nee Pistner, left in 1854 with their then three children, the youngest just six months old at the time of their arrival in New York. They, too, went to Cincinnati.

The two immigrant couples, who had known each other in Germany, were neighbors in the New World. Joseph, youngest son of Andreas Wüst, married Maria Elisabeth (Lizzie), youngest daughter of Johann K. Fix. Joe and Lizzie, both born in Cincinnati, were my grandparents. I am Maria Elisabeth's namesake.

As hard as times were, German families made sure that each male offspring learned a skill. In addition to taking whatever day labor they could find, Andreas and his brothers practiced crafts such as shoemaking and tailoring, procuring what consignments they could. Andreas learned mattress-making, a typical side industry in rural communities. Mattresses then were basically large sacks with buttoned openings, filled with straw or other stuffing material. As I looked at the home of his youth, I reflected with pride how, from this humble beginning, my great-grandfather took his craft to America and launched a thriving business.

Travel tours to foreign countries usually take us to big cities, museums, and cathedrals. Novels and histories generally take place in large populated locales. When I discovered that the planting of my roots took place in a small group of villages, deep in a forest in the very heart of Germany, I pictured generations of peaceful rustic life. I also entertained the erroneous notion that the villages of my forefathers were mostly isolated from events outside of the forest. I soon learned how wrong I was. Turmoil and distress spared virtually no one and no generation.

In studying the history of the Spessart, I discovered some fascinating stories of my own ancestors and others who shaped the rich history of the forest. I've woven the stories into this narrative of that wooded land, Spessart Forest.

Chapter 1

The Forest

Many years ago when the pathways in the Spessart Forest were still treacherous and not as heavily trafficked as today, two young apprentices were traveling through it. It was already evening and the shadows of the huge spruces and beeches darkened their narrow path. Felix, the goldsmith apprentice, kept anxiously looking around. When the wind rustled through the trees it was as if there were footsteps behind him. When the shrubs swayed, he thought he could see faces lurking amongst them. He had been hearing many stories about the Spessart. It was told around that in the past few weeks a large robber band had been attacking and plundering travelers and that there had even been heinous murders.[4]

These words from a popular early 19th-century suspense novel still resonate with the trepidation and awe with which Spessart Forest was held. Although the robber bands are long gone, the forest is yet today not a place to enter lightly unless one remains faithful to the well-marked trails.

I have driven through the Spessart mountains at night on its continuously twisting roadways and found it a harrowing experience. Although there are reflective guardrails, it is very dark on the other side of those rails. The leafy canopy is so thick that unless there happens to be an opening where the light of the moon or a star can penetrate, it is pitch black. The reflective guardrails and never-bright-enough headlights are small comfort. I did not dare think of car trouble.

I picture bygone travelers on foot or ox-drawn wagons and can imagine how foreboding they must have found the forest, especially if darkness should overtake them. Getting lost was a real danger; the pathways that led off the main trails could easily confuse a traveler. Numerous old tales and legends of the Spessart center around losing one's way in the forest.

Much of the fear was due to the very real possibility of attack by wild animals. In more modern times, Sky Phillips, a writer in Alexandria, Virginia, was a young U.S. Army wife stationed with her husband in Germany in 1946. She has never forgotten her experience with wild boars there. Phillips and her husband were quartered at Schweinfurt about 45 miles (72 km) east of Spessart Forest. Occupation regulations did not permit German citizens to carry guns, but the people were desperate for food. The Red Cross encouraged hunting parties by American soldiers who would then turn the game over to German citizens. This activity helped the Germans and also provided a pastime for the soldiers, bolstering their morale.

One day, Phillips accompanied her husband on a hunt in the nearby forest, but was herself not hunting and did not have a gun. "The wild boars were ugly, scrawny, dark grey, and mean-looking." She heard one charging and snorting through the trees and could hear its ferocity. "That's when I ran up a tree."[5]

Spessart Forest still thrives with wildlife. A mostly undisturbed forest, even in modern times, it teems with birdsong, the scampering of wild animals, and the droning of insects. Notably evident is the hammering and pecking of many species of woodpeckers, and so must it have been for centuries past. The name Spessart most likely comes from *Spehtshart*, Old German for "woodpecker forest." This old name appears in the great German epic *Niebelungenlied*, written around the year 1200. In the story, it is in this forest, Spehtshart, where Hagen kills the hero Siegfried.

The Spessart is Germany's largest unbroken deciduous forest. Today a nature park (*Naturpark Spessart*), it is roughly defined by

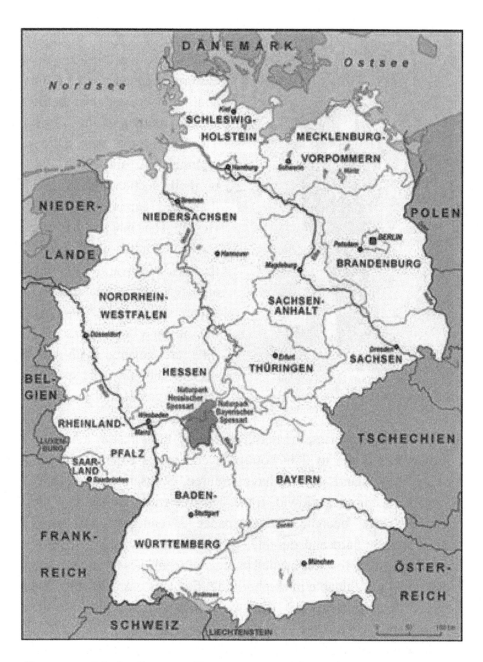

Germany with the Spessart Forest region indicated in northwestern Bavaria [Bayern].

Euroepan black woodpecker common to the Spessart region

National Geographic

the Main River as it flows southward just inside the eastern perimeter, along the southern side, and then up the western border of the forest. The Kinzig and Sinn Rivers circumscribe much of the northern section, the portion that extends up into the state of Hesse. The majority of the forest, about two-thirds, lies in the state of Bavaria. Covering an area approximately 965 square miles (2,500 sq km), the forest's mountains and hills are covered with oak, beech, and fir, interspersed with the creeks and meadows of its valleys.

Over the centuries, the nobility retained the forest as a hunting preserve, and due to tight control over logging which continues today, large stands of oak have endured. Spessart oak is highly valued and enjoys worldwide trade. The tree grows slowly; thus the growth rings become tightly packed, rendering the wood exceptionally hard and durable. Its hardness also makes it long-burning, critical for fires needed in previous centuries for mining and glassmaking. Valuable in shipbuilding, precious oak logs filled the rivers flowing westward and were shipped, primarily to the Netherlands where large trees were scarce.

Another product from Spessart Forest is the Spessartine garnet, a deep red-orange semi-precious stone. Although mined in other places throughout the world, such as in Amelia County, Virginia, the garnet retains the Spessart name, by which it was first known.

Yet today, in the early 21st century, the interior of the forest remains only sparsely settled. Going back to the time of the Frankish kings who arrived in the area by the 6th century AD,[6] and through the time of successive rulers, the nobility claimed Spessart Forest as their exclusive hunting reserve. They forbade all settlement.[7]

Early traders, however, developed two major pathways through the forest to reduce travel time between major cities and towns. The east-west trade route, Birkenhainer Strasse, which runs along what is now the border of Hesse, goes back to the Stone Age.[8] Although called a street (*Strasse*), it does not have the width of a modern street or road, but is wide enough for horses or oxen and wagon. The major north-south route, Eselweg (Donkeys' Way) was so-called because of the medieval donkey caravans that carried sackloads of salt from saltworks at Bad Orb, in the northern part of the Spessart, to Miltenberg, on the southern perimeter. From Miltenberg, situated on the Main River, boats and barges transported the salt to further destinations. Today, Birkenhainer Strasse and Eselweg are hiking trails.

In addition to traders, colorful parties of knights and men-at-arms traveled the forest roads. In times of war, army troops, friend and foe alike, used the roads. Occasionally, one saw the carriage of a nobleman or noblewoman with its fine pair of horses. Such travelers were taking a risk, even if accompanied by guards. The infamous Spessart robbers and murderers were a constant threat.

Roads through the forest generally followed mountain ridges so travelers could avoid not only swampy areas at the lower elevations but also valleys that were home to murderous gangs of rogues.

Although maintained as private hunting reserves, gradual encroachments along the perimeters of the forest began to attract some settlers. Fortresses erected by Frankish tribes, followed by walled towns, sprouted up along the Main River, from which farms started pressing against the edges of the forest valleys.

As Christianity made inroads, monasteries appeared, usually near the protecting fortresses along the forest edges. One of the first such monasteries, established in 770, was Neustadt am Main. According to legend, Charlemagne, King of the Franks, founded the monastery to house missionaries. Additionally, a few small settlements emerged near the toll-taking stops on the roads running through the forest.

The interior of the Spessart, however, remained basically unsettled until around the 12th century. Anyone daring to trespass in the forest risked being killed on sight by one of the official foresters, guardians of the hunting grounds.[9] But by the 12th century, huntsmen began to recruit workers to maintain the forest preserve and assist during hunts. Hunting had become a major pastime among royalty and aristocrats, sometimes involving very large parties, requiring a supporting labor force. To prevent workers and their homes from infringing upon the hunting area, the aristocracy settled the workers out of the way in higher locations, along the mountain ridges and ledges.

Spessart
Forest

Steinau

Jossa

Gelnhausen

Hanau

Somborn

Huckelheim

Bamberger Mühle

Grosskahl

Edelbach

Grosslaudenbach

Kleinkahl

Alzenau

Forstmühle

Mömbris

Heinrichsthal

Schimborn

Sommerkahl

Schöllkrippen

Lohr

Aschaffenburg

Waldaschaff

Rothenbuch

Mespelbrunn

Bischbrunn

Schollbrunn

Wertheim

0	5	10 kilometers
0	5	10 miles

Miltenberg

Strassendörfer (street villages) thus came into Spessart Forest. In these villages, one did not see a cluster of homes surrounded by farmland. Instead, individual properties were long rectangles laid out perpendicular to and adjoining the village street. Administrators gave each settler one of the elongated parcels, about 27 acres (11 hectares) each.[10] The parcels were adjacent to one another, the long side of one parcel next to the long side of the next parcel, and so forth, sometimes extending for several miles.

Settlers built their houses and other structures, such as stables and barns, close to the street. With homes lined along the street and lots narrow, neighbors were close enough to one another to permit a social and mutually protective village life. There were eight such villages[11] in Spessart Forest, most of them in the mid-southern part, dating back to about the 12th century.

Some of today's street villages evince their original configuration. Mespelbrunn is one such village. I have visited the famous nearby castle of the same name. When driving there, I traveled about 2 miles (3 km) along one street of houses before finally reaching the turnoff for the castle. The village is built along a ledge on a steep mountainside. Today, there are a few houses above and below the ledge in those places where the terrain would permit building, but essentially the village is just one long row of houses. While most of the farmland is gone, I could visualize just how difficult it must have been to till on those steep slopes.

There are a few vestiges of street villages in the United States. German immigrants occasionally brought the concept with them to America. One such site is the now mostly forgotten settlement of Germantown in Fauquier County, Virginia, about 8 miles (13 km) southeast of Warrenton. A group of 12 families founded the village in or about 1719. They had requested and received a rectangular tract of land, approximately 2 miles by 1 mile (3.2 km by 1.6 km). Licking

Run, a tributary of Occoquan River, ran longitudinally through it. The settlers divided the tract into long narrow equal-sized lots which ran the length of the shorter side of the rectangle, so that Licking Run traversed each lot. Thus, each family had water access and terrain with similar topography and soil conditions. One parcel was set aside for a church and school.

About the time of the establishment of street villages in Spessart Forest, economic interests slowly brought in more settlements. The nobles and lords who owned land or had jurisdictional rights over certain areas in the forest began to develop economic enterprises in those areas. Mining and glassmaking became major industries, requiring workers and settlements to house them. My ancestral villages, Grosskahl, Grosslaudenbach, and Edelbach, most likely developed because of these industries. They are close to former mines and glass factories.

The story of glassmaker Henne Fleckenstein, who lived in the 15th century, provides a typical example of how workers came into Spessart Forest. For glassmaking, workers with expertise in manufacturing glass were critical. To meet demand, authorities recruited glass workers from areas such as Bohemia, Tirol, and Alsace, where glassmaking industries were already established.

Glassmaking existed in Alsace in an area ruled by the Fleckensteins. The ruins of Fleckenstein Castle, high on a cliff, are a major tourist attraction today. The Archbishop of Mainz, ruler of much of Spessart Forest, was seeking glassmakers for Spessart at a time when the glass industry might have been suffering in Alsace, or at a time of overpopulation there and insufficient work opportunity. The archbishop offered many incentives: glassworkers would be free from additional compulsory labor required of serfs, they would be free of military duty, and they would not have to pay tithes.

It is not known if Henne was the Fleckenstein who immigrated to the Spessart, or if one of his forebears did. The surname Fleckenstein first appears in the forest in a 1406 document, in which Henne Fleckenstein is among 40 glassmakers listed as being "of and around Spessart."[12]

Henne, or one of his forefathers, obviously took the name of the lord in Alsace. Most common people did not have surnames until the 14th century and many took the name of their local lord. Although the first family surnames in Germany started developing in the early 12th century, it was a long time before family names became widespread. In the city of Mainz in 1350, only half the families had a family name.[13]

The original Fleckenstein family itself had taken their name from the cliff castle they built in 1129, calling it Fleckenstein. Historians believe that this family was a branch of the imperial Hohenstaufen dynasty,[14] which ruled as kings and emperors in Germany from 1138 to 1254.

Henne's offspring multiplied in the forest and many remained in the glassmaking business. Several founded new glassworks.[15] Because of the early arrival of the first Fleckenstein to the area, the Fleckenstein family had a substantial time to grow and expand, with Fleckenstein becoming a familiar name in the Spessart region. Both my great-grandmothers from the Spessart have Fleckenstein ancestry. Anna Maria Pistner's paternal grandmother was Maria Anna Fleckenstein, daughter of Konrad Fleckenstein. Lena Gessner's mother was Katherina Fleckenstein, daughter of Johann Adam Fleckenstein. There is insufficient documentation, however, to establish lineage back to Henne.

❦ ❦

Although many villages were established during this early period of modern settlement, 12th to 13th centuries, there was a proliferation neither of settlements nor of business enterprises. New settlements as well as new industries were strictly contained, preserving the vast majority of Spessart Forest for hunting for the noble class.

Of all the forest dwellers over the centuries, residents of the street villages probably had the hardest lives. At the higher elevations of these villages, the soil was sandy and yielded poor crops, and due to the overriding interests of the lords to maintain the expanse of their hunting preserves, villagers were forbidden from clearing more land for farming.

Because the hunters wanted the forest stocked with plentiful game, villagers were required to set out food in winter, such as piles of potatoes, to keep wild game from roaming away from the forest. So the animals remained and in their foraging soon discovered another source for food—the farms in the forest. Deer and other wildlife raided farmers' fields at night and simply feasted. To make matters horribly worse, the overlords forbade villagers from harming the wild game in any way.

Fences built around the farmlands were usually enough to keep wild boar out, but not deer. After a day's work, the farmer and his family often had to build giant bonfires, beating drums and shooting firearms to chase the animals out. The deer soon learned to ignore the noise. During growing seasons, farmers were busy day and night trying to save enough food to feed their families.

In 1793, a visiting forest official described Rothenbuch, one of the street villages: "Thereupon I soon came before a very massive oak plank fence, which, because of the red [deer] and black [boars], enclosed a poor small sandy field, in the middle of which, deep in the narrow valley, a small village lay, that had a very sorry look, and was called Rothebuch [sic]."

With poor soil, meager farming area, and foraging of deer, most inhabitants of a street village knew extreme poverty. What food they had was mostly potatoes. A popular saying of the time was that a villager ate "in the morning whole potatoes, at noon sliced, and in the evening, for a change, roasted."

After a few generations and divisions of land, most villagers had too little land to support a family, and because of deer, usually could save only part of their crops. Some villagers made formal complaints that such practices could not go on, that it would be impossible for them to hold onto house and lot. They would become homeless and their families reduced to beggars.[16]

However, the practices remained. As long as there were enough laborers to help with forest maintenance and to assist at the hunts, villagers were expendable. Some village dwellers turned to poaching. It was too tempting. They could not resist hunting some of the wild game for themselves when they were so desperate. They felt that they were taking from the forest what the forest was taking from them—their food supply. But as we shall see, poachers had to exercise much caution, as penalties if caught could be severe.

What about the very early inhabitants, before the Frankish kings claimed the forest for their hunting grounds? There is much evidence of Celtic tribes having domiciled in the forest's interior. There are prehistoric gravesites, evidence of village structures, and individual finds of Celtic tools and weapons from the Bronze and Iron Ages.

There are also ruins of several ancient ring walls (circular ramparts) which were strongholds for defense and refuge during times of attack. A Celtic ring wall found about three miles (4.8 km) south of Grosskahl, dates from around the 5th century BC. Celtic tribes would have needed refuge from enemies such as other Celtic tribes, or from foraging alien tribes.

Recent finds due to new road construction show human presence as far back as the Early Stone Age. Investigations of these recent findings are ongoing.[17]

At some point, the Celts left. They might have left when the Romans came to the area in the 1st century AD. Ruins of Roman watch towers, forts, and settlements indicate their presence up to the western and southern borders of the forest, but there is no evidence of Roman settlement in the forest. Nevertheless, their nearby presence and probable forays into the forest could have served to force the Celts out.

When their star began to wane, the Romans left, around AD 260.[18] After the departure of the Romans, Burgundian Germanic tribes entered the region. They came from the northeast, probably from an area that today contains Poland. But they were not to remain long.

The Alemanni, a Germanic tribe that the incoming Romans had previously forced out of the area, returned from the south in the 5th century and now, in turn, forced out the Burgundians. The Alemanni established a large presence concentrated in what is now Aschaffenburg, on the western edge of the forest.

Shortly thereafter, by the 6th century AD, the Germanic tribe of the Franks, which was expanding eastward from the Rhine area, came into the region. Instead of forcing the Alemanni out, however, they merged with them. This is probably, at least in part, due to the large populations of both forces. Still, the Franks were the most powerful and dominant. They ruled, and it was their customs and culture that prevailed.

Chapter 2

---•·•·•---

Overlords, Politics, and Everyday Life

My ancestral villages were not always Bavarian. From 982 until 1803, a major portion of Spessart Forest, including the villages of my great-grandparents, lay within the Archbishopric and Electorate of Mainz. The Archbishop-Elector, also called Prince-Bishop, of Mainz ruled over both ecclesiastical territory (the archbishop's diocese) and secular territory. The secular territory, a large territory in its own right, was contained within the ecclesiastical territory.

The city of Mainz is at the confluence of the Rhine and Main Rivers. The Main flows generally northwest from Aschaffenburg and then eventually turns southwest toward Mainz, providing a link between the two cities. Duke Otto of Swabia and Bavaria bequeathed Aschaffenburg and its surrounding area to the archbishopric in 982.[19] A later archbishop-elector built Johannisburg Castle, the great edifice in Aschaffenburg that overlooks the Main River. The castle served as his summer home and place of refuge in times of battle and continued in these functions for his successors.[20]

The Archbishop-Elector of Mainz was one of seven electors (later nine) and was the presiding officer of the electoral college that elected the emperor of the Holy Roman Empire.[21] He was also the arch-chancellor, or chief chancellor, of the empire. As such, he was the highest dignitary of the Holy Roman Empire under the emperor.

The Holy Roman Empire was a confederation of a wide variety of independent territories, including ecclesiastical states, city-states, principalities, duchies, and lordships ruled by archbishops, princes, dukes, and feudal lords. At the time of the Thirty Years War (1618-1648), there were more than 300 such territories, some no larger than a few square miles.[22]

There was a continual power struggle between local rulers and with the Holy Roman Emperor. Gained power, of course, was always at someone else's expense. It could be at the expense of other territories and was often at the expense of the emperor, who had to make more and more concessions. A candidate for election to emperor was expected to grant land, money, and privileges to the electors to secure their vote. There was even a word for it—*Wahlkapitulation* (*vote capitulation*).

As the emperor lost more and more power, individual rulers, especially the highly influential ones such as the Mainz archbishop-elector, became more and more powerful. By the end of the Thirty Years War in 1648, many of the territories had gained almost complete sovereignty.

An inhabitant of Spessart Forest might be directly under control of the archbishop-elector (or his regional deputy in Aschaffenburg) or under the control of a lord who either leased land from Mainz or held property in direct ownership. In some areas, the boundaries of control changed frequently. Upon awakening in the morning, a village could find itself with a different master. Or half a village could.

Before Grosskahl was so called, there was just the village Kahl, which straddled the Kahl River. Similarly, the next village south was simply Laudenbach. During the Middle Ages, those portions of the villages on the western side of the river came into a different jurisdiction when that land was leased from Mainz.

Going back to at least the 13th century, there was a triangular area of land on the western side of the river that consisted of parcels in the leasehold or ownership of various noble families, primarily the

Dieburg and Rieneck families. (The full surname for Dieburg was Ulner von Dieburg.) The leaseholds and ownerships often exchanged hands along with the rises and falls of family fortunes and interests.

The attractions of this area included its mining and glassmaking industry. It also boasted a trade route that ran north and south, connecting on the north with the major east-west trade route, Birkenhainer Strasse.

In 1665 and 1666, in different transactions, the entire triangular area came into the family of the Counts von Schönborn. Johann Philipp von Schönborn was, at this time, the Mainz archbishop-elector (1647-1673), which may have helped facilitate the deal. As the Schönborn family deepened its foothold and developed business interests on the western side of the river, naming distinctions between the western and eastern halves of the villages gradually began to take place. By 1700, the new names were well established: The western part of the village Kahl became Grosskahl; the eastern portion became Kleinkahl. *Gross* denotes large; *klein* denotes small. Grosskahl was probably larger population-wise than Kleinkahl at the

The Kahlgrund region of the Spessart, through which the Kahl River flows.

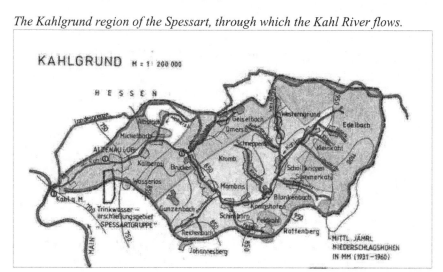

time. Similarly, Laudenbach became Grosslaudenbach and Kleinlaudenbach. Even though the area now under control of the Schönborns was part of the Electorate of Mainz, those inhabitants who came under the lordship of the Schönborn family lived under a different set of rules and regulations. While custom dictated a similarity of regulations between jurisdictions, the local lord could promulgate his own directives, as well as mete out punishments for infractions. His power had some limits. Judgments for major crimes, for example, came under the purview of the archbishop-elector's deputy in Aschaffenburg.

Kleinkahl and Kleinlaudenbach, on the other side of the river, as well as Edelbach, were under the direct control of the archbishop-elector's deputy.

Until the early 19th century, most common people in the Spessart were in some kind of bondage. Most were serfs, bound to the land where they were born and forbidden to move to another location without permission.

Peasants generally did not own land they farmed, but leased it with inheritable right of usage. Such land was called a fief. Fiefs were seldom single units, but strips of land of various sizes scattered across a larger area—the *Flur*. Although different factors could bring about the non-contiguous nature of a farmer's fief, it was primarily due to generations of dividing and redividing of the fief in accordance with inheritance laws. The different strips of land that a farmer tended could sometimes be quite far apart, adding to his burden in distances traveled, hauling his tools and other equipment. A lord could generally retake a fief only under certain circumstances, such as the farmer becoming an ally of an enemy of the lord. If a family died out, their fief reverted to the lord.[23]

For centuries, Germans practiced a three-field system of crop rotation. Each year, farmers sowed one-third of the lands in winter grain, one-third in summer grain, and left the final third fallow or used it as pasture, with manure from farm animals enriching the soil. A farmer had no choice as to what type of crop he grew, but had to conform to what the lord of the Flur directed.

Livestock was mostly sheep and cows. Besides providing milk, cows were useful as draft animals. The community as a whole often financed the maintenance of a bull for reproductive purposes. Horses were rarer except for the wealthier farmers. Horses made good draft animals but did not produce milk or appealing meat.[24]

A farmer's landlord could be a secular or ecclesiastical lord, with the right to collect taxes, fees, and rents; dispense justice; issue calls to arms; appoint the mayor and other officials; appoint the local minister or priest; exact labor for his own fields and projects; and control monopolies such as mills or breweries. The lords were to provide protection from marauders and help with food and other necessities in lean times.[25] Some lords fulfilled these responsibilities better than others.

In addition to the usual taxes and tithes exacted by the lords, higher authorities could levy special taxes. In 1551, during the Holy Roman Empire's war with Turkey, the emperor required villagers to give 24 percent of the value of their house, livestock, land and meadows to the war effort.[26]

Serfs had to obtain permission and pay a fee to move to another location, whether they wanted to move from one village to another under the same lord, or to a different territory, or to a foreign land.

Free men, such as merchants in the towns, could move without permission.

In the late-18th and early-19th centuries, there was a vast migration to Hungary or beyond to Russia. Roads vibrated with wagons heading east. Hungary was offering 50 or more acres (20 hectares) to a family to homestead and farm. Russia was offering 180 to 200 acres (73 to 81 hectares) on the Volga and Dnieper Rivers.

The mass exodus was from many regions of Germany, including from Spessart Forest. Overpopulation in much of western Europe, but particularly in Germany, was already acute. Hungary and Russia were offering land and opportunity and freedom. Individuals and families would not go as serfs but as free men. But it was not cost-free to leave. The permission fee was 25 percent of the value of all assets the emigrants were taking with them: 15 percent for buying oneself out of serfdom and 10 percent as a supplementary tax.

One of the emigrants was a Johann Adam Fix, who left for Hungary from Edelbach in 1803. Johann Adam was undoubtedly a relative of my great-grandfather Johann K. Fix, also of Edelbach, a village of about 200 people. After paying his permission fee, Johann Adam owned assets worth 227 gulden. This sum would have been about enough to support a family for a year, and was more than most emigrants were able to take with them.[27] Part of the value was undoubtedly in the goods he had with him, such as tools.

Other emigrants to Hungary included several individuals with the surname Wüst. Many of my ancestral surnames from the Spessart are in the emigration lists for Hungary.[28]

If a person received permission to relocate to another village, he had to be accepted by the new community. He was not automatically a *Nachbar* (citizen) of the new village. *Nachbar* translates as *neighbor* but its usage here is closer to *citizen*. A Nachbar had the right to use common property such as farming equipment or meadows for grazing livestock, the right to use the communal bake oven, and restricted rights to collect firewood in the forest. Communities often had plows and wagons and draft animals for common use, since most individuals could not afford them on their own. A Nachbar could also expect support in time of need.[29]

The village watched a newcomer for a period of time to make sure he was responsible, could be trusted with community property, and was not likely to become a burden. If accepted, the applicant was officially recorded as a Nachbar. If not, he was subject to expulsion from the village.[30]

A person could not marry without permission of the local authorities, who granted approval based on the applicant's ability to support a family. In the 18th century, in the area of my ancestors, the minimum requirement for a marriage permit was often ownership of property worth 200 gulden, the estimated cost to support a family for a year. Other factors affecting permission included whether both parties were of the same social class, and the applicant's trade. If there were too many shoemakers or other tradesmen, denying them permission to marry would prevent the siring of sons following in those trades.

As overpopulation started becoming acute in the 18th century, application of marriage-permission policies became more and more stringent. At first, couples found denials relatively easy to circumvent by slipping into another territory, getting married in a monastery there, and returning. By the 19th century, the state was stronger and could prevent such marriages.[31]

Mainz was trying to reign in its overpopulation, but at the same time, it wished to retain young unmarried men. The industrial revolution had yet to establish a stronghold and there was an acute demand for manpower, especially in farming communities. Unmarried young men also provided a supply of available manpower should the need for soldiers arise. Military pay was too meager to demand service of married men.

Helping to keep young unmarried men from leaving was the Mainz Land Law. Promulgated in 1755, it codified that house and land must go to children in equal parts. With some land ownership (tenureship), young men tended to stay.[32]

When a lord or territorial ruler needed soldiers or guardsmen, recruiters went to the villages, impressing young unmarried men. Sons of rich families often avoided serving by paying someone to replace them. When the demand for soldiers was great, recruiters often dipped into the lowest classes, conscripting rootless and homeless individuals. At such times, they often resorted to the worst practices, inducting vulnerable people by force.

A recruit's expectations were horrible food, poor pay, and sharing crowded beds. A common soldier was forbidden to marry while in service. When recruiting was underway, many young men fled to hiding places in the forest, some successfully.[33]

Usually a conscripted soldier served the prince or lord of the territory to which he belonged, serving as a castle guard or quelling local insurrections. He might also be part of a unit involved in a squabble with a neighboring territory, or in a battle with another European country. Or, if very unfortunate, he could find himself in a completely different part of the world.

There was the devastating time that Prince Dominik Constantin, of the Löwensteiner-Wertheim-Rochefort territory, which abutted

Spessart Forest on the south, hired out conscripted soldiers to England for service in the Caribbean. We know of the Hessian soldiers who served England during the American Revolution. Most of these involuntarily-conscripted soldiers were from Hesse-Kassel, thus the name *Hessian*.

Service in the Caribbean, though, was especially dreaded, mainly because of a high probability of succumbing to disease. For this reason, most princes and lords of territories who conscripted soldiers for use by foreign countries refused to allow their troops to be used in the Caribbean. But Prince Dominik Constantin had no such scruples.

In the mid-1790s, in the midst of the French Revolution (1787-1799), slaves in the West Indies (Caribbean) were revolting. The revolutionaries were exporting their ideals of freedom and equality throughout the Caribbean. Since many of the Caribbean islands were British colonies, and the slaves there were rising against their masters, Great Britain sought additional troops to combat these insurrections.

The British Secretary of State for War began searching for German princes willing to provide soldiers, and in April 1795, Prince Dominik Constantin contracted with the British to provide a regiment of 67 officers and 1,298 enlisted men to fight wherever the Crown might send them. The officers would have been mostly careerists, but the enlisted men were "recruited" from wherever they could be found. Recruits included poachers from nearby Spessart Forest and other *ganz versunkene Menschen* (completely wasted humans). They probably included debtors and petty criminals, some of whom might have volunteered for military service to escape their problems. Others were simply victims of impressment. Colonel Theodore von Heilimer, who had handled the German end of negotiations, and who was to be the recruits' commanding officer, later estimated that one-third of the regiment had been forcibly recruited. Colonel von Heilimer's regiment was called the *Löwensteiner Jäger* (Löwensteiner riflemen).

Authorities carefully concealed information about the conscripts' destination, knowing it would spark outrage. While gathering the conscripts in the town of Wertheim on the Main River along the southern perimeter of the Spessart, they surrounded the area with regular troops to quell potential resistance should word of the destination leak out. Ships arrived to carry the conscripts from Wertheim to Stade, on Germany's northern coast, where they would transfer to ships bound for England. By the time the recruits reached Stade, however, rumors were rampant that they were heading to the Caribbean. The troops mutinied, refusing to embark. Commanders forcibly suppressed the mutiny and managed to get the recruits embarked for Portsmouth, England.

The convoy finally set sail for the Caribbean in late 1795. While underway, major storms struck the convoy and nearly 300 Löwensteiner Jäger drowned, almost 25 percent of the regiment. Dozens more were to lose their lives in ensuing battles in the islands. Most, however, succumbed to fever. By August 1796, more than half the regiment was lost.

France had declared war on Britain in February 1793. In early 1797, Spain joined France in the conflict against Great Britain. Britain countered by striking Spanish possessions in the Caribbean. The fighting was much tougher now and much more deadly. While attacking San Juan, Puerto Rico, many of the Löwensteiner Jäger deserted to the Spanish. The British attacks ceased, but few of the Jäger ever saw their homeland again. Indeed, many were now deserters and could not return on British ships as they had come. Today, San Juan is home to descendants of these soldiers.

The Mainz elector does not appear to have hired out troops to

England, but because of the proximity of Prince Dominik Constantin's territory to the Spessart, a number of forest inhabitants ended up as "troops for hire."[34]

❧ ❧

We learn much about day-to-day life under serfdom from a 1541 proclamation by the Counts Ulner von Dieburg. At the time, the Dieburgs were lords over the villages now known as Grosskahl and Grosslaudenbach. The regulations laid out in this proclamation were specifically for those two villages as well as a portion of the nearby town of Schöllkrippen, that portion which came under their jurisdiction. Delegates of the Dieburg family were to promulgate the regulations anew every year, eight days before or after St. Martin's Day (November 11). Since peasants were more familiar with church feast days than with secular calendar dates, dates of important events were generally scheduled or recorded as the feast day, or saint's day, upon which they fell.

After centuries of common usage, the regulations were now, in 1541, for the first time, in writing. Following are selected highlights from the edict. I have paraphrased some of the excerpts, due to the antiquated language.

The Ulner von Dieburgs are lords over forest, water, and fields. They have the right to appoint and suspend court, the mayors, and all civil authorities. They have the right to promulgate orders and prohibitions as they see fit. They have the right to impound or confiscate and to punish, as has been their right from ages past.

The Ulner von Dieburgs have the right to tax and collect rent in the form of money and produce. If a man has a fief, he must pay an annual tax of one pound of flax, a cheese worth four pfennig, two hens, and the best animal from his livestock.

In addition to taxes, the lords also collected a tithe that ordinarily would have gone to the church (in this case, to the Bishop of Aschaffenburg, who served under the Archbishop of Mainz). However, an unusual provision in the Dieburg leasehold agreement with the archbishopric allowed the Ulner von Dieburgs to keep the tithe.

When the lords visit a village, about twice a year, they will overnight with the mayor. They are entitled to have their dogs and birds provided for as well.

Should it be observed that someone has been in the process of cutting a tree down in the lords' forest, but has not finished the job or yet removed the tree, the mayor or a forester [forest official] *should watch the tree for three days and three nights. If the thief comes back to finish the job and is caught, the thief's rear oxen or horses are forfeited to the lord, and the axe to the forester. But if no one comes back to take the tree, the damaged tree belongs to the mayor.*[35]

The lord jealously guarded the trees of "his" forest. To discourage pilfering of wood for resale, there were strict guidelines specifying when a peasant could take trees or wood from the forest and stringent penalties if the peasant disobeyed the rules.[36] Because of the hilly and mountainous terrain in the Spessart, there was usually a pair of oxen or horses hitched to the rear of a wagon as well as to the front. The rear animals, rigidly attached to the wagon, helped push.[37]

If the thief is observed cutting or removing a tree, the mayor and the forester should pursue him, and try to overpower the vehicle by throwing a blocking device between the back of the wagon and the rear coupling, forcing the farmer to stop. However, if they are not able to catch him before he arrives at his courtyard, he is not guilty and cannot be punished.[38]

This latter stipulation might have been to prevent commotion in the residential section of the village, stirring up of resentment among the villagers.[39]

When a fief-owner wishes to build a home or other structure, he must get permission from the mayor. He may not take more wood than needed and only as much wood as the mayor permits. The mayor and forester will go with the man to the forest, show him where he may cut the wood, and how much he may take. The serf should give the mayor and forester a half quarter of wine as their payment. The serf must fell the wood and take it out of the forest within the next two months.

If two people get into a fight that becomes bloody, they must pay a fine to the lords, to the mayor, and to each juror. If one of the party is from the Mainz jurisdiction [i.e., outside of the area controlled by the Dieburgs], *he must likewise atone in the Mainz court.*

There were also conditions to which the lord was required to adhere:

If the lords wish to sell acorns and beechnuts that have fallen in the forest, they must sell to their vassals first what they would want, before selling to others.

Acorns and beechnuts were used for livestock feed.

If a Ulner von Dieburg or his representative is given food, he will pay for it in the presence of two jurists.

All subjects had to gather and make an oath to abide by these promulgations each year at the time of their annual rereading. The gathering place was in front of "the linden tree" in Grosskahl. The lords in their turn renewed their promises to the subjects.[40] A man swore allegiance on behalf of his family.[41]

The custom of taking oaths in front of a linden tree goes back to heathen times. Freja, the chief Germanic goddess, was associated with justice, and was believed to live in a linden tree. Judges making proclamations continued to call gatherings before a linden tree until the early 20th century. When a new Mainz archbishop was installed, subjects met under their designated linden trees to swear allegiance.[42]

Chapter 3

————••❖••————

Hunting and Poaching

Among the exclusive privileges of the highborn was the hunt. Aristocrats, including knights and men-at-arms, pursued wild animals throughout the year, singly or in small parties, for sport and to hone martial skills. The game was deer in summer and boar in winter.

By the 18th century, the nobility were calling for a huge hunt once or twice a year. Preparations could take up to two weeks, and all able subjects in the forest were obligated to provide their services without pay. Authorities assigned a forest official to every village to ensure the laborers followed orders and carried out assignments.

One of the most significant aspects of the preparations was the construction of a huge cloth fence, within which animals would be penned. Large sections of cloth, the cloth made up of a very strong tear-resistant fabric, were especially ordered from Strasbourg, Alsace. Tailors (or seamstresses) stitched the pieces along a rope 160 paces (133 yards = 122 meters) long. The raglike cloth pieces fluttered, which frightened the animals and generally kept them corralled in the enclosure. The cost of the fence was enormous; it might cost 40,000 gulden.

The gamekeepers found a suitable, level location where the laborers unfurled the fence of flapping cloths, anchoring it to trees and posts to form a large enclosure with one side open. Subjects from throughout much of the Spessart then drove wild game from a large surrounding area toward the corral. Making a huge clamor and commotion, beating drums and shooting off guns, they flushed the frightened animals out into the open, herding them toward the enclosure.

At night, the workers closed the open side of the pen by unfurling more of the cloth fence, but they still had to keep watch and stoke bonfires to keep the animals from escaping. Inevitably, some of the animals, through pure terror, would jump over the quivering fence.[43]

In addition to working for no wages during the hunt and preparations for the hunt, the serfs had to neglect their own farms and businesses. Smoldering resentments led them to shirk their duties by arriving late or sending boys too young and small for the work, or they conducted their tasks indifferently. On one occasion in November 1732 near Rothenbuch, bad weather was so disruptive to their efforts that several men rebelled and stalked off to a tavern, leaving bolts of fence cloth they were transporting to molder in the rain.[44] Thanks to the general confusion, the rebellious farmers seem to have escaped serious punishment. Eventually, the forest officials managed to overcome resistance with threats and sheer force of will to get the job done.

Many of these affairs could be extravagant. In a summer hunt in 1792 near Waldaschaff, in the southern part of the forest, the hunting party consisted of Archbishop-Elector Friedrich Karl Joseph von Erthal (1774-1802), high-placed courtiers and administrators, honored guests including envoys from the emperor, Austrian archdukes, the King of Naples, and other foreign dignitaries. Ladies attended in all their finery.[45]

The presence of a ranking church member here commands attention. Until the 13th century, the Church had forbidden clergy to hunt. Then the pope granted permission for a *Stille Jagd*, which implies standing still and shooting at animals as they are forced past a shooting platform. Clergy could not, however, hunt on horseback.[46]

The party assembled and proceeded to the hunting ground in strictest order of rank and position. Arriving, they mounted a stage-type structure erected as the shooting stand.

Alongside the stage stood all the royal gamekeepers, resplendent in their full dress uniforms. Behind the stage stood the young dog handlers holding onto the leashes of the dogs. Music played, kettledrums boomed, and trumpets blared. When all was ready, the head gamekeeper gave the signal to begin. A shot rang out. Bugles sounded and whoops of anticipation pealed through the air. Workers opened one side of the cloth enclosure. The ground rumbled as the frightened deer sprang forward in full flight. Hounded by the dogs and the drivers, the deer were forced to run by the shooting platform, round and round again. The hunting party, in order of rank, took turns shooting at the fleeing animals, the women cheering with their applause. The hunters continued to shoot, until finally there was a heap of dead deer and the hunters were sated. The gamekeepers released the remaining game to the forest. In this "hunt," 236 deer were killed.[47]

❦ ❦

The nobility could hunt until they were satiated. Peasants could not hunt, no matter how hungry or poor they were. And what happened to the game the nobles killed? After the bishopric courts in Mainz and Aschaffenburg had all they could use, surplus went by boat to markets in Frankfurt.[48]

Compounding the inequity, peasantry suffered the loss of property and crops in the aristocratic chase of animals. The nobility owned the animals and could chase down their quarry wherever it went.[49] If a frightened deer ran into fields with ripening growth or into a meadow with grazing sheep, the scene turned to chaos. Thundering horses rode roughshod over standing grain, and if coming upon sheep, adrenaline-fueled hunting dogs often attacked the sheep, while the helpless shepherd could only stand by.

Many peasants hunted game illegally. They generally had little access to meat even if they could afford it. City markets were too far. Forest wardens constantly prowled for the illicit activity and meted out penalties accordingly, for poaching went on year-round and was indiscriminate—illegal hunters killed female and male game alike.[50]

Punishments were harsh. Until the 18th century, poachers apprehended in the Mainz territory could be sent to the Venetian galleys, never to be seen again in the Spessart. The unfortunate men were chained together with Turks captured in skirmishes with Venice's rivals to the southeast. The last poacher in the Mainz territory thus dispatched was in 1716.[51] Another common practice was to cut off the thumb of a miscreant to make it near-impossible for him to operate the noose-snare used for trapping deer.[52]

A new law in 1731 specified that for a first offense, a poacher would be sentenced to a year of hard labor. The next offense carried a sentence of exile, often to Australia. Those such punished were taken to the Netherlands, from whence the Dutch transported them to that distant land, along with other banished convicts.

In the face of these penalties, full-time poaching was rare. But there was one who dared it, becoming a folk-hero whose legend residents of the Spessart celebrate to this day.

Johann Adam Hasenstab was born in 1716 in our oft-mentioned street village, Rothenbuch. His family and friends called him Hannadel. His grandfather, Karl Hasenstab, was a gamekeeper, which was an honored and desired position. Karl's son Christof, Hannadel's father, did not step into this job, perhaps because he was a younger son. Instead, Christof became a woodcutter, earning much less income than a gamekeeper. This, plus a tiny piece of farmland, was just barely enough to sustain his family.

Then Christof died. He was 27. Fatherless at an early age, Hasenstab was the oldest child with two younger siblings. As a lad, he was fortunate to acquire a position as helper in the forest, but he also poached on the side. At first, it was probably small game such as hares—also off limits—but he soon graduated to larger game. The gamekeepers became aware of Hasenstab's side activity and fired him.

Hasenstab continued poaching on into adulthood. He was skilled and caught animals with relative ease. He hid his weapons in the forest, in tree cavities or under rocks. People sometimes heard gun shots, but he hunted at times and in remote places where he was likely to go undetected, or where he would have time to get away. To evade capture while carrying game from the forest, he found places to conceal it. He partnered with a farmer who would later fetch the carcasses and load them in his wagon, hiding them under produce. Hasenstab repaid the farmer by sharing the meat.

He sold the game he caught to innkeepers, farmers, and even to parish priests. Like other residents, a village priest did not have a local or legal source for buying meat.

The officials were extremely anxious to catch Hasenstab and subsequently, he had many close calls. During one of his escapes, he made it to Bronnbach Monastery, just outside the forest to the southwest, and outside Mainzer territory. He remained there in asylum for some time. The monks trained him in medicine and the use of herbs and salves, hoping that Hasenstab would become a monk himself and stay. However, he eventually returned to the forest.

Members of many professions, especially of the traveling professions, wore a particular set of clothes or costume so that their occupation was readily identifiable. Disguising himself as a barber-surgeon and traveling from place to place, Hasenstab earned some money using his skills as a healer. This gave him a cover while resuming poaching activities.

As a roving barber-surgeon, Hasenstab's status was that of a lordless traveler, and as such, he never would have gotten permission to marry a legal resident. If there was any movement in the social order of the time, it was usually downward. At the top of the pyramidal social order were the sovereigns and lords, then the free citizens or townsmen and officials, with the serfs at the bottom. Off the pyramid and below everyone else were the riffraff, vagabonds, beggars, and peddlers who had no lord, no land, and no home. They included rootless laborers, discharged soldiers, gypsies, and uprooted Jews.

This hardscrabble group often formed bands and roamed the region. Some took up a traveling trade, such as scissors sharpener or barber-surgeon. Or they stole. Or they peddled and stole. Because of the often shady dealings in which band members participated, a special language eventually developed among them—*Rotwelsch* (thieves' argot). It consisted of an olio of words and phrases, including many Hebrew words that the Jews among them contributed. Today, one can still detect words and phrases from this colorful language in the local speech.[53]

Due to discrimination against Jews, much of it based on fear of competition, there were few means of making a living available to them. Jews lived under many restrictions, especially with respect to land ownership and trades and businesses in which they were allowed to participate. As a result, many found themselves in the circumstance of being wanderer-beggars.[54]

In the ranks of the peasantry, as with Jews, whole families could join the homeless class. If an illness or other catastrophe befell the main provider, the family might end up as beggars, or they might go to the forest to dwell with other displaced persons in a hidden camp.

Hasenstab was one of the rootless. Because of his popularity and derring-do, he most likely had plenty of liaisons, but for a long while, no wife. He finally did marry, however. His bride was Eva Maria Werner, daughter of a traveling crockery and tableware salesman. She was also of the rootless class, but Werner's father must have had some success as a salesman, for she brought a dowry of some valuable objects, one a marvelous ring with a blue stone she presented to Hasenstab.

In this time of superstitions and wild tales, many legends arose surrounding the ring. The peasants believed it to be magic. Because of Hasenstab's uncanny ability to escape his pursuers, they were convinced he could become invisible by merely turning the ring. They further believed that water nymphs dwelling in the springs and fountains of Weibersbrunn, a village southwest of Rothenbuch, had given the ring to Werner. (Sagas of water nymphs were widely told throughout the region.)

Ring or no ring, the authorities did eventually capture Hasenstab. During the ensuing shootout, in which he was surrounded, he sustained a gunshot wound in the foot that left him limping ever after. In accordance with the new laws, the judge sentenced him to hard labor. He was confined at night and labored during the day, chained to a wheelbarrow.

There must have been some attendant circumstances because he remained in custody for more than the one year prescribed by law. After some years, Hasenstab escaped. He might have convinced one of the guards to help him get his chains off and escape with him. The soldier guards were themselves poorly fed and housed. Hasenstab was now 40 years old.

There was a desperate effort to recapture him. With no standing police force, community administrators had to assume the responsibility of hunting down outlaws, forming posses as necessary. In Hasenstab's case, they also called for military forces who arrived from Mainz and quartered in people's homes. The soldiers made frequent unexpected patrols, and searched all homes and outbuildings. They apprehended any person without a permanent place of residence and every foreigner without a pass. A foreigner was anyone whose place of residence was outside of the Mainz territory.

The authorities called Hasenstab the *Erzwilder* (the *Arch Poacher*). Soldiers and posses spared no effort in finding him. They even set bloodhounds on his trail. But find him they did not, enhancing his reputation of having supernatural powers, especially regarding his power to become invisible. People reported that the bloodhounds either ran from him howling or licked his hands.

Local citizens made up the posses. Without a doubt, many of them knew Hasenstab well, but somehow they never recognized him. Or if they did and gave a direction in which he had taken off, a search in that direction would turn up nothing.

Hasenstab finally was able to escape to a foreign land, that is, to the other side of the Main River on the southern border of Spessart. He was now in the Würzburg bishopric. Hasenstab was safe. His pursuers would not cross over the border to continue the search. The Mainz soldiers had no authority to pursue him there. Each of the more than 300 territories of the Holy Roman Empire jealously guarded their dominions.

Our poacher reentered the forest, going to the village of Schollbrunn, which he established as his home base. Although Schollbrunn was in Spessart Forest, it was in a particular area that did not belong to Mainz. Schollbrunn is an example of a village or town straddling two completely different territories, not just two different jurisdictions within a territory. Schollbrunn had about 82 homes. Half of this small village belonged to the bishopric of Würzburg and was Catholic. The other half belonged to the Earldom of Wertheim and was Protestant. To which territory the village belonged was a source of continual strife, both sides claiming the whole village. They came to some mutual agreements on how to administer the village but the issue of ownership remained unresolved.

Hasenstab walked around freely. He could walk across the street and be in a different territory, yet be safe in both. And just a short climb up a steep road put him back in Mainz territory. He soon began poaching again, although not in the territories of the village where he now lived, for he needed a safe haven. He poached in the Mainz district and then slipped back into Schollbrunn.

This was all very embarrassing to Mainz. To catch the "Arch Poacher" became a high priority. Once again, the chase was on. Finally they caught him. It was 1770; Hasenstab was now 54. They took him to Aschaffenburg and this time the judge sentenced him to lifetime exile to Australia. But in late autumn of the same year, rumors started circulating that he was back in Spessart Forest. And indeed he was. He might have escaped at some transfer point or again cajoled someone to let him go. He could not have gotten to Australia, for he never would have made it back.[55]

But events were closing in on our poacher. A reward was set up for his capture, dead if that was the only way his captor could take him, but preferably alive. Now Hasenstab was mostly on the run. (He and his wife had not lived together for some time.) A gamekeeper, Johann Sator, newly assigned to the village of Bischbrunn, made it his overriding objective to catch Hasenstab. Bischbrunn is not far from Schollbrunn and close to the area where Hasenstab hunted when he ventured into Mainz territory.

Finally on June 3, 1773, Sator caught up with him. He shot and killed Hasenstab. According to tradition, Sator testified that he had called, "Halt!" and that Hasenstab raised his gun to him, but that he (Sator) was able to get off the first shot. (If he had given a different story he might not have gotten the reward.)[56]

Sator's reward was 15 gulden. He became well-known throughout the forest, and the Mainz authorities held him in high esteem. He eventually received the position of head forester for his district. The peasantry, however, denounced his deed, the killing of their hero. After Sator died, many tales sprung up about his restless soul. There were sightings of his ghost roaming through the forest or through the rooms of the forestry headquarters.

Hasenstab had a simple burial in the Breitenbrunn cemetery, south of Schollbrunn, without fanfare and without a headstone. His friends and admirers, however, soon erected a stone cross near the spot where he was killed.[57] Still today, locals visit the site of the cross, often leaving flowers.

Almost 200 years after Hasenstab, there was another "hero-poacher" in the forest. Known only as the *Bamberger Mühler* (miller), he was the owner of the Bamberger Mill at the source of the Kahl River, a short distance northeast of Grosskahl. At that time, around the time of World War II, there were two owners, however. Around which owner does the story revolve?

According to the story handed down, the Bamberger Miller poached for game and gave it to the poor. The story continues that the authorities finally caught him, but because his was a major mill and the community vitally needed the milled grain, the judge gave him a sentence of jail which he was to serve for a certain number of Sundays. Every Sunday he went about 17 miles (27 km) each way, probably by bicycle, to the jailhouse in Aschaffenburg.[58]

Who was this miller? For many years up to 1939, Alois Markert and a neighbor, Leo Kilgenstein, co-owned the mill and shared milling rights.[59]

In 2009, I met Karlheinz Markert, Alois's grandson and the old mill's current owner. He was only 10 when his grandfather died, and he did not have the opportunity to learn all his grandfather's stories, but he had heard that Leo was once caught poaching and went to jail. So it appears that Leo Kilgenstein might be the Bamberger Miller.

Alois Markert, however, was also a poacher (fairly common during this time), and had a close call himself. He had shot a large deer with a wide antler spread. The police pursued him to the mill, Alois just having time to slide the deer into the water behind the mill's water wheel. The police searched but found nothing.[60]

Today, Spessart Forest is mostly a state-owned nature park, with about one-third of the forest under individual or community ownership. Individuals with the requisite training and who are properly registered may acquire hunting permits for specified forest areas.[61]

As for the Bamberger Mill, today it encompasses a guesthouse, restaurant, and a brook which supplies fresh trout for the restaurant.

Chapter 4

————•••⁙•••————

Customs and Practices

The many beliefs, customs, and practices of its inhabitants are a living part of the forest's history. Echoes and remainders of old traditions to this day evoke the lasting vibrancy and charm of Spessart Forest. Similar customs and beliefs existed throughout Germany and Europe, of course, but in an isolated region, they could take on an especially prominent role.

One of the most visible reminders of age-old traditions in the Spessart is the *Bildstock*. It is a type of memorial. It can also be a type of shrine. It can serve as thanks for deliverance of a community from some disaster such as a pestilence, or as atonement, or as a place of devotion. Since there is no good translation for it, I will use the German word. The pronunciation is similar to *"bilt-shtok,"* with stress on the first syllable. If an accident or violence took a person's life, individuals or a community usually placed a Bildstock on or close to the site of the happening. It was a memorial as well as a type of plea or prayer to ward off future occurrences. We often see roadside memorials in the United States at sites of fatal accidents, but they are usually temporary.

A Bildstock is permanent and usually sculpted out of sandstone, the Spessart's native stone. Those in the Spessart date back as far as 1585[62] and one is as recent as the 1980s.[63] They have different forms but usually consist of a cross, with the horizontal part of the cross abbreviated (or omitted) so that the whole has the appearance of a column. At the top piece of the cross there is generally a devotional carving or image. If the Bildstock was erected because of a tragedy, it generally includes a short description of what happened, the date

Bildstock in Sommerkahl [left], erected in 1609 after the deaths of several miners. In Edelbach, a bildstock is built into the façade of a house to commemorate the accidental death in 1842 of a young man who died during roughhousing in the front yard of the house.

of the event, and the name or names of the people who died.

The Spessart is dotted with *Bildstöcke* (the plural). They stand along forest pathways, on edges of fields, on sides of streets, in village centers, in private yards, and even in lumber yards. Once placed, a Bildstock is generally left undisturbed, life going on around it. Some older ones have deteriorated and only parts remain. Often the lettering has worn away.

High on a hill in Edelbach, a Bildstock was dedicated to the memory of Sebastian Gessner, a brother of my great-grandmother, Lena Gessner. One day in 1892, long after the emigration of his sister to America, Sebastian was out with his wagon and oxen. He was under the wagon tending to a stuck or broken wheel when something spooked the oxen, causing them to lurch forward. Sebastian, caught under the iron-rimmed wheel, was killed.[64] When I visited the site in 2003, a couple walking nearby knew all about the story.

A wooden cross has replaced the original Bildstock, which had badly deteriorated. Due to its high location at the edge of an open field where the accident occurred, the sandstone structure suffered more than normal exposure to weather. The local community collected funds and replaced it. When visiting it, I noticed, in an adjacent tree, someone had placed a small figure of an angel facing the memorial as if gazing upon it. It gave me a warm feeling to know that a live memory of my long-ago relative yet remains. I also thought of the sadness that his sister, far away in America, must have felt when she received news of the tragedy.

Another Bildstock in Edelbach is encased in the wall of a private home. A schoolhouse had once stood next door to the house, and in 1842, during a church festival held at the school, several young men started hijinks and roughhousing. One threw a stone that tragically killed one of the other young men. Panicked, the guilty party quickly paid someone else to take the blame, then fled to America. Upon arriving there, he sent an explanatory letter accepting blame. The victim of the incident had died in the front yard of the house next door to the schoolhouse, and the owners of the house permitted the Bildstock to be built into the wall of their house.[65]

A second visual reminder of past customs is the community bake oven. Few of the older ovens survive, but two yet stand in the Kahlgrund region. The Kahlgrund, home to my ancestral villages, consists mainly of Kahl Valley, which follows the Kahl River. One of the ovens, built in 1827, is preserved in the town of Kahl am Main and the other in the village of Niedersteinbach, neither still in use. Made with fieldstones, the upper part of each oven tapers to a point, with an opening at the top to vent the smoke. Standing outside, women shoveled their loaves onto a grate large enough for baking 10

Community bake oven

loaves of bread at once, each loaf about 1½ feet (46 cm) in diameter.[66]

Communities continued to build bake ovens until the 1930s.[67] Newer ones consisted of small buildings with oven grates indoors, where the baker was out of the weather and there was counter space for setting the loaves to cool. One such oven, occasionally opened for community events, is in the village of Erlenbach, about 4 miles (6 km) southwest of Grosskahl. During a local festival in Erlenbach, I had the opportunity to indulge in one of its freshly grilled frankfurters.

The ovens provided an efficient way to bake large quantities of bread, the main food staple. Günther Pistner of Edelbach, a boy during World War II, remembers the villagers using the old stone oven in Edelbach during and after the war, and that it remained in use until about 1960. Eventually it deteriorated and finally collapsed.[68]

Use of the ovens was strictly organized. Each household had to adhere to its scheduled baking time. The oven was usually close to the village center so that it would be convenient to most homes, and was also near a water source in case of fire. Typically, the family living closest to the oven was responsible for ensuring that villagers complied with the regulations and was also expected to settle disputes. The first person to use the oven for the day brought the brushwood for the fire.[69]

Men of the family came to pick up the finished loaves, bringing wagons or wheelbarrows for carting the bread home. The loaves had to last two to three weeks before the baking of the next batch. To protect the bread from mice and other vermin, the family wrapped the loaves in wire filament and hung them from attic rafters in winter and from the basement ceiling in summer.[70]

‌‌❦ ❦

When it came to medical treatment, peasants seldom saw a doctor. They believed in their familiar folk medicines, which were also cheaper. Very few school-educated doctors practiced in the interior of Spessart Forest, even in the towns. This might have been due at least in part to the fact that people probably would not have gone to them anyway. Lothar Schultes, a local historian in Schöllkrippen, related that when a member of his ancestral family was in critical need of a doctor in 1826, the patient had to be taken to Aschaffenburg for treatment.[71]

Peasants tried home remedies first. A common remedy for pain was a stocking filled with hot boiled potatoes placed where the pain was located. Homemade drinks and salves made with goose fat or rabbit fat were healing aids for other ailments. If home remedies failed, almost every village had a midwife or woman skilled in the use of special herbs, ointments, and what foods to eat. She gathered certain herbs only during a full moon. She recited prayers or chanted magic formulae while administering the medicaments. The midwife or healer charged less than a doctor and was more apt to accept farm products as payment. Dealing with many patients, the healer probably did develop some proficiency at her craft.

Male healers, such as barber-surgeons, were rarer. Johann Adam Hasenstab, the "Arch Poacher," traveled from village to village as a barber-surgeon, the cover for his criminal activities as a poacher of wild game. However, he actually had some practical training in the use of medical remedies, and people came to him for healing. A shepherd, who acquired medical knowledge in caring for animals, might also provide healing services.

When all efforts failed and it appeared a person was dying, family members hung the root of a hazel shrub over the patient's bed to help ward off death. If death did come, family members opened the windows in the room where the person died, covered mirrors, and stopped the clock if there was one. They also lit a candle.

These rituals were meant to appease the spirits. Open windows permitted the person's soul to escape. Mirrors were covered so the person's soul did not get trapped in the mirror or pull someone else's soul with it through the mirror. The stopped clock helped prevent bad luck coming to the household. At the time of death, the deceased began his eternity where there is no time. By stopping the clock, his soul could move on; otherwise his spirit could remain and bring misfortune to the family. A candle was lit to thwart the entrance of evil spirits, which came in the dark and could cause another death. The members of the household observed all these precautions while the body of the deceased remained in the house.

Since there were no mortuaries in the villages, the body of the deceased remained in the house until burial. When the coffin-bearers bore the coffin to the cemetery, they positioned it so that the feet of the deceased faced away from the house—the person's spirit must not have a chance to look back into the house and seize the soul of another occupant, thus compelling him to follow the deceased into death. Most villagers joined in the funeral procession, the men wearing tailcoats and top hats. Four girls in white dresses carried lit candles and accompanied the coffin. After the burial, a church service was held for the deceased, followed by a funeral feast. Individuals took pride in laying money aside for their funeral feast.[72]

❦ ❦

Just as with the exacting care to keep demons at bay following the death of a family member, the same care was taken to protect newborn babies. A newborn was baptized at church as soon as possible, usually the day of its birth, or early in the morning, if the baby was born at night. Until the baptism, evil spirits could snatch a child's soul from its body, causing death.[73]

To protect a baby before its baptism, family members kept a light burning by it, as they did with the deceased, since harmful spirits came in the dark. No baby clothes hung outside whereby an evil spirit could observe that a baby had been born. As throughout much of the world today, a baby boy was dressed in blue. The belief was that demons were much more likely to snatch baby boys. The heavens nullified the power of the demons, and since the heavens are blue, the color blue would give the baby more protection.[74] (In many Arab countries today, households paint their doors blue to ward off malevolent spirits.)

The reason pink developed as traditional for girls is unclear. Pink is a delicate color, so people might have used it for girls as a counterpart to the traditional blue for boys. Also, it might have been an easy and inexpensive dye to make. A type of berry called the sloe berry produced a pink dye.

The baptism party consisted of the baby's father, the godparent or godparents, and the midwife. The baby's mother remained at home for 14 days, after which the priest would bless her and she could then take part in public life again. The blessing was a formal and joyous occasion. It took place after the Sunday sermon, at the altar in front of the assembled congregation, with the baby's mother accompanied by the midwife and other attendants.

The godparent was usually an aunt or an uncle, but almost always a relative. The godparents alternated between the father's side for one child and the mother's side for the next child. The child invariably took the name of the godparent. I did not find one exception in my ancestral family. The godparent bestowed his or her name as a gift to the child. If a child died, the next child of the same gender usually received the name of the child who had died, most likely with the same godparent.

Godparents had a special relationship with their godchildren. On New Year's Day, godparents visited their godchildren, bringing them a special gift. The traditional gift was a shortbread cookie, formed in the shape of a boy's leg for boys and in the shape of a doll for girls. They also visited on Easter, again bearing gifts, such as a chocolate Easter rabbit or Easter eggs, and sometimes an article of clothing. When a child started school, godparents supplied the school satchel. They provided their godchild's outfit for his or her First Holy Communion. When a child was confirmed, the Confirmation sponsor took over the gift-giving. The sponsor's present was usually a watch, probably a pocket watch. Both godparents and Confirmation sponsors were very important figures in a child's life.[75]

What did our forefathers in the Spessart wear? Typical dress for a male peasant consisted of pants and a smock, all homewoven, mostly of a mixed weave of linen (made from locally grown flax) and wool, an especially sturdy fabric. For everyday wear, clothes were a drab practical color. Women wore long skirts and long-sleeved blouses, simply cut with an open neck. A full-length apron covered the skirt front. Women might also wear a bodice or short close-fitting jacket. They typically wore their hair smoothly combed to the rear and then pulled up into a knot on the top of the head. A flat cap tied around the chin held the knot in place. For women, outer jackets or coats were not customary. Rather, wool shawls or capes provided protection against rain and cold. Sundays, a man traditionally wore a long coat with tails, with breeches and stockings, before long pants became common. Local communities had their own traditional costumes for church and festive occasions, such as their particular style of hat, color and pattern of clothes, and embellishments.[76]

Villagers often made their own shoes, woven from straw. They wore wooden shoes for grubby work, such as working in barns.[77] If a person was fortunate enough to own leather shoes, he or she studded the bottoms with nails and applied a horseshoe-shaped metal piece by the toes to save the soles. Leather shoes generally passed to the next generation.[78]

Women in the family did extensive patching of clothes. They made "new clothes" from old bedspreads and curtains. The fabric of old adult clothes became children's clothing. One saw the same frugality after World War II when there was an acute shortage of money and fabric throughout much of Germany. The red fabric of Nazi flags (after the removal of the Nazi symbol) turned into much-needed clothing.[79]

There was no general conformity of measurement. When there was standardization, it was usually only within a particular jurisdiction. There were differences of measurement between the Mainz archbishopric-electorate and the leasehold territory governed by Schönborn, which included Grosskahl and Grosslaudenbach. In other words, there was a different set of measurements on either side of the Kahl River. This was particularly true when measuring length. For example, one unit of measurement, the *Schuh* (shoe) was equivalent to 11.32 inches (28.75 cm) in Mainz and 11.96 inches (30.38 cm) in the Schönborn territory.

The *Zoll* (inch), in the Mainz territory, was equivalent to 1.1 inch (2.8 cm) as measured today. An inch was also roughly measured as a *Daumenbreite* (thumb width) or the width of twelve ripe barley kernels laid side by side. The Schuh was 10 Zoll.

Following the shoe unit was the *Rute* (rod), equivalent to 12 Schuh. Builders measured construction sites and farmers measured fields in rods. A long piece of dry wood was marked off with 12 shoe lengths, with a groove or nail at each shoe length.[80]

This system of measurements remained basically intact until the late-19th century when the new German Empire joined with other countries in 1875 to adopt a general uniformity of measurement.[81]

Chapter 5

Industry

The main industries in Spessart Forest up to the mid-19th century were mining and glassmaking. With its long-burning hardwoods, plus the necessary water and raw materials, the forest allowed both industries to thrive.

Because of their proximity to centers for both mining and glassmaking, my ancestral villages were in an important economic area. Transporters (carters) hauled products by cart and wagon to large trade centers. Boats and barges carried goods via the Main and Rhine rivers to far-away reloading points such as in Cologne and to seaports in the Netherlands for further shipping throughout the world.[82]

We can imagine the sounds and sights so different from today. Oxen and hauling vehicles covered the roads, amid the hammer sounds and emanating chimney smoke of the foundries, with the back-and-forth shouting of men.

Mining in the Kahlgrund, the area of my ancestors, went back to the middle of the 15th century. Possessing a wealth of ore and mineral deposits, the area was especially rich in copper. Lead and silver were also mined, and eventually cobalt and iron as well.[83] The two main tunnels of the copper mine Hilfe Gottes (God's Help) were just north of Grosskahl, within a short walkable distance. A whole community of miners settled within the village. A miner's home was usually identifiable by a hammer and mallet symbol above its door.[84]

Copper mining in the region, however, was labor-intensive, for copper here appeared in combination with other minerals and elements, such as lead, zinc, arsenic, and sulfur, which made it difficult to process and smelt. Further, the sulfur dioxide fumes created during the smelting process caused extremely unhealthy working conditions.[85] The noxious fumes could lead to chronic respiratory problems and to bronchitis. Exposure to this dangerous environment began early, since many miners began as young boys. The ore going to the pits generally traveled through tight galleries that only young boys could fit into.[86]

Glassmaking in the Kahlgrund goes back to at least the middle of the 11th century. The oldest documented glass production site in the forest is a glassworks on Batzenweg (Weg = path) near the village of Kleinkahl, in 1050.[87] Spessart Forest became one of the most significant early centers of glass production in Germany,[88] and much of the production was in the Kahlgrund.

The Archbishop-Elector of Mainz availed himself of new business—and riches—by establishing a center for glassmaking in Lohr, on the eastern edge of the Spessart. He eventually opened several branches in the interior of the forest. For these burgeoning enterprises, he recruited practiced glassmakers from outside the area, especially from Alsace.

The interior foundries, however, impinged on the hunting area for the nobility. The glassworkers soon found themselves under unusual restrictions. An ordinance of 1406 declared that the workers must vacate the foundries from St. Martin's Day, November 11, until the following Easter.[89] They overwintered in Hain and Laufach, just south of Schöllkrippen. Enforcing this regulation was a ban on the erection of permanent living structures in the vicinity of the kilns, though by 1450, this was widely ignored and small villages clustered near the works. The archbishop at last tolerated their existence and opened a parish for them at Wiesthal.[90]

Glassmaking required felling trees wholesale for firing the furnaces, which led in one odd way to new settlements. As one area became denuded, the heavy logs had to be dragged from farther away, and eventually, the glassworks moved to a new location with accessible timber. The cleared area might then become farmland, with a new village arising in the abandoned complex.

This is how the village Edelbach, where my great-grandfather Johann K. Fix was born, came into existence. There had been a glassworks in the location. After the area was stripped of its trees and the glassworks had moved, Edelbach sprang up. The name was formerly *Ödelbach*, the first part of the word coming from the Old German *Ödland*, meaning empty land.[91]

The area to the north of Grosskahl is in the drainage basin of the Kahl River,[92] with numerous tributaries, and thus an ideal location for glassmaking. Glassmaking and mining operations on the west side of the Kahl River, including the area around Grosskahl, were generally under the control of the Counts of Schönborn. Industry on the east side of the river, including the area around Edelbach, came under the regulatory control of the Archbishop-Elector of Mainz.

Under these two regulatory bodies, independent enterprises sprang up, although probably more so under the Counts of Schönborn. Mainz preferred to own its own factories, employing directors to run operations.

One of the enterprises that sprang up under the Schönborn counts was a glassworks established by my seventh-generation ancestor, Johannis (Hans) Adam Hubert and his sons-in-law, Kaspar Scheinast and David Scheinast. (I count my father as first generation.) The brothers Kaspar and David married two of Hans's daughters, Dorothea and Katharina Hubert. I descend from Kaspar and Dorothea through my great-grandmother, Lena Gessner.

Lothar Schultes, a local historian in Schöllkrippen, alerted me to the story of my ancestors' glass factory. The account of their endeavor provides much insight into how entrepreneurs could establish a business, the competition, and the sometimes outright ruthlessness between competitors.

On October 11, 1761, Hans Adam Hubert, and Kaspar and David Scheinast, along with Abraham Mann, a man from near Fulda, north of the forest, made an application to the Schönborn counts to establish a glass foundry in an area a short distance north of Grosskahl. Hubert and his sons-in-law all lived in Grosskahl. Hubert, whose main occupation was as a miller, had a mill on the Kahl River.

In their petition, Hubert and his sons-in-law claimed to be learned glassmakers. Whatever the actual level of their expertise was, the business did require someone with significant knowledge and experience. They recruited Mann, who was such an expert, to join them.

The applicants agreed to certain payments for the wood they would be taking from the forest for fuel. The petition specified the amounts they would pay per measure of wood, depending on the type of wood they took. They sought permission to burn brushwood and fallen branches for ashes, needed in making potash, a major ingredient in glassmaking, and requested meadow grazing rights for up to four draft animals that would be hauling the wood.

For the foundry grounds, the four men asked to lease three

morgen (a little less than two acres), and requested permission to build a road through the woods for the transport of wood to the foundry and for bringing in other necessary materials.

Hans Adam Hubert, who would be the principal owner and foundry master, put up as security the land where his mill was and transportable goods from the mill up to a total value of 1,000 gulden. (We have already seen that in the mid-1700s, 180-190 gulden was about the minimum amount to support a family of five for a year.)

The Schönborn counts, or their representatives, approved the construction of the foundry. Permission was granted for the manufacture of window pane glass and *Hohlglas* (hollow glass). Hollow glass most likely included bottles, such as medicinal or liquor bottles, and drinking vessels.

Three and a half years later, in 1765, Franz Michael Hoffer was now the resident expert, having replaced Mann sometime in the intervening years.[93] Hoffer had worked for twelve years as a smelter at a glassworks in Bohemia, and also had experience with the making of mirrors.[94]

At this time, in his own name, possibly without the other men's knowledge, Hoffer petitioned to construct a foundry to produce mirror glass. Following the fashion which had taken off in France, mirrors had become very popular and there was a huge market for them. As events unfolded, Hoffer's ambition and tactics were to have a critical impact on Hubert and the Scheinast brothers.[95]

The Mainz archbishop-elector would have looked askance at the presence of another mirror factory competing with his own. In addition to his other glass factories, in 1698, the elector had established in Lohr a factory for mirrors.[96] He followed with branches in other locations of the forest, including in the Kahlgrund, but outside of the Schönborn area. Another mirror factory would be in direct competition with his firm.

The archbishop-elector was lord over the Schönborns, and they leased their land from him. He had the evident right to approve or disapprove a new glass foundry. However, Mainz declined to make an issue of it. For 100 years, the Counts of Schönborn and the archbishop-electors of Mainz had been involved in a land dispute. Any Mainz interference in the area was prone to bringing on suits and counter-suits.

Therefore, Hoffer would not be meeting Mainz resistance in his request. On April 3, 1765, to buffer his petition for a mirror factory, Hoffer informed the Schönborn representatives that he had already lined up a merchant in Nuremberg, who had ready cash to buy mirror glass for resale.

Simultaneously with these developments, Hans Hubert registered a complaint with the Schönborn representatives over his inability to acquire ash, used in glass manufacturing. Mainz households outside the Schönborn area were given directives to supply or sell ash only to Mainz factories. Schönborn residents, on the other hand, refused to sell Hubert the material despite the generous offers he made, and his own labor force could not produce the copious amounts needed.

Hubert was completely baffled. He stated to the authorities: "[*Ich*] *weiss aber die uhr sach nit warumm, ob es aus passion geschieht odter behalten sie selbst und streuen soche auff die wiessen.*" ("[I] don't know the reason why. Is this a passionate happening or are they keeping the ash to spread on their own soil?") Ash, made from fallen branches and other scrap wood, made a good fertilizer. But it also provided additional income to the peasants when they sold it to glassmakers. Adding his voice to the complaint, Hoffer stated that if the overlords did not issue an order for households to sell them ash at a fixed price, they may have to close the foundry. This might in fact have been exactly what he wanted.

Gerhard Kampfmann and Stefan Krimm, the authors of the book

referenced here, speculated that Master Hoffer probably had a hand in the shortage of ash. Otherwise, they argued, why would he be making plans for building his own mirror glass foundry which would require even more potash? It was most likely that Hoffer wanted to ruin Hubert and push him out. With Hubert's business closed, Hoffer would not have his competition. The authors claim it is probable that Hoffer pressured the Schönborn subjects not to provide the materials by promising higher prices in the future when he would have his foundry.

Another reason for Hoffer to push Hubert out of business is that he wished to acquire the business himself. He feared that he wouldn't get the permission to build a new mirror factory and that it would be easier to get authorization to convert the old foundry into a mirror-producing factory.

Just 10 months later, in February, 1766, Hoffer was in possession of the Hubert foundry.[97] During those 10 months, Hoffer had managed to buy out Hubert and the Scheinasts, who were now near bankruptcy. Hubert and his sons-in-law eventually received a satisfactory, if partial, settlement from Hoffer.[98]

With his share, David Scheinast built a flour mill in Kleinkahl, on a street now called Mühlgasse. Today, the mill is a private residence.[99] But David returned to glassmaking.

The Mainz elector had built a large foundry around the year 1768 in a location about 1.8 miles (3 km) southwest of Jossa in the northern part of Spessart Forest. It manufactured window glass and other glasswares. The factory was called Emmerichsthal, named for the then archbishop-elector, Emmerich Joseph von Breidbach-Bürresheim (1763-1774). This firm, instead of having a hired manager, was leased out, with Mainz getting a share of the profits.

In 1773, the elector was searching for a new leaseholder to take over the works. He asked David to take over the leasehold. David, however, preferred to return to the family's old foundry—Hoffer was now gone—which had fallen into disuse, and, to revive it with Kaspar. But Mainz convinced him to lease and operate the glassworks in Emmerichsthal by offering money toward the rent and other concessions. David leased and ran the firm until his death in 1783.

For the next two decades, the family managed to hold onto the lease. The lease-holder changed between David's two sons-in-law, sometimes one, sometimes the other, until they both died. David's two daughters had fully participated in running the foundry, but the leaseholder apparently had to be male. After they were widowed, the sisters petitioned to take over the leasehold with another partner (male). Mainz, however, decided to open the leasehold to bids, and an outside businessman named Karl Beck proffered the highest bid, acquiring the leasehold in 1805.[100]

I do not know what my direct ancestor, Kaspar Scheinast, did immediately after the sale of the foundry to Hoffer in 1766. In 1777, however, Kaspar built a large house in Kleinkahl, and began a cement-making business on the property. The house, at Kahlerstrasse #24, still stands.[101] When I last saw it, it was undergoing extensive renovation. Hubert most likely went back to running his mill.

We might wonder how Hoffer fared after he acquired the jointly-held firm from Hans Hubert and the Scheinast brothers. After acquiring the old foundry, he did indeed request to convert it to mirror-manufacturing, and by March 4, 1766, he received permission to build a new foundry for mirror glass.[102] Still, it appears that after all his effort, Hoffer did not convert the old glassworks nor build a new mirror plant. He went elsewhere.

Several glass factories had sprung up in the Sinntal area of Spessart Forest, north of Grosskahl. A group of noblemen investors in Kassel owned one of these factories, not far from Emmerichsthal. As with owners of other glass foundries, they were finding it difficult to find a master glassmaker to run the firm. Master glassmakers were demanding 1,000 gulden and more per year in salary. The Kassel lords felt fortunate to find Hoffer who, on August 22, 1766, accepted the position for 900 gulden, plus benefits such as free living quarters. He may have decided the assured income of 900 gulden was preferable to beginning his own business.

By the end of 1774, the lords in Kassel watched profits decline and fired Hoffer, only to reinstate him on May 12, 1775.[103] No doubt, they had had difficulty in finding a replacement.

❦ ❦

The Hubert/Scheinast/Hoffer glass foundry was one of the last significant enterprises in the Spessart in which the owners were also the operators. At the dawn of the industrial age, these small independent industries were dying out, and larger conglomerates were coming in with hired managers to displace individual owners.[104]

In these changing times, outsiders with investment capital installed a major glassworks in 1786 just north of Grosskahl near my ancestors' old foundry. The new facility employed up to 80 glassmakers. They made many items, including bottles, drinking glasses, mirrors, and chandeliers.[105] Some of the buildings are still standing.

The glassware produced in the forest was generally green in color, sometimes quite dark in hue, due to iron impurities in the raw materials. Such glass was called *forest glass*. This was a fairly typical color for everyday glassware at the time. Better glassware required a more expensive process with added chemical elements to make it clear.[106]

It was the heyday of the mirror. News of the Hall of Mirrors at Louis XIV's chateau at Versailles drove a craze fueling demand. Keen competition prompted a rapid expansion of production in the Spessart. Nobility everywhere wanted these household accoutrements, and as merchants grew prosperous, they too coveted looking glasses as symbols of wealth and influence. The price of a good mirror at the time was easily equivalent to the worth of a middle class car in Germany today.

From 1698, when the Mainz archbishop-elector founded the mirror-glass industry in Lohr, through the mid-19th century, exports of Lohr mirrors went to the Americas, Asia, India, and all of Europe. The elector's mirrors were of such quality that people the world over viewed them with awe. Johann Wolfgang von Goethe (1749-1832), once noted in his travel journal, "I have seen mirrors from Lohr."

Many myths grew up around mirrors. Because they gave such clear reflections, people believed mirrors could see and even speak, and that when they spoke, it was the truth,[107] as did the mirror in the fairy tale of Snow White. Feeding this fancy, manufacturers began embellishing their frames with allegories, mythical figures, and mottoes.[108]

While men conducted most of the glass-manufacturing, women undertook peripheral duties such as washing waste glass to recycle for further use and packing finished products in straw. Children of glassmakers helped with tasks after their eighth year.[109]

As with mining, glassmaking contributed to serious health problems of the workers. Inhaling silica dust during the blowing process worked havoc on lungs. The particles clung to and irritated the lung lining, leading to a build-up of scar tissue and gradual loss of lung capacity.

Worse was the effect of mercury used in mirror backs. Poisoning by this element caused dizziness, shakes, coughs, skin lesions, stomach pains, and loss of hair and teeth. Managers rotated workers around the production rooms and gave frequent breaks, but the toxin took its inevitable toll. Many thus afflicted desperately stole some of the mercury to sell to traveling peddlers in exchange for dubious nostrums that might cure them.

Amid these conditions, a new director, Tabor, arrived at Lohr in 1788. He applied an iron fist, and many of his subordinates simply fled, causing him to institute drastic measures. If a runaway was caught, he was flogged in front of the others as a warning.[110]

Tabor himself was acting under threats to his future. Facing desertions in his work force and an unceasing requirement to produce in an atmosphere of cutthroat competition made him fear for his livelihood. All his rank and privileges were at stake, including, most likely, spacious quarters in the Lohr castle.

Most laborers in other fields did not try to escape or leave their jobs due to the difficulty of finding employment elsewhere. Experienced glassmakers, however, were in high demand, and other glass firms often tried to coax them away with promises of higher wages and better conditions. In 1786 and 1787, a group of Frankfurt merchants started investing heavily in a complex under consideration by the Sternheimer brothers. With the promised windfall from Frankfurt, the brothers obtained license to build a plant on the Main River, just inside the western edge of the forest. Its mirror foundry, part of the complex, sorely needed a master mirror maker, and they soon found one.

In 1789, Friedrich Herteux was a highly skilled mirror specialist at the Rechtenbach foundry, a branch of the archbishop-elector's Lohr works. The Sternheimers lured him away with an immediate payment of 80 gulden and a future salary of 1,000 gulden a year. Telling no one, Herteux left his foundry in the middle of the night. The practice of enticing away workers continued at Rechtenbach until it finally closed down in 1798, in part because of the loss of skilled hands.

This episode bespeaks the rise of private corporate industry over traditional enterprises owned by royalty or ruling authorities. With the Napoleonic reforms soon to come, industry continued its shift toward new entrepreneurs.[111] Capitalism, pure and simple, spelled the end of an older economic order.

In addition to mining and glassmaking, there were the traditional industries, most significantly milling. There were three main types of mills: grain mills, oil mills where plant life such as the seed of the rape plant was pressed into oil, and sawmills. Again, my Gessner ancestors were part of a local industry that made it into the annals.

My great-grandmother Lena Gessner was not only descended from the glassmakers Hans Hubert and Kaspar Scheinast. She also descended from a long line of millers who operated a significant mill, Forstmühle (Forest Mill), on the northern edge of Schöllkrippen.

Forstmühle was in the Gessner family for 142 years that I have been able to establish, and probably for much longer. The Gessner family possessed the mill at least as early as 1695, when my eighth-

Castle in Schöllkrippen, now the town Rathaus.

generation ancestor, Adam Gessner, was recorded as the miller at Forstmühle in the baptism record of one of his sons. Adam did not own the mill outright but had the inheritable rights of operation and all the benefits that went with it. An official survey in 1837 shows a Christian Gessner as the owner, 142 years after the record showing Adam Gessner as the owner.[112] I do not know when the family finally sold the mill, but it was after 1837.

For much of the history of the mill, its immediate overlords were the baronial family von Dalberg, domiciled at Hofgut Reuschberg. Reuschberg mountain lies in the area between Kleinkahl on the north and Schöllkrippen on the south. (Kleinkahl is across the river from Grosskahl.) The Dalberg manorial estate lay at the foot of the mountain in the market center of Schöllkrippen.

The Gessner family probably came into actual ownership of the mill around 1815, shortly after the annexation of this part of the former Mainz archbishopric-electorate to Bavaria. Subsequent to Napoleon's reforms in abolishing serfdom and the continuation of these reforms by the states after Napoleon's defeat, holders of properties with overlord ownership generally had the option to buy the properties from the lords. The *Hist-Atlas von Ba*yern (*Historical Atlas of Bavaria*), probably commissioned by Bavaria, was published in 1815. It stated that Forstmühle was ruled by the archbishop of Mainz (an apparent mistake), which the Baron von Dalberg, not to be denied the proceeds of a sale, immediately disputed.[113]

Gessner family's former mill complex: Forstmühle.

The mill compound naturally could not support all the Gessner offspring. My last direct ancestor who was owner of the mill was Heinrich Gessner, who died in 1814. One of his sons, Johann Jakob, Lena's father, was a cabinetmaker. Johann Jakob was born in Forstmühle, but moved to Grosslaudenbach, a short distance away, most likely when he married Katherina Fleckenstein, who lived in

Grosslaudenbach.

The mill had originally been a flour mill, later a sawmill.[114] The compound is now a family residence, but contains several old buildings that were undoubtedly there during the time of Gessner ownership. As I stood outside the gate, I could hear the pleasing sound of rushing water. The old channeling still brings water to the property.

Forstmühle was in operation until 1987.[115] In the years immediately after World War II, it and another sawmill in the area comprised the most important industry in the Kahlgrund.

It is interesting to note that there was another nearby mill also under long-term ownership of a Gessner family. This one was in Sommerkahl, just to the east of Schöllkrippen. It was a grist mill that belonged to this Gessner family from 1752 until 1848, when a son-in-law took it over.[116] There was probably a tie between the two families. Perhaps an offspring from the Forstmühle Gessners was able to acquire an existing mill in Sommerkahl or to establish a new one.

Today, most residents of Spessart Forest work outside the forest. The current local economy in the Kahlgrund includes farming, apple-growing, and lumber yards.

Chapter 6

Rogues High and Low

Dangerous criminals—thieves and murderers—were a constant in Spessart Forest. Traveling through the forest was perilous, for nobleman, trader, or commoner.

Because of its density, thieving bands flocked to the Spessart, where they lived in hidden camps. They used the concealment of the forest to ambush their victims and then escaped easily with their booty under the same cover. With no local or village police forces, pursuit of miscreants was a sometime thing, and attempts to organize citizen search parties met resentment due to the intrusion on the immediate concerns of everyday life. The common cutthroat was not alone in these depredations. There was a time when the local knights became marauders themselves, taking refuge in their castle fortresses, proof against justice or retaliation.

The years of the robber knights, at the end of the Middle Ages, in the 14th and 15th centuries, were a particularly violent time. What happened to the golden age of knights? Previously, the empire had relied heavily on knights to form the core of its armies. Those who showed valor and success in defeating the enemy could expect substantial rewards. The most sought-after goal was a fiefdom with castle and villages, generating a steady income in farm produce, rents, and fees. With such a prize, the knight became a landed lord. In return, he was bound to serve the noble who granted him his fief and be ready to answer the call to battle at any time. Knights might also acquire castle-fiefdoms through services to their overlords, such as ably administering a lord's property or territory. The number of "knight-castles" in Germany eventually reached about 10,000.

By the late Middle Ages, however, knights were becoming outdated. Monarchs were favoring standing armies with professional soldiers, who usually made up the officer corps, and recruiting mercenaries and conscripting young men when needed. As knights became obsolete, the sovereigns and overlords who had granted the fiefdoms were now demanding payment from the knights in lieu of military service. At the same time, states were gaining more power and ability to exact taxes and tribute from the knights, who had to mortgage their land to meet the new burdens. Their means of livelihood was slipping away as they began losing their land and source of income.

Knights and their men, heavily armed, began scourging the highways and waterways, robbing and plundering, returning to the safe havens of their castles. In a time when there was little organized law and order, their reign of terror was virtually unrestrained.[117]

The Kahlgrund, the local region of my ancestral villages, boasts the remains of four knight-castles. The castles stood on rises above the Kahl River, along the portion of the river after it passes Schimborn and turns toward the northwest. Castle Hauenstein, two miles (3.2 km) west of Schöllkrippen, was particularly prominent. It was a fortress-like structure, located by a tributary that flowed eastward from the Kahl River. Near the end of the tributary, the water was dammed with an earthen wall, creating a moat around the castle. The Counts of Rieneck probably constructed the castle in the late 13th or early 14th century and most likely built it to protect the newly cleared and cultivated area surrounding it. They also most likely built the other three castles along the Kahl.

There had been a long-running conflict between the powerful Rieneck family and the Archbishopric-Electorate of Mainz. Both Mainz and the Rienecks had been striving to bring this part of the Kahlgrund under their own control. While imperial land lay to the west of this portion of the Kahl, Mainz claimed the land on the east side, a claim disputed by the empire and by the Rieneck counts, who were expanding their agricultural enterprises in and around Spessart Forest.

Disputed claim not withstanding, Mainz leased land to the Rienecks on the east side of the river, but objected to the extent of agricultural land they were developing on the leased land. Such expansion required the importation of farmers to clear and work the land, and the building of castles to protect the newly farmed land and its harvests. The Rienecks were building too strong a presence, which threatened Mainz. The castle-fortresses jeopardized the elector's control over the Kahl River, which was paramount to controlling the land along the river. And when the Rienecks brought in farmers, they brought in "king's men," peasants who were imperial subjects. The increasing imperial presence added to Mainz's discomfort.[118]

The term "king's men" instead of "imperial subjects" was used at this time. When the German electors chose the next emperor, he was the emperor-elect and bore the title "King of the Romans" until the imperial crowning took place.[119] The pope was to do the crowning, usually in Rome. For political or logistical reasons or because of pressure of events at home, the trip to Rome seldom occurred. Therefore, the emperor-elect was usually simply known as the king. (After 1530, the emperor-elect proclaimed himself emperor.)

To retain their leaseholds and the use of imperial subjects as laborers, the Rienecks walked a fine line between the interests of the empire and those of Mainz. By allowing the archbishop-elector judicial authority over the villages, and thus control over their activities, the Rieneck counts mollified the elector's representatives sufficiently to renew their lease—but just barely.

The rivalry between Mainz and the Rieneck Counts finally erupted into armed conflict, lasting from 1260 to 1271. Mainz was victor. One of the concessions that the Rienecks made was to allow the marriage of Rieneck Count Ludwig III's daughter Elisabeth, with a substantial dowry, to Ulrich I, an ally of Mainz. Ulrich was the imperial administrator of Hanau, on the northwest boundary of the Spessart and close to the area in question. The dowry included the city of Steinau as well as other substantial land holdings. Ulrich even assumed the Rieneck heraldic crest, much to the consternation of the Rienecks. With this power base, Ulrich's descendants gradually acquired much of the land in the western part of the Kahlgrund, including land held in leasehold from Mainz. Castle Hauenstein came into the Hanau holdings.

A knight, Werner Kolling, had served as the magistrate of Hanau for many years. In 1375, Ulrich V of Hanau appears to have granted Hauenstein Castle to Kolling, for he ordered Kolling to build an addition to the castle as a suitable living area, into which Kolling and his family subsequently moved. He received a fiefdom along with the castle. Unrest and lawlessness had been escalating, and Ulrich V seemingly wanted more armed presence in the area.

The land available for agriculture had become insufficient to support the growing population in the region. Lords as well as laborers were suffering. Mainz had been getting stronger and presumably better able to extract fees and taxes, adding to the overall burden of the inhabitants as a whole. Fighting and plundering was occurring on a daily basis. The Rannenberg family, whose members were leading court officials in the area, should have been enforcing law and order, but were participating in the lawlessness themselves.

Because of their reduced income and increased burden, knights and other lords were, in turn, demanding more and more service from their laborers and higher percentages of their produce. Workers started leaving, with or without permission. Caught in a bind, the knights and other noble families began seizing men in nearby towns right from their homes and forcing them to perform feudal services for them, even though many of the men were free, not subject to bondage.

Hanau was either too weak or unwilling to intervene. The emperor-elect, King Wenceslaus, mostly absent, likewise had neither the power nor the will to take action. By way of inheritance, Wenceslaus was also the king of Bohemia, where he was King Wenceslaus IV (not to be confused with the "Good King Wenceslas" of song, a king from an earlier period). Because of critical problems in Bohemia, he domiciled in its capital, Prague, and took little interest in events in the German territories. Indeed, in Germany, his nickname was *der Faule* (the Idle).

By 1389, crime had escalated dramatically. The robber knights, Kolling among them, were wielding unrestrained terror. They attacked ships on the waterways, and merchants and pilgrims on the roads. The two major trade routes through Spessart Forest, Birkenhainer Strasse and Eselweg, were completely unsafe.

The Archbishop-Elector of Mainz, Johann II von Nassau (ruled 1396-1419), alarmed at the violence as well as the severe damage to the trade economy, appealed to the imperial forces in the area to intervene, but to no avail. He built a castle of his own in the Kahlgrund as a show of force and to protect his holdings there. (Castle Alzenau was completed by 1400.) He used his political power to get King Wenceslaus deposed as emperor-elect, while contriving to get someone of his own choosing elected. Many of the other electors were likewise concerned, since robber knights were creating havoc throughout much of Germany, especially in the southwest, which includes Spessart Forest, where states generally had more trouble maintaining order. Wenceslaus was deposed on August 20, 1400. On August 22, Rupert III of the Palatinate became the new emperor-elect, the new King of the Romans.

Meanwhile, from 1395 to 1399, Mainz and several other bishoprics combined military forces to combat the problem. But the final decisive action in the Kahlgrund did not come until 1405.

In 1404, the new king dispatched 232 troops to march from Frankfurt into the Wetterau, a large area stretching from Frankfurt to the Spessart. There were many knight-castles and bastions of robber knights in the region. Because of the extent of crime and devastation the knights were creating, there was widespread interest in the outcome of the military action. Several towns and cities, including Mainz, Speyer, and Worms, sent delegates to accompany the troops, lending their moral and visual support. The knights and their gangs came to a quick end. Many died in the fighting. The captured met summary executions, mostly by hanging.

After cleansing the Wetterau of its errant knights, the small army went after other strongly entrenched families who were also participating in the lawlessness. In February 1405, the troops finally marched into the Kahlgrund. They first attacked the three castles situated directly on the Kahl River, defeating the knights and their retainers holed up in the castles. Castle Hauenstein, the strongest and most troublesome, was last. In May 1405, the castle was taken and the Hausenstein knights, including Werner Kolling and his son, were captured and hanged.

Mainz razed the knight-castles in the Kahlgrund to prevent their future use as strongholds. In the ensuing years, every stone disappeared, scavenged for use elsewhere. For Castle Hauenstein, however, the elector gave orders to leave a part of the castle compound (possibly a separate building—a non-defensible building) unharmed as residence for the two Kolling widows and their families. Werner Kolling's granddaughter Kunzele Kolling married Georg (German for George) Geyling, whose descendants continued to live in the home on the castle grounds until it was destroyed during the Thirty Years War (1618-48). All that remains today of the former castle complex is a cellar and parts of connecting walls to a barrel vault, possibly the entrance to a short tunnel for transporting goods from the waterway or for use as an escape route.[120]

Although the robber knights were gone, the forest was never safe. Through the centuries, certain times were more perilous than others, such as during the Thirty Years War, but danger always lurked. Finally, after a series of attacks in the early 19th century, a concerted effort to capture villains and bring them to justice helped abate much of the lawlessness.

Population, poverty, and joblessness had been escalating dramatically. People who were already marginalized dropped off the economic pyramid altogether. Many turned to thievery and joined bands of the similarly rootless and homeless.

Villainous attacks began occurring one after the other. A noteworthy spate of attacks in and around the Spessart took place between January 1807 and February 1811.

On January 12, 1807, robbers broke into the house of the Geisstlitz mayor and severely wounded three people. On February 4, 1807, they beset a guest house in Dettingen. This time the robber-murderers killed one person and severely wounded another. On September 6, 1809, a coach traveling near Steinau was attacked. At the end of September 1810, bandits assaulted a Nuremberg merchant and his fellow travelers as the party journeyed along a trade route through the forest. On December 13, 1810, a robber band from Frankfurt attacked a farmer as he was driving his wagon to his home in the forest. The thugs followed him until he reached the seclusion of the trees, where they mugged him, stealing his goods. On January 8, 1811, a robber band assailed a mail coach by Gelnhausen and robbed two French military officers who were part of Napoleon's then occupying authority.

The attack on the guest house in Dettingen on February 4, 1807, is an example of how ruthless and bold the bandits could be. A band of approximately 16 robbers, mostly young and armed with pistols and short sabers, sneaked into town under cover of darkness. Cutting the rope to the church bell so that no one could sound an alarm, they used a thick timber from a nearby building site to smash down the front door of the inn. Using the same battering ram inside, they knocked down the doors to the inner rooms. Having heard the commotion at the outside door, the guests and family had locked all the interior doors and cowered behind them, but to no avail. The robbers tied up the owner, his wife, and the owner's father. One of the guests, a priest, was murdered. They shot a servant in the face as he ran into the street, but he survived.

The townspeople must have heard the shots and commotion, but armed members of the gang had remained on watch to prevent any attempts at a rescue. The thugs escaped with money and many gold and silver objects. When they reached the edge of town, they celebrated by shooting off their guns. Most had not bothered with a disguise.[121]

The authorities managed to capture one suspect in the attack, Peter Eichler. He never confessed and evidence was insufficient to convict him. Under the new Napoleonic code, the criminal process was to be public and the courts could not use torture to extract confessions. However, there were still many means of torture. Reluctant to release Eichler, the court kept him chained for three years in a damp chilly cell in the Aschaffenburg jail, which broke his health. The authorities then transferred him to a prison in Mannheim, where he died a year later, in 1812.[122]

Mostly though, the authorities were helpless. The small towns and villages in the forest simply did not have means for sufficient patrols or stakeouts, or even to make effective pursuit of the evildoers. Finally, a robbery and murder on May 1, 1811, on a mountain road southeast of Spessart Forest, provoked a determined action. The authorities organized a dogged pursuit until at last they caught the robber-murderers. At least one of them, *Schwarze Peter* (Black Peter), had probably also taken part in the bloody attack in Dettingen.[123]

Hauled to Heidelberg, the culprits were tried and most of them beheaded. Executions then were not just for murderers but also for especially notorious thieves and robbers.

This successful pursuit and capture was a beginning in clamping down on runaway crime in the area. By 1814, there was substantially less criminal activity in the forest and in the region. More cooperation between territories and increased border control developed, while armed escorts for postal wagons became standard.[124]

Chapter 7

———···•⦂•···———

Castles and Forest Tales

Castles and castle ruins abound in Spessart Forest. As my ancestors walked to St. Katharina Church in Schöllkrippen, they would have passed a castle on their way through the town. It is a smallish castle, but appealing with its round corner towers and simple lines. Recent renovations (2002) have exposed structural designs that indicate the original castle might date back to 1200 and, if so, probably served as an assembly place and lodging for hunters.[125] Subsequently rebuilt and enlarged, it has had many uses over the years. It served at different times as a private residence for nobility and wealthy merchants. Eventually, the Mainz electorate acquired it for an administrative building, the use which the Bavarian kingdom also gave it after this area went to Bavaria. After World War II, the castle became a home for repatriates streaming in from the east. The castle now serves Schöllkrippen as its *Rathaus* (municipal building).[126]

Two of the most beautiful castles in the Spessart are the one in Lohr, on the eastern perimeter of the forest, and Mespelbrunn Castle, in the southern part of the forest. The Lohr castle now houses the Spessart Museum. The Counts of Rieneck originally built it in the 14th century as a military stronghold. Added onto and modified, it had become an imposing residence by the end of the 15th century. The earliest known Count Rieneck, Count Gerhard of Rieneck of the late 11th century, held offices within the Mainz archbishopric-electorate. Through imperial bestowals and advantageous marriages, the Counts of Rieneck gradually increased their territorial holdings. By the end of the 13th century, they owned or held lease rights to much of the Spessart. When the last Rieneck count died in 1559, Lohr and most other Rieneck holdings went to the Archbishopric-Electorate of Mainz, which took over the castle and gradually gave it its present appearance.[127]

The most famous and arguably the most beautiful castle in Spessart Forest, if not in all of Germany, is Mespelbrunn Castle, a European jewel. Descendants of the original family still live in one wing of the castle.

Hamann Echter was the Mainz archbishop-elector's representative in the town of Aschaffenburg. In 1412, as an award for his services, the elector bestowed upon him property at a place called Espelborn, now called Mespelbrunn. The nearby street village of Mespelbrunn had already existed for 300 years. The property included a pond in a small valley where Echter built his house. But the house was not a safe haven. Spessart Forest, wild and virgin, teemed with bandits and marauding soldiers. Many of the plundering soldiers had spilled over into this part of Germany from Bohemia, site of the on-going Hussite wars (1420 to 1434), a revolution that had broken out in Prague. The Echters needed a stronger structure.

In 1427, Hamann Echter, son of the first owner, started rebuilding his father's house. The resulting structure was a fortified castle with walls, towers and a moat that incorporated the pond. But it was now more of a fortress than a comfortable home. Ensuing generations remodeled the defense structure, giving it the style of a Renaissance manor. They retained the original round watchtower and the moat. Today's appearance is much as it was in the mid-16th century. Its remote location surrounded by thick forest helped save the castle from damage during the Thirty Years War and World War II.

In 1648, the male line of the family died out and the last member of the family, Maria Ottilia Echterin, married Philipp Ludwig of Ingelheim. By grant of the emperor, the two families, Echter and

Ingelheim, combined their names and coats of arms.[128]

❦ ❦

No story of a forest can be complete without its fairy tales. For many of the tales handed down to us, the world will be forever thankful to the brothers Grimm, Jacob and Wilhelm, who grew up in Spessart Forest. They were born in Hanau, and in 1791, when Jacob was six and Wilhelm five, they moved to Steinau. Their father had taken a position as a jurist in the small town on the northern edge of the forest. The father's death in 1796 left the family near destitution, but with help from family members, both boys left the village in 1798 for Kassel and then Marburg and the higher education that might merit them civil service positions and thus means of supporting the family. When their mother died in 1808, Jacob returned to Steinau.

The two brothers gathered tales they had heard at home, and also collected stories in other locations, particularly from acquaintances in Kassel, as well as from other sources referred to them. The origins of most of the stories are unknown today, as well as how far the stories traveled before reaching the locale where they were recorded for posterity. Over time, many took on the elements and flavor of the local environment where they landed.

Many tourists to Germany have travelled the Fairy Tale Road. The "Road" stretches 370 miles (595 km) from Hanau, where the Grimm brothers were born, northward toward the city of Bremen on the north coast of Germany and is purported to go through the many different locales of the story-tales. To be sure, a group of city officials and business people devised it. It is an economic boon to the communities with stopping-off points where the different tales "happened." It doesn't appear that the locational evidence had to be

Grimm Brothers childhood home in Steinau.

substantial.

Dr. Karlheinz Bartels, a pharmacist, historian, and fable researcher, relates the rationale for the different designated locations:

Schwalm Valley is the designated site for the story of Little Red Riding Hood. According to Dr. Bartels, this honor is based on the fact that the traditional costume for women in the village included a small cap that was sometimes red.

The city of Marburg claims the story of Hansel and Gretel. A well-known artist, Otto Ubbelohde (1867-1922), did much of his painting in Marburg. His works often used scenes from the Grimm story collection, including from "Hansel and Gretel." This, plus the fact that the Grimm Brothers had gone to school there, allowed Marburg to make its claim.

"Sleeping Beauty" is set at Sababurg Castle in Reinhard Forest, mostly due to the romantic appearance of the castle. Another city, Cochem an der Mosel, also claims the story of Sleeping Beauty for their castle, Reichsburg.

The site of Bremen for "The Musicians of Bremen" is a complete misnomer as the musicians—a donkey, a dog, a cat, and a rooster—never made it to Bremen. The action of the story takes place in a robbers' house in a forest. Certainly a location in the Spessart, often called *Räuberwald Spessart* (Robbers Forest Spessart), would have more significant claim to the story.[129]

And what is the site for the treasured tale of Snow White? The town of Alfeld, in the state of Niedersachsen, became the designated site because of the seven mountains there. A Grimm edition of the story has the wicked stepmother traveling over seven mountains to the home of the dwarfs.

Dr. Bartels has made strong arguments for Spessart Forest as the location of the Snow White story. He shows the relationship between the core elements of the story and characteristics of the Spessart. Admittedly, Dr. Bartels is from Lohr, but his arguments bear weight and have gained some acceptance. Alfeld itself no longer claims to be the setting for the story, although tourists yet flock there to see the tale's locale, and many road signs in Alfeld still depict Snow White and the dwarfs.[130]

One of the story's most important elements is the magic mirror. Glass production, as we've seen, was a major industry in the Spessart, from where manufacturers exported glass products to locations throughout the world. By the 18th century, glassmakers in the Spessart, specifically in Lohr, were also producing glass panes and mirrors. Mirrors became highly decorative, and after the French fashion, contained embellishments with mottoes inscribed within. One popular motto adopted from the French, and inscribed in French, was *"Elle brille â la lumière"* ("She is as pretty as the light.") People started calling such mirrors *Sprechende Spiegel* (talking mirrors). These "talking mirrors" acquired the reputation of "always speaking the truth," and were undoubtedly the inspiration for the stepmother's talking mirror.

Clear panes of glass also figure into the tale. Glass producers made glass boxes such as small storage cases, often called coffins, out of the new glass panes. Such glass cases would have inspired the glass coffin in which Snow White was laid to rest.

And very importantly, where did the beloved dwarfs and their little cottage come from? Mining was the other major industry in Spessart Forest, and in the story, the dwarfs are miners. Miners were usually small men and often boys, a necessity due to the low tunnels and narrow galleries in which they worked. Because of perpetual poverty in the Spessart, people were generally small, but mine workers had to be especially small. To protect themselves from falling rocks, they wore hooded caps and cape-style throws. Further, the nature of their work and the low tunnels eventually caused miners to develop bowed backs. With their small size, bowed backs, and hooded caps and throws, they may have had the appearance of dwarfs. And because of the especially prevalent poverty of miners, their houses were generally small.[131]

As for the seven mountains, one can easily find a chain of seven mountains in the Spessart. Lastly, apple trees have been a constant in Spessart Forest for generations. For the poisoned fruit given to Snow White by her wicked step-mother to be an apple would have been natural.

Spessart Forest also figures in the famous tale of Siegfried. As already noted, the epic poem *Nibelungenlied,* usually translated as *The Song of the Nibelungs* and which has gradually assumed status as the German national epic, gives us the story of Siegfried and his murder in Spessart Forest.

Written around the year 1200, *Nibelungenlied* is based on Old Norse legends. Although the poet is unknown, researchers have determined that he came from the Danube region in what is now Austria. In the 19th century, the story became a source for the third of four operas in Richard Wagner's cycle: *Der Ring des Nibelungen* (*The Ring of the Nibelung*).

Worms on the Rhine River is the setting for much of the story. After the Alemanni tribes forced the Burgundian tribes out of the Spessart region in the 5th century, one of the Burgundian tribes, as related in the epic, settled in Worms.

The villain Hagen slays Siegfried while he is drinking from a spring in Spessart Forest during a day of hunting. The edge of the forest is about 40 miles (64 km) east of Worms, a little far for a day's hunt. Using poetic license, the poet most likely chose a well-known forest, one with a deep foreboding reputation.

We often think of witches as part of the fantasy world. What would Halloween be without at least one witch? But up until early modern time, belief in actual witches was indeed strong, with often horrendous consequences for accused victims. Superstitions and external pressures erupted into one of the ugliest chapters of European history, and Spessart Forest witnessed some of the worst atrocities of the witch persecutions.

Chapter 8

---•••⋅⁝⋅•••---

The Witch Trials

The inhabitants of Spessart Forest could not escape one of European history's most horrific episodes in the craze over the occult, the supernatural, and the inexplicable, a frenzy driven often by the worst examples of human greed, vengeance, and outright hysteria. Between the years 1560 to 1670 at its most manifest, witch trials took place at hitherto unknown levels, leading to a furious orgy of bloody and mindless persecution, most of it directed at women.

Recent studies give an estimate of about 50,000 legal witch executions in Europe, of which 25,000 were in the German-speaking territories.[132] These numbers do not include those who fell to murderous mobs or to otherwise illegal procedures which would bring the total deaths in Europe to a much higher number, some estimates being 500,000 or more.[133]

Communities in the Spessart had some of the highest rates of witch burnings per capita. One of the hottest beds of witch persecution in the forest was about seven miles (11 km) northwest of Grosskahl. From just 1601 to 1605, the magistrates of the Freigericht jurisdiction tried and executed 139 witches—126 women and 13 men—by burning at the stake. Two more women died in prison as a result of torture. Two were set free.[134] They may have been set free, but women released were often so broken, bodily and mentally, that they never became totally whole again. A number of villages belonged to the jurisdiction of Freigericht. In the seven largest, victims ranged from about 5 percent of a village's population to almost 10 percent.[135]

To heap injury upon injury, the convicted had to pay all expenses of incarceration and execution. This included wages, plus food and drink, for court personnel, jurors, scribes, guards, torturers, and the executioner. The victims paid for maintenance of the jail and torture equipment and for the very wood used to burn them. The courts set costs and fees as they saw fit. Inn- and tavern-keepers could also expect much personal enrichment, for there was often extensive gorging by prison and court officials at the prisoner's expense. The many spectators who gathered for the executions, making merry, indulged in refreshments in these same inns and taverns. A newly coined phrase popular at the time pronounced: "There is a new alchemy, the making of gold and silver from a witch's blood."[136]

If not collected from the victim, the victim's family was responsible for payment of the fines and fees. In the Freigericht village of Albstadt, payment averaged 931 gulden per witch.[137] Fifty gulden at this time bought six cows. Needless to say, most families could not meet the obligation. They became impoverished and lived thereafter in bitter need. Many had to leave their home towns and try to earn a living elsewhere, contributing to the rising number of migrants and vagabonds. These new outcasts survived on whatever occasional work they could get, and by turning to begging and thievery.[138]

As in Freigericht, Aschaffenburg judges came to realize the extreme profitability of prosecuting witches. Nikolaus Reigersberger, the mayor of Aschaffenburg, the administrative seat for the Kahlgrund, was the town's chief prosecutor of witches from 1624 to around 1652. By the time his judgeship was over, he owned several houses, including his still-standing home at number 41 on Dalberstrasse, in Aschaffenburg. This was in addition to vineyards and other property acquired.

Emboldened, the authorities began welcoming accusations against wealthier women, especially those who owned inns. It was easy to denounce them by accusing them of poisoning the food or for some other evil act. The female guesthouse owners who had been making a fat profit off the executions were now in danger themselves.

Several times when I visited Spessart Forest, I stayed at a guesthouse in Aschaffenburg called "Zum Goldenen Ochsen," the

House of Nikolaus Reigersberger, judge and chief prosecutor of witches in Aschaffenburg, 1624 to c. 1652.

oldest part of the hotel going back to the 16th century. During the witch craze, a former owner of this hotel was one of the executed victims. The court confiscated 3,332 gulden from her property.[139]

The conviction rate for accused witches was at least 95 percent. Torture was the means. The general prosecutorial process of an arrested suspect began with an oral interrogation. If the suspect claimed she was innocent, she was subject to stripping and examination for a devil's mark. A mole sufficed. If she had such a mark, which was generally the case, the torturer stuck a needle into it. If it did not bleed, this was evidence she was a witch. (If not stuck completely through, a mole seldom bleeds.) After this, she wore the prison garb provided, usually a white linen shift. She could not wear her own clothes for she might have magic hidden in them to help her thwart the court.

If after the needle test, the accused still maintained her innocence, the "painful interrogation" followed. The torture was horrendous and almost always resulted in a confession. The torture proceeded in stages. First there was the showing of the instruments that would be used. If this failed to bring forth a confession, the torturer usually attached thumb screws to the thumbs or clamps on the calves. The accused had another chance to confess. If not, the torturer slowly began to tighten the vises, and continued until blood started flowing, sometimes gushing.

The next torment followed. Two men stretched the unfortunate over a ladder, heavy weights hanging on her until her joints were dislocated. If that was not enough, hoisting could follow. Her hands tied behind her back, the torturers hoisted the victim by the arms until her arms were turned out of their joints.

Sadly for the victim, a simple confession seldom satisfied the court. Some accused witches confessed straight-out. Knowing what was coming, they preferred death. But the magistrates wanted names. This was often due to the demands of the populace who, in their frenzy, clamored for a thorough cleansing of witches. It was also due to the magistrates realizing the profitability of convicting witches. So the torture continued until their suffering quarry named her accomplices and kept naming them.

This practice often had a terrible escalating effect. In 1611, a seamstress in Aschaffenburg, Elsa Strauss, named accomplices who then in turn were tortured and named further accomplices. The result was that 66 people besides Elsa burned at the stake, all women.[140]

The courts kept the trial records secret so that word did not get out prematurely as to who the named accomplices were. If the records were public, people would learn of the accusations against them and might flee before the arresting officials came. Further, the holding cells generally were not large enough to accommodate many prisoners at one time, so they could not pick up all the suspects at one time. After one group of suspects had their trials and speedy executions, the authorities went after the next batch.[141]

❦ ❦

Belief in witches and burning of witches goes back to pagan times. In the early Middle Ages, the Catholic Church, at first, struggled mightily against such thinking. The Church wanted to strengthen the Christian faith by getting rid of all remnants of heathenism. It taught that witches did not exist and tried to eradicate all belief in witches. Belief in supernatural powers was belief in powers rivaling God's.

But the belief was impossible to eradicate. In the vast expanse of territory, the Church could not effectively control actions by local governments or angry mobs. Unable to erase the belief, the Church and, under church influence, many rulers pushed for milder sentences. Hrabanus Maurus, the Archbishop of Mainz from 848 to 856, tried to encourage the exiling of witches rather than executing them.[142] Other rulers exhorted courts to prescribe punishments such as a fine or a day in the stocks.

The struggle against the persecution of witches was a see-saw process. While some rulers pushed for tolerance, others pushed for eradication. Those pushing for eradication referred to the Old Testament, particularly to Exodus 22:18. "Thou shalt not suffer a witch to live." (Some versions of the bible say "sorcerer.") Alfred the Great of Wessex (reigned 871-899) used this reference in imposing the death penalty on women who were believed to commune with sorcerers or magicians. The French king Charles II (reigned 840-877) decreed "that witches had caused illness and death in different parts of his realm, and should therefore—men and women alike—be put to death according to law and justice, together with their accomplices and supporters."[143] Advocating tolerance, Desiderius Erasmus (1466-1536) of Rotterdam, a Catholic priest and humanist, argued that taking the bible verse literally was an error. The source was ancient and could have a completely different meaning. It could be referring to some type of poisoner.[144]

In the Middle Ages and in the early modern era (1500-1800), the words *witches*, *sorcerers*, and *magicians* had various meanings. Early sources sometimes seemed to use them interchangeably. It is difficult today to determine precisely what the differences in meaning were. Accusations against some victims, particularly men, were for sorcery rather than witchery. Basically though, they were all performers of evil magic.

When, by the 11th century, the Catholic Church began attacking heresy, there was a gradual change in its position regarding tolerance toward witches. In 1227, Pope Gregory IX formalized the process of prosecuting heretics through the establishment of the Inquisition, instituting special courts for the finding, conviction, and execution of heretics. In 1252, Pope Innocent IV authorized the use of torture as a means toward conviction of heretics.[145]

In 1320, Pope John XXII authorized the Inquisition to prosecute sorcerers (or witches) in addition to heretics. John XXII was himself "obsessed with fears of sorcery and thought himself to be the victim of a number of magical plots."[146]

The stage was now almost set for the full-scale official prosecution of witches. But it was still primarily the Inquisition courts that carried out the trials. Most territories were not yet aggressively prosecuting witches and they were also resistant to inquisitors coming in and arresting and prosecuting people in their realms. So time passed, with sporadic persecutions and mini-crazes, either officially or by mob action when a group of determined people dared to do so. Taking the law into their own hands was not risk-free, for mob participants put themselves in danger of capture and execution.

❧ ❧

Official action against witches progressed only slowly. But there was one Dominican priest to reckon with, Heinrich Kramer. This man appears to have been a mad but cunning mastermind who knew how to manipulate people and had no inhibitions about doing so. As an inquisitor, Kramer had met with opposition wherever he went because of his brutal tactics, unlimited torture, disregard of law, and distorted reports. Hampered by such resistance, he had prevailed upon Pope Innocent VIII for help, requesting a papal bull to give him and fellow inquisitor, Dominican Jacob Sprenger, specific authority to prosecute witchcraft, as part of the Inquisition process in German territories. On December 5, 1484, the pope issued the bull, *Summis Desiderantes Affectibus* (*Desiring with Supreme Ardor*), ordering the German ecclesiastical provinces to cooperate with Kramer and Sprenger in this enterprise.

Kramer still met with resistance. He went to Innsbruck, the capital of the duchy of Tyrol, the northern part of which was a German territory. Papal bull notwithstanding, he soon ran afoul of the senior cleric and secular authorities there, who ejected him.

Kramer then retired and commenced his great mischief. He wrote a step-by-step guide for the prosecuting of witches, which he later titled *The Malleus Maleficarum* (in German, *Hexenhammer*— Witches' Hammer). In his guide, Kramer gave arguments supporting the existence of witchcraft and urged the necessity of a campaign to eradicate it. The manuscript detailed how to identify, interrogate, and destroy witches. In its instructions on unearthing witches was a list of their typical crimes, including sexual consorting with the devil, defilement of the communion host at the Sabbath, and using malignant powers to cause crop failures, livestock deaths, and injury to humans.

The guide contained complete instructions on carrying out the prosecution and effective methods of extracting confessions. Kramer further declared that to eradicate witchcraft, authorities must abandon legal inhibitions. In other words, many of the actions he advocated were against both papal and imperial law, but the current crisis of witchcraft required drastic measures.[147]

Kramer associated witchery with women. He wrote, "All witchcraft comes from carnal lust, which is in women insatiable."[148] He believed that since women by nature were more susceptible to demonic influence, the pursuit should be mainly against women.

The first publication of the book was in 1486. Learning of it, the Church banned the book just four years later, but the damage was done. Kramer had cleverly included the papal bull in the preface. The municipal courts now had what they needed. They not only had an effective guide for the legal process against accused witches, including torture, but the prosecutorial process had the seeming blessing of the Church.

In addition to the clever placement of the papal bull, the *Witches' Hammer* contained mendacious claims of widespread support. Kramer also appears to have fabricated the support of his supposed co-author, Jacob Sprenger. Sprenger, a leading ecclesiastical figure, his former colleague and superior, bitterly despised Kramer. In fact, Sprenger later expelled Kramer from Alsace, which was Kramer's own homeland.[149] Although many historical sources name Sprenger as Kramer's co-author, that seems unlikely. Kramer probably used

Sprenger's name to give his book more clout, gambling correctly that he would get away with it.

There had been previous publications by Christian theologians attempting to prove the existence of witchcraft and encouraging its eradication. But Kramer's book provided a systematic approach for achieving these goals and the seeming authority to do so. He was aiming his book for readership among prince-bishops and their law courts, but the town councils of smaller communities were also buying it and buying it in large numbers. Local magistrates and court officials were generally not highly educated[150] and unlikely to examine closely Father Kramer's actual authority. The book enjoyed continual reprinting, in other countries as well as in Germany.

After publication of the *Witches' Hammer*, witch persecution gradually increased until it reached its peak years in the latter half of the 16th century. Kramer's guide was used widely as the core source for prosecution, including in the region of Spessart Forest.

It was cited even in the American colonies when Salem, Massachusetts, took up the furor over witches in its midst, in 1692 to 1693. In the mid-20th century, a professed belief in devil worship, by British author Montague Summers, traced its origins to this malign work.

By the 16th century, the official prosecution process against witches was moving away from the Inquisition courts to the secular courts, but there was no let-up in the prosecutions.

In 1532, the Holy Roman Emperor Charles V issued *Constitutio Criminalis Carolina*, the imperial criminal code. The *Carolina* provided clearly defined rights to the suspect. The court must submit every sentence of execution to a high court or a law faculty for review before they carried it out. It further stipulated that the courts could use torture for obtaining confessions only when there was clear evidence of guilt. Torture was not for extracting confessions on the basis of mere denunciation or suspicion.[151]

The emperor, however, did not have the power base or arms long enough to counteract flagrant violations of imperial code. The courts condoned, even ordered, unrestricted torture on the flimsiest of evidence. Executions were swift, often without review, especially in smaller communities where the reviewing body would most likely be at a distance, which could cause a delay in the executions. Larger cities and towns had easier access to higher legal courts and faculties, but in this frenzied time, the legal courts were frequently little more than rubber stampers. With Kramer's "Witches' Hammer" for a guide, many courts ignored code. Flouting the law facilitated the widespread persecution of witches.[152]

The "press" contributed to the frenzy. The new movable type, invented by Gutenberg in 1440, was making possible the rapid dissemination of publications harping on the dangers of witchery.[153] Posted broadsides further helped in working up furor. The woodcut industry was busy churning out the popular images of witches and Witches' Sabbaths, where rituals with the devil took place.[154]

Many theologians, both Catholic and Protestant, added more fuel to the fire with their fiery sermons against witchcraft. Although there were people, at least among some of the higher social and educated strata, who did not believe in witches, there were many influential leaders who had such beliefs ingrained in them. Indeed, some education institutions fostered them.

The witch mania came into full swing. Witch hunts accelerated, and the most tenuous circumstantial evidence sufficed. Even children's testimony was acceptable.[155]

There were several common concepts of the interaction between demons and witches. One was that devils recruited witches by promising material rewards and sexual pleasure. According to this belief, a devil, usually in the appearance of a good-looking young man, would appear to a potential recruit and woo her. A formal ceremony would follow in which the new witch devoted herself to the devil and she received the powers with which she could carry out his plans—doing harm to her neighbors, the community, and the world. The ceremony might take place at the annual Witches' Sabbath held in a secret place, most often on a mountain, timed to be on the same night as a Christian festival night. The Sabbath was a wild orgy. There was naked dancing, sexual intercourse between the witches and the devils, and no restrictions on behavior. Children could be present, either as participants or to be sacrificed. Male witches participated as well. The devil in the form of a woman might have recruited them, or a female witch could have done so.[156]

Women comprised 80 percent of witches executed in Europe.[157] In the Freigericht jurisdiction in the Spessart, 89 percent were women.[158] In addition to the general identification of witches with the female gender, there were many other factors stacking the odds against women. Women lived in a highly male-oriented society. Society and churches, Catholic and Protestant, considered them to be useful only for bearing and rearing children and keeping house. They were also spiritually weaker.[159]

Due to their inferior status, women were easier targets. An elderly widow with little income was in special danger. Unable to completely support herself, she may have begged for food or help from neighbors or even turned to petty thievery such as pilfering wood for her stove. People already living on the margin themselves saw her as a burden. And she had no male protection. Old widows were among the first victims.

Healers, who were mostly women, were also common targets. Their practices added to their mystique. They gathered herbs at midnight, reciting prayers and chants. They mixed salves and liquids with mysterious ingredients. The rituals were probably, in part, a way of enhancing the healer's reputation for possessing special skills and knowledge. During the coming witch craze, these practices often had a very unfortunate interpretation. Healers with their magic potions were responsible for every kind of misfortune. If a baby was stillborn or died shortly after birth, the midwife (most healers were also midwives) could become immediately suspect. During the witch furor, midwives feared to carry an infant to church for its baptism as was the custom, for fear the baby died on the way and blame fell on them.[160]

When interrogators forced the accused under torture to name accomplices, she named other women almost exclusively.[161] This might have been due to the general association of witches with women, and it did not occur to them to name men. The intimidation factor could also come into play. The jail, or more likely dungeon, was hellish. It was dank, airless, and cold. The jailers, torturers, interrogators, and judges were all men. The accused woman was miserable and defenseless. Alone and terrified, and completely at the mercy of this male cadre, her sense of being of the weaker gender could only have been intensified and she may have shrunk from accusing men.

Men, however, did not escape accusations, especially as the craze wore on. They were sometimes the husbands of convicted witches. Such husbands became social outcasts, with people shunning them, and thus they became more vulnerable. But judges often suppressed accusations against males. There was a need for male laborers, especially in the fields.[162] The judges might also have had some worry about accusations against men getting closer to home.

❧ ❧

Many factors contributed to the witch craze. The Reformation, following upon Martin Luther's posting of his *Ninety-Five Theses* to a church door in 1517, and the subsequent Counter-Reformation, created much religious tension and social turmoil, and frequent bloody conflict.

The growing social unrest, as well as the economic pressures of a growing population, collided with some of the worst weather conditions to hit the world. Called the Little Ice Age, extremely cold weather descended upon Central Europe. Some of the worst weather was in the 1430s and the 1480s, but the core long-sustained phase began in the early 1560s and proceeded with little relief, reaching the harshest years in the late 1620s. These years are also the years of the most extensive witch hunts.

There were long cold winters, late frosts and hailstorms, deep freezing of lakes and waterways, and extensive stormy periods. Of the years 1584 to 1590, only two saw fertile growth in the fields. There were large hailstorms so fierce they wiped out farmland and killed great numbers of livestock. On May 24, 1626, a citizen of Stuttgart recorded in his diary that a hailstorm had dropped about a meter (3.3 feet) of hailstones. The year 1628 barely had a summer.[163]

Years of continual cold caused years of ruined crops. The price of food went up and people starved. Famine was widespread and disease followed. Farmers did not have the variety of seed that we have today, that could withstand extreme conditions.[164] Infrastructure was so poor that there were little means for transporting foods available in one area to another. The fear of death was real.

People who had to go outdoors suffered serious frostbite. Even indoors, hearths could barely provide the needed heat. Homeless people froze to death. Prowling hungry wolves began entering villages, effecting pure dread.

The weather was beyond anything anyone had ever experienced or even heard of. People believed that unnatural forces had to be causing such abnormal weather.[165] What else could be responsible except evil magic? The populace rose up and demanded the rounding up and execution of all the witches who were causing the calamity. As the unnatural weather persisted, so did the demands for witch persecution. (One witch testified under torture that she caused the severe storms by taking buckets of water high into the sky and dumping them.)

Neighbors turned in neighbors. If there had been an argument with a neighbor, and then a child died or the milk cow dried up, the person suffering the harm was convinced the neighbor did it through evil magic. Slights and jealousies came to the forefront. The climate of suspicion was pervasive, and spilled over from town to town.

Many suspicions of witchcraft, however, never went to court. People were afraid to get involved. There was also the danger that they themselves would become suspect.[166] People tried to counteract the effects of evil spells with such measures as making signs of the cross, burning bonfires, and marking symbols on their doors to ward off evil spirits.

But in the growing atmosphere of desperate fear, people became bolder in their demands. In dire straits, they knew of no other way to regain control over their lives but to have the witches eliminated. Pressure from the populace forced authorities to act. If they ignored the demands, mob action and a breakdown in order were sure to follow. Officials of the lower courts in particular feared for their own lives.

De laniis et phitonicis mu⸱
lieribus ab illustrissimum principem dominum Sigismundum
archiducem austrie tractatuo pulcherrimus

Witches making bad weather
Frontispiece from Ulrich Monitor, De
Laniis et Phitonicis, *Cologne, 1489.*

God was far away in heaven and the world was the realm of the devil. The people could do nothing about the devil, but they could eliminate the witches who were doing his work.

Although belief in witches and their power was widespread, most people realized that there were also many accusations against innocent people. But these same people often felt that to get rid of all witches, it could not be helped that there be some spilling of innocent blood.

In Aschaffenburg, during the years of 1603 to 1629, 231 executions of witches took place. That was about seven percent of the estimated population at that time. These are the known executions—many records are missing. Most victims were burned alive at the stake. They were taken to the gallows-mound in the section called Damm, in the northern part of the town, where they burned.

Some of the condemned in Aschaffenburg were beheaded, which was an unusual means of executing a witch in a Catholic community. The beheadings were not public but occurred in the same chambers where the tortures took place. Imperial regulations required that all executions be public, including beheadings.[167] Did these victims actually die under torture and the authorities did not want it known? Were they so badly broken by torture, they wouldn't be able to walk to the stake? We can only guess.

Public executions helped placate the populace. The lust for

A map of 1592 showing a Kahlgrund witch-burning site as a gallows [center left] *to the south of Somborn, spelled Sonborn.*

vengeance brought excited and boisterous crowds. Executions were great popular events.

Death by burning is one of the most horrid ways to die. Sometimes prisoners escaped the actual pain of burning if, for example, the executioner garroted them before the flames were able to take hold. Or, if the fire was very large, such as when prisoners were part of a large group going to the fire at the same time, carbon monoxide poisoning could overtake them before they experienced the anguish of the flames.

If the fire was small, however, the convicted burned for some time before death came. As the flesh burned, fluids and salts leaked from the damaged tissue. This resulted in loss of circulating blood and oxygen and brought burn shock to the body. Eventually the fire got large enough so that the victim suffered smoke inhalation and a searing in the lungs from the super-heated air.[168] Finally, death brought an end to the suffering.

Contemporary depictions usually show smaller fires. They show a pile of wood mixed with sticks or straw arranged around the feet and calves of the condemned. The high cost of wood was a probable factor in limiting the size of the heap. The authorities sometimes granted permission to the family or friends of the condemned to add additional wood at their cost to bring death sooner.

During the time of the Inquisition, the common method of execution of condemned heretics was the fire. Since a witch was also a heretic because of her pact with the devil, burning followed as the accepted means of execution.

Death by fire extinguished the evil presence. Blooding a witch, that is, destroying her blood by fire, nullified her power.[169] In Gelnhausen, a Protestant town on the northern edge of the forest, the sentence was often decapitation instead of burning. The authorities took care to completely burn these bodies as well, so as to ensure that no part of the body survived to allow the whole to resurrect itself and that the witch's power was completely gone.[170] They then gathered the ashes into a container and buried it.

Gelnhausen, an old and picturesque walled town, became Lutheran in 1543. It is included here because it is an example of witch persecution in a Protestant community near Spessart Forest. Gelnhausen lies about 8 miles (13 km) northwest of Grosskahl. Communities in the Spessart were predominantly Catholic at the time, as they are today, but there were some Protestant villages and towns, especially along the northern border of the forest. Protestantism had made many inroads into the northern area of

Germany.

Most Protestants, like Catholics, believed in witches. It was a belief so deeply seeded that it was not one of the issues when the Reformation came about. Martin Luther (1483-1546), was a firm believer in witches and the need for their eradication. His beliefs and extensive writings on the subject formed part of the basis for prosecution in Gelnhausen. Like others, he thought that the weaker nature of women made them more susceptible to communion with the devil.

In Gelnhausen, the prosecution of witches proceeded in a manner similar to that of other communities, that is, in violation of imperial code. It too used Dominican priest Kramer's *Witches' Hammer* as its guide. One difference from the nearby Catholic communities is that in Gelnhausen, the judge frequently assigned decapitation as the death penalty instead of burning.

In July, 2009, I happened to be visiting the Spessart when Gelnhausen was holding its annual witch tour. The tour began at the *Rathaus* (town hall) which is located on a prominent hill in the town. It is where the trials took place and possibly also the tortures. We wound our way through the narrow streets of Gelnhausen down to the tower and dungeon that housed the accused.

Accused witches in Gelnhausen were imprisoned in the airless cellar of this tower.

The three-story witch tower was a defensive keep and an armory in earlier times; later, the windowless and doorless lower level was used to house prisoners. The accused witch was led up an outside staircase leading to the second story some 13 feet above ground. Here there was hole in the floor through which jailers most likely lowered the prisoner to the pitch-black enclosure below. Down went the captive by rope and back up again to face a court or torture session and finally for the last trip to the scaffold. The opening was known as the *Angstloch*, the *anxiety hole*.

When the first phase of witch trials in Gelnhausen began in 1574, most women went free. As the witch craze grew and the public demanded more action, acquittals became increasingly rare. Court officials here had also become adept at circumventing imperial law.

In 1597, Clara Geisslerin, a Gelnhausen widow, died after several sessions of torture. She had confessed to being a witch during the first session and named her accomplices. Then she recanted, denying everything she had said. Nevertheless, the officials rounded up the women Geisslerin had named, even though they could not now prosecute them because their accuser had recanted. However, by using intimidating oral questioning techniques with the women, a mix of congeniality and threats, they succeeded in getting one of them to report the utmost misdeeds committed by Geisslerin. Armed with this new accusation, they again threw Geisslerin under torture.

During a subsequent torture session, lasting several hours, she made an elaborate confession. But this time she did not recant because she had died—not at the hand of overzealous torturers, however. On August 23, 1597, the court recorded her official cause of death: "The devil did not want her to reveal anything more and so broke her neck." The town burned her body and buried the ashes.[171]

The law required that a person could recant anything he or she admitted during torture. But as we see from Geisslerin's case, the interrogators found ways to circumvent the law. Imperial code also dictated that there was to be no repetition of torture. A common way around that was to record a torture session as a continuation of torture rather than a repeating of torture.[172]

The Würzburg bishopric was just to the east of the Mainz archbishopric-electorate. The seat was in the city of Würzburg, which lay about 15 miles (24 km) to the east of the forest edge. Some of the most horrendous abuses during the witch craze took place there and Würzburg has earned its own chapter in the world's annals of witch-hunting.

The trials of Würzburg are included here because they provide a nearby example of the leading figures of a city initiating many of the accusations. Generally, accusations came from the lower levels of the populace. In this case, as in some other capitals, the rulers grasped the opportunity of the general frenzy to get rid of many of their own enemies.

Between the years 1616 and 1631, 1,200 people—men, women, and children—were burned at the stake.[173] The population of Würzburg in 1617 was approximately 11,500 people.[174] Although some victims were university students or vagrants passing through, most were residents of the city. Almost 10 percent of the city's population died for witchery. As the hysteria exploded, victims came from all levels of society, including nobles, councilmen, priests, and laborers. Adolescents and youngsters even of age three were put to death.[175]

Children likewise suffered accusations of consorting with the devil and, at least for girls, of having intercourse with the devil.[176] Executing children along with their parents had an advantage of saving the community from the burden of additional orphans. Most people were unwilling or too afraid to take in the children of condemned witches. The children became social outcasts and had little hope of future marriage. Some went to orphanages, or joined bands of other outcasts. An additional advantage to executing children of condemned witches was that the court had a less-muddy claim to all the family's possessions.

❦ ❦

In a determined drive to reform itself and halt the propagation of Lutheranism, Rome gathered forces after the Council of Trent (1545–1563) to launch a Catholic Counter-Reformation, spearheaded by some of the brightest intellects among its clergy. Unfortunately, these were accompanied by zealots who would delimit Protestant advances by resort to force and subterfuge. By the second half of the 16th century, reversing religious change in northern Europe was a chancy proposition. Some bishoprics were Catholic in name only, with many of their leading subjects having undergone conversion. Whole towns and duchies had followed Luther, and members of some families were now on opposite sides of the divide. Communities had professional and social ties that cut across the new confessional partitions, and the new demographics could not be easily disentangled.[177] The religious Peace of Augsburg in 1555 established the principle that a local ruler decided the form of religion within his territory, with certain guarantees, not always honored, for adherents of a different creed.

The Mainz archbishopric, within which lay the largest portion of Spessart Forest, was part of a swath of ecclesiastical territories housing much religious unrest. A large portion of the swath bordered on Protestant territories to the north, influencing and contributing to the significant Protestant population within their own borders. It eventually became a path of terror running half-way across central Germany, where many of the worst clerical abuses of the Counter-

Reformation took place. It ran for about 190 miles (306 km) from the Bishopric of Trier in the west to that of Bamberg in the east, with Mainz and Würzburg lying in between. The Bishopric of Cologne, which lies 90 miles (145 km) northwest of Mainz, was also one of the hotbeds of persecution. The bishops of these five territories earned the moniker: the "witch-bishops." There were, to be sure, other hotbeds of persecution in Europe, especially in southwestern Germany. But these five bishoprics together provided one of the heaviest concentrations of unbridled witch persecution.

New factions arose to campaign for one side or the other in the competition for souls. The near fanatical spirit of several of the bishops emanated from the Jesuit University of Ingolstadt in Bavaria, where preachers trained to attack the Protestant faith, and also, often enough, those within the Roman tradition who disagreed with them. Maximilian I of Bavaria (ruled 1597–1651) founded The Catholic League, a loose confederation of Catholic German states, in 1609, to counter the Protestant League of the previous year. The League effectively lobbied in getting clergy of their choice appointed to various bishoprics, those clergy influential in hounding all enemies. Pope Urban VIII (reigned 1623–1644) disdained the religious zealots of Germany[178] but had as little control over events as did the Holy Roman Emperor in Vienna.

There were also Protestant evangelists, such as from Wittenberg, Geneva, and Zürich, representing the Lutheran trend and the newer Calvinist theology, who were no better in having reason prevail and were likewise borne along in the craze.[179]

Julius Echter von Mespelbrunn, born in the beautiful Mespelbrunn castle, became bishop of Würzburg in 1573. He fairly succeeded in eliminating Protestantism in his domain by banishing Lutheran preachers and decreeing that all public officials and teachers must be Roman Catholic.[180] He helped whip up the frenzy over witches and used the hysteria to eliminate objectors and political enemies, eventually seeing off some 300 witches before his own natural end in September 1617. His successor, Johann Gottfried von Aschhausen (in office 1617–1622), was not the same zealot and oversaw far fewer executions, but Philipp Adolf von Ehrenberg, next in line from 1623 to 1631, raised the ante again, though he preferred to keep some distance between himself and the actual proceedings against his subjects.

The archbishop-electors of Mainz were among the "witch bishops," and there were an estimated 1,800 executions within the electorate between 1590 and 1630. Here, unlike in Würzburg, the trials were usually the result of initiatives at the town and village level rather than emanating from Mainz itself. The rulers in Mainz often opposed the proceedings and their methods, but they could do little in face of the momentum of mania. The electorate was large, spread-out, and fragmented, not even contiguous in many places. Over time, towns and local court districts had attained considerable rights of self-government and legal administration. Spessart inhabitants, in the middle of the malefic tumult of the day, suffered accordingly.[181]

Wider events overtook the insanity at the time of Ehrenberg's death in 1631, the point at which the witch persecutions in the region declined heavily. Attention refocused with the arrival of Swedish troops who took Würzburg that year. The Thirty Years War had arrived. The rampaging soldiery brought with it the horrors of war and a plague outbreak that could not be ascribed to poor defenseless denizens of the town.

Many of my ancestors migrated into the Spessart and into the Kahlgrund after the Thirty Years War, which ended in 1648. Some of my ancestors, however, dwelled in the forest during the horrific period of the witch persecutions. The surnames Gessner (a great-grandmother's line) and Stenger (a great-great grandmother's line) were common names in and around my ancestral villages during the time of the witch trials.

Mespelbrunn Castle

I sometimes think about the terrible anxiety these forebears must have felt during this period. Accusations could come at any time. When arresting officials came into a village or neighborhood, the atmosphere had to have been thick with fear, waiting to see whose house they would visit.

Many people thought the witch persecutions were horribly wrong. Most, especially those who lived in the communities where the frenzies were rampant, were probably too afraid to speak up. Likely, there were many whom we do not know about, those who did speak up and died as a result. But eventually some voices got stronger and louder, gaining weight by the early 17th century.

Numerous publications objected to the persecution and advocated the cessation of witch trials. The opposition publications began as early as the 1490s. One of the first well-known objectors was Johann Weyer (also Wier), a Dutch physician. In his 1563 manuscript, he presented every argument he could gather to show that witchcraft was an impossible crime. He concluded that "the women accused of witchcraft were not guilty, that they must therefore not be burned to death and, finally, that burning witches was an enormous crime in itself. Those who participated in such activities, lawyers and authorities included, were nothing but murderers."[182]

Other influential writers against the persecutions included Cornelius Loos, a priest and humanist of Dutch origin, and Adam Tanner, an Austrian Jesuit and professor of mathematics and philosophy. These writers often wrote anonymously because of the danger in speaking out against the trials. To question the existence of witchcraft or to appear to defend witches was heretical and evidence that such speakers or writers were likely witches themselves.

Cautiously, instead of speaking out against belief in witchcraft, some writers began to argue against the lawlessness of the persecutions according to the rules of the imperial law code. By speaking only within terms of the legality of the prosecution process, they hoped to avoid prosecution themselves. But even this was not foolproof protection.

The protestor who had the biggest impact in helping to bring the witch hunts to a close was Friedrich von Spee, a Jesuit priest, born in Kaiserswerth on the Rhine River. In his 1631 book, *Cautio Criminalis* (*Precaution for Prosecutors*), Spee wrote against the remorseless use of torture and other abuses. He argued that admissions and denunciations procured in such manner were totally unreliable. He wrote against the manipulations, the lies and promises by jailers and executioners, and the virtual impossibility of acquittal. He declared that witch-hunters were the disastrous consequence of Germany's religious zeal. The treatment of accused witches was cruel and illegal.[183]

But Spee took his denunciations an important step further. Instead of speaking in generalities, he attacked in detail the many different tactics and "proofs of guilt" from the time of arrest to torture and execution. He showed the illogic and injustice of each step. He wrote in a clear, uncluttered manner, with a sarcastic wit that held a reader's interest. One of the "proofs" or evidences of a witch's guilt was whether she showed fear or not. Spee wrote: "And lo, now a new proof is gained against her by this other dilemma: either she then shows fear or she does not show it. If she does show it (hearing forsooth of the grievous tortures wont to be used in this matter), this is of itself a proof; for conscience, they say, accuses her. If she does not show it (trusting forsooth in her innocence), this too is a proof; for it is most characteristic of witches, they say, to pretend themselves peculiarly innocent and wear a bold front."[184]

One of the book's avid readers was Johann Philipp von Schönborn. When he became archbishop of Mainz in 1647, he strongly enforced an end to all witch trials in the archbishopric. Although witch trials continued elsewhere in Germany, Spee's book had a conclusive effect in Mainz's territory.[185]

Spee had written the book anonymously, but because of the actual trials from the prince-bishoprics he cited, showing his familiarity with the cases, contemporaries soon surmised who the author was. The author was then a professor at the Jesuit college at Paderborn, 99 miles (159 km) northeast of Bonn. The witch commissioners at Bonn tried to catch the author, but his superiors at the college protected him. The Bonn commissioners openly threatened Spee with torture and execution. One of their members, a lawyer, Heinrich von Schultheis, declared that Spee was more dangerous than the witches and they should treat him as harshly as the witches.[186]

Bringing witch trials to an end did not bring belief in witches to an end. There were still violent mob actions and lynchings. But the coming of the Thirty Years War brought new hardships and a drastic change of threat.

Chapter 9

———————...•⫶•...———————

The Thirty Years War (1618-1648)
What it Wrought

The new immigrants trekked onward. They led and pulled wagons and carts filled with all their belongings, struggling over badly-rutted roads. They passed broken wagon wheels and shafts along the side of the road, rusting pieces of armament, sometimes the carcass of a horse rotting since the war.

When it rained heavily, the ruts and deep holes filled with water and mud in which the wagons got stuck. Peter Wüst gathered limbs and branches and shoved them under the wheels of his wagon to ease its pulling out. At night, the weary travelers made fires as best they could with wet wood and then huddled under the wagons, sparingly eating of their provisions. When it stopped raining and the morning sun came out, their spirits rose. Then it turned dry. When very dry, clouds of dust stirred up, giving signals to robbers. Staying grouped together provided the best assurance of safety, but it was no guarantee. Ruthless and large roving bands of ruffians and ex-soldiers had the advantage. From chance encounters with others, the travelers heard many grim tales of attacks.

Finally, after weeks of traveling, the immigrants entered Spessart Forest. Eventually, Peter and his party separated from the others and headed in the direction of Grosskahl. Their trail gradually narrowed, becoming a path that in many places was so overgrown with vines and brambles and intruding tree roots, that it virtually disappeared. They passed through deserted villages. Peter could see rambling weeds and woody vines weaving through the ruins and creeping out of half-standing houses. As they left the villages, he saw neglected farmland that the forest was rapidly reclaiming. Here and there were small graveyards, with only fieldstones marking the graves, giving no indication of who lay within.[187] Evidence indicates that Peter Wüst, my seven-greats-grandfather and earliest known Wuest ancestor, emigrated to the Spessart from Alsace shortly after the war. I am imagining his entrance into the forest.

The Thirty Years War had ended, but much of Germany lay ravaged. The German-speaking states had been the main battlefield and had suffered miserably. The population of Germany fell from approximately 21 million to about 13 million—more than one-third of the population having perished,[188] many by direct battle action, many by marauding and plundering soldiers, but most through starvation and disease. The statistics are even worse for the men. Up to one half of the German male population died.[189] Soldiers and mercenaries succumbed in huge numbers in battles and skirmishes, as well as falling victim to the diseases that spread throughout the armies.

Some areas of Germany suffered much more than others. As with the witch persecutions, the region of Franconia, covering the northern portion of modern-day Bavaria and the region containing Spessart Forest, came to be in the thick of action. For Spessart Forest, most estimates put total losses at 75 percent of the population.[190]

The war began in 1618 in Prague, the then-capital of Bohemia, but it soon spilled over the country's borders. Villagers at home began to hear rumors about a far-off war. Those rumors and reports intensified. Finally, people could no longer ignore the war. Recruiters were coming in, gathering up young men for the emperor's army. Farmers were compelled to hand over large numbers of their oxen and horses and weapons.

But the war was still far away. Or so people hoped. In a time with virtually no news media, the forest's inhabitants relied on sketchy reports from travelers passing through or from other villagers returning from a town or city. The atmosphere was electric, the uncertainty and unrest contributing to the mass hysteria that resulted in the horrendous witch persecutions which were still in full swing.

Then it hit. The first inkling a village or hamlet might have of the nearness of the war was when they were suddenly overtaken. A resident who for some reason had not been home would return, spotting smoke curling up as he approached his village, soon finding his family and all others tortured and butchered. As he stood there in dismayed numbness, he might have heard the peaceful far-off church bells of another village, a village still undisturbed and unaware.

It was not disciplined armies marching in unison who brought the war. Many of the soldiers were conscripts, inducted officially or simply dragged off by whatever military members they were unlucky enough to run into. Most were mercenaries.

There were no particular uniforms. Officers and high-born soldiers rode horses, astride with chest armor over their colorful clothes: velvet jackets and lace collars and high boots. Muskets were slung over their shoulders and swords dangled from their belts. Lesser soldiers were mostly on foot, often barefoot or with feet wrapped in filthy rags. Some had mules or horses they had stolen. Their apparel was a patchwork of tattered clothes, rope holding up their britches. They carried homemade weapons such as scythes or wooden clubs, or possibly a sword or a pistol acquired somehow. But they all strove to wear great broad-brimmed hats, with long plumes waving in the air.

For most, pay was meager or in arrears or non-existent. Soldiers were to take care of themselves. That meant looting and extortion and lawlessness. There was rape and wanton destruction and torture and murder. Expectation of plunder drew many vile and brutal men into the armies. These marauding soldiers ranged far and wide, often ahead of the army they were with, catching villages and victims completely by surprise. Friend and foe suffered alike. It did not matter whose side someone was on.

The soldiers attacked villages and hamlets first, due to their isolation and lack of protection. If, on the way, they passed a farmer in the fields, they might kill him simply out of rage that he was not fighting, or abduct him to be a soldier. A kidnapped Catholic often ended up in a Protestant army. A seized Protestant, or Jew, for that matter, could find himself fighting in the Catholic imperial forces.

A forewarned village would flee or stand ready to fight with scythes, threshing flails, and dogs, maybe guns if they still had some. If the village successfully thwarted the attackers, the assailants moved to the next village, maybe a smaller one. Frustrated by failure in one village, they could be especially merciless in the next. The marauders drank much and their crazed murder-lust was often alcohol-fueled.

Grosskahl (then part of Kahl) was in an area of high vulnerability, although by the end of the war, virtually no village in the forest remained unscathed. Grosskahl, lying just two miles (three km) south of Birkenhainer Strasse and near a north-south trail descending from it, was in easy striking distance for roaming attackers. Birkenhainer was a main transiting route for virtually all armies fighting in Franconia or marching through to other destinations.

❧ ❧

The Thirty Years War, part religious strife and part power struggle, became primarily a power struggle as more and more countries and territories entered the conflict. Before the war, and as the Counter-Reformation continued, tensions between Catholic and Protestant territories and rulers had been heating up. Finally, a 1618 incident in Prague lit the fuse that touched off the war.

The Bohemian Protestants had been granted a *Letter of Majesty* in 1609 by the Catholic king, guaranteeing their religious freedom. Moreover, the letter permitted them to build churches on royal land, where many of them lived and worked as serfs. Some lived and worked on royal land that had been ceded to the Catholic Church. The Letter of Majesty was not clear as to whether this ecclesiastical land acquired through ceding was included in "royal land," but the Protestants proceeded to build churches on these lands as well. That action remained unchallenged until 1617.

In 1617, two Catholic bishops of Bohemia decided to test the ruling. They closed or destroyed Protestant churches on Catholic church land in their jurisdiction, and several burghers who protested the action were arrested. Protestant leaders made vehement complaints to the emperor, Matthias. Matthias, however, was gravely ill and his spiritual advisor took it upon himself to send back a sharply-worded rebuke to the protestors.

On May 23, 1618, an inflamed group of Protestant nobles broke in on a meeting of the emperor's representatives in Prague; the meeting was taking place in Hradschin Castle. Seizing two of the regents, the attackers threw them, along with their clerk, out of an upper-story window of the castle. The fall was about 56 feet (17 meters), but fortunately, none of the three men was seriously hurt.

Fearful they had gone too far, the Bohemian nobles issued a letter the following day, explaining their actions, and declaring it was the local representatives they were angry with and not the emperor. But it was too late. The emperor saw their actions as an act of open rebellion, and one of the worst wars in the history of the world commenced.[191]

While the imperialists were mobilizing, Protestant-Bohemians went on the offensive, carrying the conflict throughout the land. They ejected the Catholic bishops and seized church land. They deposed their elected king, Ferdinand, the emperor's cousin. They called upon the Protestant Union for help against the mobilizing imperial army. In exchange, they invited the head of the Protestant Union, Calvinist Frederick V, the Palatine prince-elector, to be their king. The Palatinate was a large territory and electorate in western Germany. In November 1619, Frederick was crowned King of Bohemia, although his reign was to be short.

Portions of Austria which were heavily Protestant joined the revolt against the imperialists. Hungary entered the fray. An ambitious Hungarian Calvinist prince, Bethlen Gabor of the Transylvania Principality, promised to help the Bohemians in exchange for titles, rewards, and an annual tribute from Frederick V, upon the latter becoming King of Bohemia. Bethlen was ambitious, but as in Bohemia, he feared that repressive imperial religious policies would play out in Hungary.

Countries and territories entered and pulled out of the conflict, based on fears of consequences of someone else gaining too much power and endangering their own state; on ambitions of rulers for political gain; or on promises of spoils of war, including wealth, titles, and land.

Poland aligned itself with the Habsburgs, the ruling imperial family which was seated in Vienna, but the Ottomans, garnered by Bethlen Gabor, marched in and defeated the imperialists who had entered Poland. The Hungarian army, meanwhile, was driving out the Habsburg forces that had entered Hungary. It looked like the Protestant forces were victorious, and the war might not last too long.

A turn in the conflict came in November 1620, at the Battle of White Mountain near Prague, where the Bohemians met defeat. The imperial family had appealed to King Philip IV of Spain, another Habsburg, for assistance, and he sent an army to help the emperor.

Although Protestant, Saxony also intervened on behalf of the emperor. The Elector of Saxony, John George I, feared growing strength in Bohemia, just to the south, with the powerful Frederick V as their king. He also saw that imperial reaction to Frederick's acceptance of Bohemia's kingship endangered Protestant lands throughout Germany, and hoped that siding with the emperor would help redeem Frederick's error. In a treaty with Ferdinand, Saxony was guaranteed religious freedom, and as typical in the many different alliances forming, was promised spoils of war, in this case, Lusatia, a part of Bohemia to be annexed to Saxony after Bohemia's defeat.[192] The emperor was now Ferdinand II, Matthias having died shortly after the outbreak of hostilities. Throughout the war, Saxony, mindful of its interests, was to switch back and forth.

Catholic Bavaria entered the war on the side of the imperialists, partly in exchange for the coveted electoral title that belonged to the Palatinate.

After the White Mountain Battle, Frederick V lost everything: the Palatinate as well as the new kingship of Bohemia. He went into exile in Holland, although he made a few more attempts to regain his possessions. Frederick and the Bohemians had hoped that Frederick's father-in-law, James I of England, would help with money and troops, but the British Parliament declined to help.[193]

The Duke of Bavaria helped repulse the rebellious regions of Austria. Meanwhile, Ferdinand made peace with Transylvania by granting Prince Bethlen Gabor additional territory in Hungary, although a firm final peace with Gabor did not come until the mid-1620s, when the Transylvanian prince was "old and weary."[194]

The imperialists were now in the ascendancy. They ventured farther afield, doing battle and gaining more and more control over Protestant territories in northern Germany, thus making the Protestant Danes nervous. They feared for their own sovereignty as a Protestant nation. In addition, the Danish King Christian IV had holdings, and therefore economic and political interests, in northern Germany. In 1625, Denmark entered the war, only to meet defeat.

Protestant losses in northern Germany finally aroused Sweden, which had been occupied in a war with Poland, to enter the conflict. Like Christian, the Swedish king, Gustavus II Adolphus, alarmed at the growing power of the Holy Roman Empire, feared that Catholic aggression would encroach upon his country. He also wanted to obtain an economic foothold in the northern German states which fronted on the Baltic Sea.

Between 1630 and 1634, the powerful Swedish-led armies drove the Catholic forces back out of the northern territories, and began a grand sweep of Catholic territories to the south. The Protestant forces, however, met a major defeat in September, 1634, at the Battle of Nördlingen, in Bavaria.

France had been providing financial support to the Swedes, but now, alarmed at their losses, directly entered the conflict. France was a Catholic nation but with the growing power of the Habsburgs to its north, south, and east, it joined sides with the Protestant forces. (The imperial Habsburg family had managed through political marriages and early deaths of royal spouses to gain control of both Spain and the southern part of The Netherlands.) France declared war on the Holy Roman Empire in August 1636. Widespread fighting ensued, with neither side gaining an advantage.

Events in France, however, were soon to transpire to help bring the long war to an end. In 1642, Cardinal Richelieu, the Chief Minister of France, died. A year later, King Louis XIII died, leaving five-year old Louis XIV on the French throne. The new chief minister, Cardinal Mazarin, facing an internal domestic crisis, began working to end the war. Both sides were low in funds and it was becoming apparent that no side could hold a lasting advantage. Peace talks began in Westphalia.

This is a condensed overview of a war which was a complex affair, with multiple layers of fears, motivations, and alliances playing out among each of the many different participants. It serves to provide a background for describing how the war played out in Spessart Forest.

The period of the early 1630s, when the Swedish forces were in their ascendancy and the war was at its height, is also the period when the Thirty Years War entered the Franconia region, and subsequently Spessart Forest, with full impact. The residents of the forest had felt it before. By the early 1620s, marauding soldiers from troops marching through had already brought a good deal of misery to the forest. Now things were to get much worse.

In the fall of 1631, Gustavus laid siege to Würzburg, just east of the Spessart. His forces then proceeded to capture major cities and towns on and near the perimeter of the forest, including Hanau, Frankfurt, and Aschaffenburg. When the Swedes entered Aschaffenburg, the governing seat for Grosskahl, the leading citizens and ruling classes had already left, taking high-value goods with them and leaving the inhabitants to their fate. But there were enough funds left as well as food and drink that the town was able to persuade the Swedes to spare the town from an assault.[195]

Aschaffenburg may have been temporarily safe from destruction, but small villages in the interior of the Spessart were not so lucky. In the campaigns in Franconia, the victorious Swedes and the routed imperial forces continually transited the forest, bringing with them plundering and disease. Gustavus posted occupation forces in towns and fortresses seized and left his soldiery encamped in the forest. As the demand for food grew, soldiers sought farther and farther for an undisturbed village. Many soldiers had their families with them back at the camps. These dependents also required food. Able family members and other camp followers often did their own pillaging. A giant wave of destruction spread over the land. Although the Swedish forces were well-organized, provisioned, and trained, at least at the outset, they absorbed great numbers of less-disciplined men into their ranks, including defeated enemy troops who joined them as soldiers. As the war wore on and provisions ran out, Swedish forces likewise participated in the plundering.

Inhabitants who survived often did so by hiding in dense woods far off the byways and scrounging food from the forest. People hid in caves, concealed huts, and even mine tunnels. They furnished their shelters as best they could with animal pelts and whatever household items they could improvise. In spring, if they were able, they stole back to plow and plant their fields, and then again in autumn in hopes of a harvest. Livestock were kept in caves or mines, and when safe, herded out to pasture with all their bells removed.

Though some better-off individuals escaped the territory, most villagers had no means of flight. A family moving by foot or cart soon met with soldiers or a gang of rogues who would kill them and take everything. Due to the ongoing general mayhem eclipsing any kind of law and order, gangs of outlaws increased, becoming additional sources of danger. Some fugitives did make it to walled towns, but then suffered later when the armies and plunderers and diseases began entering those towns.

Although the emperor's troops had taken back Franconia after the Nördlingen battle in 1634, the Protestant forces were still strong and the fighting continued. Fighting entered directly into the Kahlgrund. Freigericht, west of Grosskahl, became a significant battlefield, the surrounding area suffering much damage.[196]

The presence of the emperor's forces brought as much misery as that of the Swedish forces. When the Swedes were in control, they had demanded money and goods from the already-destitute residents, and now the imperial army was demanding more of the same. Seemingly oblivious to the impossible burden on the local people, they further laid waste to fields, destroyed harvests yet remaining, and burned villages in order to starve out the Swedes still in Hanau.[197]

Disease eventually took the greatest toll, in the towns and in the villages. The populace was in a tragically weakened state. All foodstuffs were gone. Means for keeping warm were also gone. If soldiers needed firewood for their campfires, they simply took it and hauled it away. After they depleted the woodpiles, they tore down wooden fencing and outbuildings. When these were gone, they tore down the houses, whether or not people were still in them. Starving and with insufficient heat and protection from the elements, residents were highly susceptible to the deadly diseases coming through, mostly via the soldiers.

The living, weak themselves, buried their dead quickly and simply until there was no one left to do the burying. Churchyards had long since become insufficient for all the burials. Designated areas in common acreage became burying grounds.

As noted, estimates put average loss of life in Spessart Forest during the war at about 75 percent. The Kahlgrund was almost completely depopulated.[198] According to a well-known story handed down, the entire population of the village of Laudenbach, later divided into Grosslaudenbach and Kleinlaudenbach, died, except for one small boy. Nearby foresters in the service of the archbishop-elector heard him crying and rescued him.[199] In Schimborn, a village of 17 houses, also on the Kahl River and southwest of Grosskahl, only two people were still alive at the end of war. In Erlenbach, just to the east of Schimborn, the entire population died and not one house still stood at the war's end.[200]

Aschaffenburg, too, eventually felt the full impact of the war. The emperor confiscated goods and foodstuffs everywhere for his armies. Famine ensued in the town and disease followed. Typhus, scurvy, bubonic plague, and dysentery raged. The town's two cemeteries could hold no more bodies. In the winter, when the earth was frozen, the town's people mostly incinerated the bodies. At one point, designated inhabitants gathered 500 bodies from streets and houses, stacking them up by the town's gates, and then burned them like cordwood. By the end of 1635, only 150 households still existed, hardly one-fourth of the town's population at the beginning of the war. Many orphaned children helplessly roamed the empty streets. When Mainz sent an order to Aschaffenburg to strengthen its fortifications, there were too few able-bodied men to carry out the order.[201]

By 1644, the peace process had finally begun in Westphalia, in northwestern Germany, but there was yet no slackening of misery in the Spessart. While the peace talks dragged on, sporadic battles continued, with each side jockeying for a stronger position in hopes of better terms in the final treaty. This meant tens of thousands of soldiers needing to take care of themselves. Marauding, plundering, murder, and rape continued unabated.

At last, on October 24, 1648, Catholic and Protestant parties signed the treaties and the Thirty Years War ended.

What did all the fighting and misery and death bring? Individual territories in Germany gained more sovereignty, limiting the strength of the Holy Roman Empire and decentralizing German power, thus further loosening ties between Germany and Austria. The Habsburgs were still in Spain and The Netherlands but much weakened. France and Sweden emerged as the strongest countries in Europe, both gaining territory.

The horrendous destruction by mercenaries during the war influenced the eventual building of well-disciplined national armies.

The large-scale religious bloodshed that had accompanied the Reformation and Counter-Reformation ended. There would still be isolated religious battles but no more large-scale religious wars. The Peace of Westphalia provided that the religion of territories and countries would be designated as they were in 1624. After much debate and negotiation, 1624 had emerged as the *normative year*, the year with the most acceptable distribution of the three recognized faiths: Catholic, Lutheran, and Calvinist. Those belonging to a different religion than the official religion of their state could leave with all their possessions if they chose. If they preferred to stay, they could do so without persecution, although there were other forms of discrimination. Imperial courts would settle all disputes between the faiths, and neighboring powers could not intervene.[202]

❦ ❦

The Mainz territory had suffered a large proportion of the war's human loss. Even after the return of some of the former inhabitants who had escaped and survived, many areas within the archbishopric-electorate were drastically devoid of people. The archbishop-elector, Count Johann Philip von Schönborn (ruled 1647-1673) was desperate to rebuild his population and regain the territory's tax base. He campaigned vigorously for new settlers.

Just prior to the signing of the Westphalian peace treaties, Schönborn decreed on October 14, 1648, that those people who were willing to accept devastated farmland and to cultivate it would be free from paying rent and free of all other payments and taxes for a period of two years, except for "the tenth," the 10 percent of produce due annually. There would also be a reduction in the usual entry fee for homesteading in a new village. Farmers, handworkers, ex-soldiers (even foreign), all were welcome. They had only to be diligent workers, agreeing to clear the land of overgrowth and rebuild the houses and barns.[203]

Schönborn had to compete with other territories and principalities, of course, as many places had suffered huge population losses and were offering similar incentives. He never did get as many settlers as he desired, but many did come.

Glassworkers from Bohemia made the move to Spessart Forest, hoping for opportunities not available at home. With the abundance of raw materials available and Bohemian know-how, glass factories sprang up in the forest in large numbers. Italians immigrated in, many settling in Vormwald, on the eastern edge of the Kahlgrund.[204]

But most immigrants to the Spessart came from Alsace and Lorraine, especially Alsace. As an archdiocese, the Mainz archbishopric had an extended area of suffragan dioceses. Schönborn put the word out in many of the parishes of these dioceses,[205] including parishes in Alsace. As elsewhere, Alsace had experienced heavy damage and loss of life. But there might have been areas in Alsace where circumstances existed preventing opportunity in the local area.

My seven-greats-grandfather, Peter Wüst, most likely was one of these Alsatian immigrants. Wüst is today a well-represented name in northern Alsace, the Bas Rhin region, and was also so before the Thirty Years War. The name Wüst does not appear in records for the Kahlgrund or the surrounding area until after the war. In 1650, Peter Wüst bought a house and property in Kahl. (At that time, records did not differentiate between Grosskahl and Kleinkahl.) Peter bought eight and one-half morgen (about 5.3 acres) of farmland and nine morgen (about 5.6 acres) of meadow.[206] He had probably arrived a year or two before, cleared the property and improved it as required, and now could purchase the rights to it. The purchase would not have been on a freehold basis, but rather, gave him the rights to work the land and pass the tenure rights to his children under the normal terms of serfdom.

I believe that the ancestor of my great-grandfather Johann K. Fix also came to Spessart Forest at the end of the war, and that he likewise came from Alsace. Like *Wüst*, the name *Fix/Vix* occurred in the same areas of Alsace as did *Wüst*, and I have found no reference to the Fix name in the forest prior to the war. But my original Fix immigrant probably settled elsewhere in the Spessart. The earliest information I have for this branch is from a marriage record for Christoph Fix in 1668 in Heinrichsthal, about 3 miles (5 km) south of Edelbach. His father's name was given as Peter. Peter Fix was probably the immigrant to the forest. My Fix ancestors descending from Peter remained in Heinrichsthal until my forefather Johann Anton Fix (1728-1786) moved to Edelbach at some point, probably when he married.

We can imagine the daunting tasks both the Peters faced when they arrived. Long neglected, much of the agricultural land had reverted to forest. In the villages, houses were without roofs, and walls were tumbling down. Fences were gone or lying broken, and barns were gone or half-standing.

Before departing their previous homeland, the immigrants would have been careful to secure or barter for those items they knew they would need. In the war-ravaged areas, there was a dire scarcity of pots and pans and farm tools, and no easy means of acquiring them.

Traveling priests, carrying their own church implements with them, held services in badly damaged churches. Any kneelers—there were generally no pews—had long disappeared for fuel; windows were unprotected from rain, snow, and wind. The altar was sometimes a kitchen table. The priests relied on farmers for shelter and food, candles for the service, and sometimes for a farmer's cottage itself for holding the service if there was no standing church. The few surviving former residents saw a new mix of attendees. Along with the newly-arrived immigrants were vagrants and rootless ex-soldiers. Even vagabonds and soldiers had had religious upbringings. For many, circumstances had forced them into the lives they had recently led. They now joined the others at church services.

Law and order returned only slowly. People still had to practice caution in their daily movements. Danger lurked everywhere, especially in the shadows of the forest. And there was a new threat.

Amid the onerous conditions, the wolf population in the forest had surged to new heights. Spine-chilling howls echoed up and down the Kahl valley. People ventured out at night at their peril and, in winter, when the predators were at their hungriest, daylight offered no safety. Inhabitants kept careful vigilance over the farm animals and seldom permitted their children to go outdoors. Those who had to go out at night carried torches before them.

Prior to the war, there had been an effective struggle against wolves. Because they killed wild game, fouling hunting sports, authorities had had a strong interest in controlling their population. But this came to a halt during the hostilities, allowing the wolves to increase unabated. They continued to menace man and beast through the end of the 17th century. But the immigrants persevered through all, setting new roots in this ancient forest.

Chapter 10

————···•⦂•···————

Religion and Schooling

For centuries, inhabitants of my ancestral villages had attended services and received the sacraments at St. Katharina Catholic Church, in Schöllkrippen. The origins of the church go back to at least 1184. The current structure, in the gothic cross form, replaced the older church sometime in the 14th century. The church suffered much damage during the Thirty Years War, but restoration did not begin until 1702, 54 years later. In the bleak and halting recovery from the hostilities, people were busy recouping livelihoods and homes. The delayed church reconstruction featured new embellishments, including an onion dome for the tower.[207]

On the east side of the church is the cemetery. Space there is limited. A family in this part of Bavaria generally leases a burial site for 25 years at a time. Leaseholders diligently maintain their plots, each with its own distinctive landscaping. Headstones list multiple names, more than any one plot site would accommodate—new burials are stacked on older ones with a layer of dirt between. Coffins are of pine, which usually disintegrates, and with time, the ground subsides enough to accept the new arrivals.

German cemeteries I have visited are beautiful to walk through. After family members visit a gravesite, they leave a customary red candle burning, white if a child is recently deceased. Lanterns burning throughout a cemetery are a wondrous and peaceful sight. I'm not sure how long the candles burn, but they seem to last at least several days. A memory that will never leave me is of once strolling through a small cemetery on a mild winter night with dozens of red

St. Katharina Church in Schöllkrippen

lanterns flickering in the snow.

If a family does not renew its lease at the end of 25 years, it is assigned to someone else. Slightly marring the beauty of the Aschaffenburg cemetery is the presence of yellow tabs affixed to the stones, reminders that a lease is about to expire. Families move away, of course, and might let their plots go. During the mass emigrations of the 19th century, whole families sometimes left, leaving no one to maintain or to pay for the plots. Any members remaining were often too poor to renew the leases. In the cemetery at St. Katharina's, there are no visual markings or cemetery records for any of my ancestors.

If there had been stone markers, they are long gone. People who give up their plot, voluntarily or involuntarily, have permission to take their headstones. However, they generally do not. With no particular place to store them, the stones simply disappear over time.

In times of acute poverty when people were struggling to keep their homes from crumbling around them, headstones could become part of a house foundation.[208]

While churches were in the larger communities, small chapels often sprang up in the more rural areas. They were places of worship where villagers and travelers could stop for prayer and meditative

Heilig-Kreuz-Kapelle [Holy Cross Chapel], Grosskahl, around 1932

rest. For centuries, the Holy Cross (German: *Heiligkreuz*) Chapel has stood directly to the west of Grosskahl. In the early 15th century, a knight, Friedrich Geipel of Schöllkrippen, who had extensive land holdings in the area, built the chapel at the foot of Habersberg Mountain on the trade route leading northward.[209]

The Holy Cross Chapel was a favorite destination for pilgrimages which originated from St. Katharina's or from churches in the Westerngrund region, west of the chapel.[210] A pilgrimage was a great event. The priests heading the procession were dressed in their finest vestments, followed by the altar boys swinging incense burners or proudly carrying religious banners, crucifixes, and other objects of veneration. After a mass in the chapel, the participants held a festival. Besides a spiritual experience, pilgrimages were a welcome opportunity to socialize and to break the tedium of perpetual toil.[211]

There have been several rebuildings of the chapel. By 1600, the first structure had fallen into disrepair. Renovation and enlargement followed, probably with the financial help of the Ernstkirche parish, where St. Katharina's is located. Local village authorities had promised to keep it maintained, but by the end of the 17th century, the structure was again in a dilapidated state. The construction of yet another new chapel took place, completed in 1698.[212] The new chapel had a small bell tower for which one of my probable lateral ancestors, Andreas Wüst, donated the bell.[213] (The brother, for example, of a direct ancestor, is a lateral ancestor.)

Over time, this chapel too fell into disrepair and its doors closed in 1814. But the villagers missed their chapel. Next to the chapel ruins was a manufacturing complex for making roof tiles.[214] In 1840, the owner of the manufactory built a new chapel. Although, like the others, eventually falling into a ruinous state, this chapel stood until 1982, when the inhabitants of Westerngrund replaced it with the current chapel on the occasion of their 700th centennial. Annual pilgrimages to the chapel continue to take place.[215]

Andreas Wüst, the bestower of the bell for the chapel completed in 1698, no doubt closely related to my direct ancestor Peter Wüst who settled in Grosskahl in the mid-17th century. Andreas, of the bell, also lived in Grosskahl, which does not appear to ever have had more than 300 and some inhabitants.

Engravings on the bell depict a religious scene. Also engraved are the year 1696 and the inscription:

Andreas Wüst laest sie Giesen
Johann Conrad Roth aber Fliesen

Loosely translated with some interpretation of the spellings, it seems to say that Andreas Wüst let it be cast (paid for the material),

Johann Conrad Roth let it flow (did the pouring).[216] (Another source gives the date on the bell as 1697.)[217]

The bell, which now, more than 300 years later, hangs in a grotto in the village of Edelbach, has had its own little saga. A new St. Josef Church in Kleinkahl was nearing completion at about the same time as the shuttering of the Holy Cross Chapel in 1814. The

The bell donated by Andreas Wüst hangs in the latticed bell tower in a grotto in Edelbach.

community did not have the money for a bell for their new church. The bell from Holy Cross was a natural choice. Its time in the tower of St. Josef, however, was short. The bell was too small, the tone too weak. Inhabitants of Kleinkahl and Grosskahl could hear it, but not the other villages of the Kleinkahl community. It then went to Edelbach.

The Edelbachers hung the bell on their workhouse and proudly rang it every morning, midday, and evening. It hung there and served the community for over 100 years, until 1940, when it fell victim to World War II. The army confiscated it with the intent of melting it down for war material. But the bell survived.

In 1948, Edelbach received notification that the bell was at the port in Hamburg, and they could come and get it if they wished. The story is that two individuals took the train to Hamburg to retrieve it. The community coffers had no money but the people were so elated to get their bell back, they donated what they could for the trip. Although the bell had suffered damage, a metalworker was able to repair it. Now there is an additional engraving on the other side of the

St. Josef Church in Kleinkahl

bell. This inscription reads: "J. E. Weule 1949". Weule was the repairer, probably at no cost, and saw no reason not to give himself some permanent credit, the same as Wüst and Roth had done in 1696.

In the fall of 1949, the bell again hung on the workhouse, until 1965 when the community made a wooden tower for it at St. Mary's Grotto in Edelbach. It hangs there today.[218]

The new St. Josef Catholic Church in Kleinkahl held its first mass in October 1814. After centuries of attending services at St. Katharina Church in Schöllkrippen, the villagers finally had their own church. No more the one-hour walk to Schöllkrippen. Most people dutifully attended church, even if it was at a distance. It could be strenuous and exhausting, especially for the elderly and families with small children.[219] St. Josef served the cluster of five villages: my ancestors' three villages (Grosskahl, Grosslaudenbach, and Edelbach), plus Kleinlaudenbach and Kleinkahl, the most central of the five.

St. Josef can thank Napoleon for its existence, at least in part. While in control of much of central Europe, Napoleon had appointed Karl Theodor von Dalberg, lately the Archbishop-Elector of Mainz, as Grand Duke of the newly formed territory, the Grand Duchy of Frankfurt, which included Aschaffenburg, from which Dalberg ruled.

Dalberg was a progressive ruler. He worked diligently at improving the lives of the inhabitants of his duchy, which included the Kleinkahl community. He encouraged and helped implement more efficient farming methods. He sought ways to counteract the failing of industries that was already taking place, and promoting cottage industries, among others. He worked at the betterment of school and church institutions.

In 1809, Dalberg approved funds for a church in Kleinkahl. Count von Schönborn, lord of Grosslaudenbach and Grosskahl, contributed to the funds. The villagers also helped. They dug the foundation, planned for buying the interior furnishings, and accepted responsibility for all future maintenance.

After some delays, the ground-breaking finally took place in 1812. The villagers were ecstatic and held a big festival. Then further delays followed, due to a shortage of funds caused by the upheavals of the ongoing war, followed by the departure of Dalberg when Napoleon lost in 1813. Some of the wealthier parishes in the area stepped in, lending funds to finish the structure at least to the point of being able to hold services. At last, in October 1814, the parishioners were able to welcome the church dignitaries arriving to consecrate the new house of worship. St. Josef's first mass took place in a church which had only the barest necessities and with only a temporary roof covering the tower. But the joy of the parishioners was everywhere in the air. Following the service, there was a great celebration.[220]

Thereafter, a priest came from Ernstkirche for mass on Sundays and holy days, after which, he provided catechetical instruction. He also came to perform marriages and baptisms. On Tuesday, March 2, 1848, he presided over the wedding of my great-grandparents, Johann K. Fix and Anna Maria Pistner. The cleric could always count on a parishioner to invite him in for refreshment before his hour-long trek back to Schöllkrippen.

There were many reasons the villagers would want their own church. As in so many European settlements, the church was the focus of village life. Not only religious activity, but festivals and celebrations centered on the structure.

In 1818, four years after the consecration of the church, the clergy at the cathedral in Aschaffenburg provided funds to St. Josef for a large bell and an organ. In 1819, the tower top was completed.[221] By 1826, the community converted some land behind the church to a cemetery, where the congregation has since interred its deceased. Prior to 1826, they buried their departed at St. Katharina's. (At St. Josef's, as at St. Katharina's, there are no physical markers or records of any of my ancestors.)

Most of the inhabitants in Spessart Forest were Catholic, although, as we have seen, there are some towns and villages that were mostly Protestant, especially near the northern border of the forest. Many of the glassmakers who immigrated into the Catholic areas of the Spessart to man the glassmaking factories were Protestant. In an 1834 list of employees at the large glassworks just north of Grosskahl, 20 of the 95 workers were noted as being Protestant.[222] Possibly there was a different fee or tax schedule for Protestants, or perhaps the notations were for some type of census. Although there were insufficient Protestants in the area to have a church and pastor, Protestants in Schöllkrippen built a *Bethaus* (prayer house) in 1880.[223]

The Jewish population in Schöllkrippen went back to at least the early 17th century[224] (in Aschaffenburg, to at least the year 1300[225]). The Jews formed a class of businessmen, shopkeepers, and livestock dealers, usually living in larger cities or towns rather than the forest villages. Their children attended the local school and received religious instruction from a rabbi once a week in their own neighborhood.[226]

In 1829, the Jews of Schöllkrippen built a synagogue. Unfortunately, it fell victim to Krystalnacht, also known as the Night of Broken Glass. On the night of November 9, 1938, Nazi brown shirts stationed in Aschaffenburg under the Hitler regime entered Schöllkrippen to carry out a series of attacks against Jews, their homes and shops, and their synagogue. A commemorative sign now marks where the synagogue once stood.

❦ ❦

Many historical religious customs are associated with the Catholic populace in the forest. A small museum in Schöllkrippen has changing displays on the history and old customs of the region, including some of the religious practices. Several displays in particular caught my interest.

Schluckbilder (pictures to swallow) were religious images (usually of St. Mary) printed on a paper-like edible substance. They came in a sheet of maybe a dozen or more such images, each a little larger than postage-stamp size. Their use was common in the mid-19th century as spiritual blessings. A person carefully tore off one piece and then swallowed "the blessing" while praying.[227] The custom has its origin in an early Christian pilgrimage practice. The early pilgrims thought of the edible pictures as spiritual medicaments. If a pilgrim became ill while underway, the usual medicines were not always available, and Schluckbilder were easy to carry.[228]

Liturgischen Spielzeuge (liturgical toys) were miniatures of those items that the clergy and altar boys use during a mass. A set of these miniatures usually included a chalice, a paten (plate to hold the Eucharistic bread), a crucifix, bells, incense burners, a bible, candle sticks, and many other items. Parents sometimes bought a set of liturgical toys for a boy they hoped would become a priest.

Set of liturgical toys, part of the Schöllkrippen museum collection.

Every Catholic home in the area kept ready a table-top crucifix and two candle holders, reserved for the last rites, the sacrament of extreme unction. These items were made of pottery, wood, or silver, depending on what the household could afford. The priest brought the other necessary articles and a communion host for the dying person. When approaching the front door of the home, an altar boy preceded the priest, ringing a bell, signaling the presence of the Eucharistic host. Men took off their hats and caps, while women curtsied and murmured prayers.[229]

In bygone times, churches usually did not have pews. People stood during the service. Perhaps there were kneelers to kneel on. Wealthier people could usually buy or rent a kneeler with armrests or maybe even a bench. The priest walked around while giving the sermon so that the parishioners could hear him more easily.

Men stayed on one side during the service and women on the other. Men stood on the side which had a statue or painting of St.

John the Baptist and which was usually to the right of the altar (when facing the altar). Women were on the other side, where there was a depiction of St. Mary.[230] This custom continued in many German-speaking Catholic churches in the New World. My father's older sisters remembered their parents speaking of the separation of men and women in their church in Cincinnati.

Eventually some churches began to install benches. This was not necessarily for the comfort of the churchgoers. There was frequently a problem with some male parishioners not going to church. They might choose this time when everyone else was at church to go hunting–that is–poaching. People would not be around to observe them. Of course, this was not in complete secrecy. It was difficult to keep church attendees from hearing the occasional shot.

The oldest section of this building, the Sackhaus, in Schöllkrippen, dates to 1473 and today houses the local history museum.

When churches had benches, it was easier for the priest to see who was missing. Later, the priest sent word to the truant to come see him. He might assign reciting several rosaries as a penance, plus he might threaten the guilty party with the withholding of communion and confession.[231]

In earlier centuries, clergy, especially the higher clergy, often had mistresses. Although banned, there was a time when it was fairly common. Early Mainz archbishops were no exception. The position of religious lord and secular lord over a vast territory was a powerful one, and members of leading noble families vied for the office. Holders of the office had to be ordained clergy.

Some who took the clerical vows did not necessarily have the calling, nor did they necessarily intend to lead a chaste life. Citizens at this time, however, generally accepted the mistresses, for the union between a high-born cleric and one of the town daughters helped to unite the various strata of society.[232]

One of the most interesting stories concerns the wife of Hans Kile (or Kyle). Kile lived from 1418 to around 1485. Meegen had been the mistress of the Mainz archbishop Dietrich Schenk von Erbach (ruled 1434-1459). She became pregnant. The archbishop arranged for Kile, a forester, to marry the pregnant Meegen.[233] Erbach thereafter organized a new forestry administration for Spessart Forest, headquartered in Schöllkrippen, and promoted Kile to *Laubmeister* (head forester) of the Spessart. In this position, Kile became one of the most important officials in the forest. He answered to the forest authority in Aschaffenburg, but he ruled over an extensive area of the forest. Among his powers, he could grant or deny permission for industries such as glass foundries and mines.

Erbach constructed many buildings in the town to accommodate the newly-generated activity and the increased population associated with the new center of forestry. The construction included inns and pubs, storage buildings, mills, and rebuilding and enlarging the town's castle. Erbach gave Kile and his wife control over the new building complex and the right to the substantial revenue that it created.[234]

The archbishop set up this dominion over the building compound as an inheritance, but not as an inheritance for Kile's offspring. He wanted the inheritance to go through his child, who turned out to be a daughter, Dorothea. The documents specified that Hans and Meegen Kile's first daughter would inherit the group of buildings. Dorothea was Kile's legal daughter since he married Meegen before the girl was born. Dominion over the buildings would continue down the line, always going to the oldest daughter. If there was not a daughter, the son would inherit, but then it would go to that son's first daughter. It was not until more than 200 years later, in 1670, that Dorothea's blood line ran out. Control over the property then reverted back to Mainz.[235]

As elsewhere, churches were usually the earliest institutions in the forest, and schools were among the latest. As of 1800, there was still no school in the Kleinkahl community and most inhabitants could neither read nor write. Larger communities had schools going back to the 17th century, but this was often not the case in rural areas.[236]

There was a short period in the late 18th century when children in the Kleinkahl area did learn some basics. At the roof-tile-making factory next to the Holy Cross Chapel, a recluse named Konrad Bommersheim had made a make-shift home. He had some education and offered to teach the basics, probably for some small compensation. Many children from the area came to him for reading, writing, and arithmetic. But this ceased after Konrad died in 1785.[237]

The Mainz archbishop-elector had declared in 1758 that all children must go to school from their 7th through 13th year, and must attend school from St. Martin's Day (November 11) to Easter. This would free them up for the crucial work periods on the farms, especially harvest time. Children started helping with the heavier duties at age 8 or 9. (The 7-year attendance obligation continued after this area of Germany came under Bavarian rule and lasted until 1938, when the requirement became 8 years.)

The Mainz decree further specified that each family contribute a set amount per child for the teacher's pay, and households would take turns hosting him for meals. The community must provide wood for heating whatever served as a schoolhouse, where the teacher also lived and worked at some side industry for additional income.[238] Not all communities could comply—they simply did not have the means. Schooling for children in the Kleinkahl community (including the children of the workers at the glass foundry outside of Grosskahl) began only in the early 19th century.

When instruction for children in the community began in the 19th century, the first school was in a private home at house #28 Grosskahl. Then classes were held in a guesthouse at #23 Grosskahl. At the time, addresses consisted of the village name only and a house number. The first teacher also worked as a weaver and he wove between lessons. It was not until 1818 that the community got its first formally-trained teacher. Before that, the schoolmaster was someone with only a modicum of education himself.

In 1821, Kleinkahl was finally able to build a regular schoolhouse. Built on the other side of the courtyard from St. Josef Church, it had two large classrooms on the first floor. There were living accommodations for two teachers on the second floor. Authorities in Aschaffenburg had granted a loan for the building. The repayment terms of the loan plus interest were 200 gulden per year for 23 years. The villagers shared in the labor to build the school and were responsible for its maintenance.[239]

The Kleinkahl community's first schoolhouse, built in 1821.

At the time the school opened its doors, there was a population of 1,377 people in the Kleinkahl community: five villages and the glassworks compound. The first enrollment was for 196 students. In 1821, one teacher earned 296 gulden; a second teacher made 80 gulden.[240] Perhaps the second teacher had less experience or was the teacher for the girls. Boy students were in one room and girls in the other. Conditions were probably far short of modern standards. Josef Rossmann (now deceased), a former resident of nearby Albstadt, once reminisced about his first day of school in 1867. There were 87 children in one room; the students sat on primitive wood benches without backs; and a rough wooden board served as a place to write on.[241]

Kleinkahl now had its school, but had trouble repaying its loan and fell behind. To settle the matter, Aschaffenburg made them an offer they could not refuse. The authorities would reduce the payment to 80 gulden a year for the remaining years of the loan and forgive the rest, provided the community made the payments on time. Kleinkahl accepted the offer and presumably made good on it.[242]

I had the fortunate opportunity to see the school records of my two great-grandfathers, Andreas Wüst and Johann Fix. Hans Rosenberger, a local resident, saved several of the early school record books from destruction. He had heard that they were in the process of being thrown out and asked for the ones that were still left. Not only I, but many of his friends and neighbors have genuinely appreciated the rescue of those books.

Although Herr Rosenberger was only able to save some of the books, they covered several years of schooling for both of my great-grandfathers. It was a thrill to see some human aspect of these two ancestors whom I never met. They were both deceased long before I was born. Now here were some handwritten pages from the 1820s and 1830s making them real, more than 175 years later.

Most of Germany used the 1 to 6 grading system, with "1" being the highest grade. Teachers graded students on ten different subjects and aspects of conduct. With help from some native-German speakers, I am able to roughly describe them. They are: *Fähigkeiten* (ability), *Schulfleiss* (diligence in school), *Häuslicher Fleiss* (homework), *Fortgang* (progress), *Christenthum* (religion), *Lesen* (reading), *Schreiben* (writing), *Rechnen* (arithmetic), *Sittliches Betragen* (moral behavior), and *Gemeinnützige Kenntnisse.*[243] This latter category roughly translates to common sense, including behavior such as that in the classroom and on the school grounds, in other words, general deportment.

Older children were urgently needed at home to help with household chores or in the fields. Children aged 12 or over had the option of finishing their last years in *Sontage Schule* (school on Sundays). In this program, the child went to school only that one day of the week, right after the church service.[244] Both Andreas and Johann finished their school years in this manner. They each went until the age of 16, having attended school a few years more than the state-required minimum. This was probably a trade-off for attending school on Sunday only.

Andreas began school at age 7 in 1823, just 2 years after the new school opened. For the first couple of years, he earned mostly 1's, 2's and 3's. There was one exception, a 4 in reading when he first started school, but he quickly began to improve. At age 9, he earned all 1's, with a couple of 2's in *Fortgang* (progress). The grade book containing the years 1826 to 1830 is missing. The book with years 1831 and 1832, when Andreas was 15 and 16 years old and going to school only on Sundays, shows all 1's except for a 2 in 1831 for *Gemeinnützige Kenntnisse.* Perhaps there was a little mischievousness on his part such as cutting up in class or not paying attention. There was a notation that he could use improvement in this area.

Johann did not have quite the stellar grades that Andreas did. The book for when he was 7 and 8 are missing. For ages 9 to 11, he had only a few 1's, earning mostly 2's and 3's. He also received the lower grade of 4, in all three years, for this *Gemeinnützige Kenntnisse* category. (I hope he was not too much of a trouble maker.) At age 12, he began to improve. In his last four years, he received all 1's and 2's.[245]

Although girls were required to go to school as well, the grade books I saw seem to indicate they did not go as long during the year and were more likely to finish at age 14 rather than age 16, even if they were going to *Sontage Schule*. I did not find school records for either of my great-grandmothers. Maria Magdalena Gessner would have been 7 years old in 1832, and Anna Maria Pistner would have been 7 in 1831. Although some of the record books for some years had both girls' and boys' grades in the same book, other years seem to have had separate books for girls' grades. These books, unfortunately, are missing. I found no records at all for girls in the 1830s, though I did find school records for two sisters of Andreas in the 1820s.[246]

Chapter 11

—···•⃟·›⃟‹⃟·•···—

The Villages go to Bavaria

Although ruling for only a short time, Napoleon completely and lastingly changed the landscape of central Europe. By 1802, he had thrust directly into the heart of Germany. With his military and regulatory interventions, Germany's approximately 375 separate principalities, free cities, and duchies were drastically reduced to around 40.[247] This was accompanied by reforms which went a long way toward a more rational administration along the French model. Church influence being vastly diminished, civil rule was no longer an ecclesiastical domain. The French emperor completely recast the legal system in a transparent code manifest to high- and low-born alike. Upper class privilege fell prey to a new, efficient tax system, and the emperor's free-trade policies undercut the power of the powerful, exclusive artisan guilds. Serfdom was abolished.

Karl Theodore von Dalberg, newly installed Archbishop and Elector of Mainz, was a great admirer of the new French system. Long frustrated with the calcified regime of multiple states with jealously guarded rights and different legal codes and even currency, Dalberg willingly assented to the Napoleonic reforms and won great favor, being named Grand Duke of the new Duchy of Frankfurt in 1806. The Mainz archbishopric was reduced to a small holding and remained a church office only. Napoleon decreed that after Dalberg's death, the position of Grand Duke of Frankfurt could only go to a civil authority, in this case, Eugene de Beauharnais, Empress Josephine's son.[248] Aschaffenburg became the center of the new duchy, which included the villages of my ancestors.

Still facing hostile Prussia and Austria, in July 1806, Napoleon formed the Confederation of the Rhine allied against them. A member of this coalition of 16 willing German-speaking states, now under Napoleon's "protection," had to renounce any allegiance to the Holy Roman Empire. In Vienna, Francis II acknowledged reality and declared the thousand-year-old institution dissolved, thereafter ruling as head of the Habsburg domains in southeastern Europe and Italy.

Napoleon's reign in Germany was to be short. The French emperor's ascendancy in Europe ended October 16-19, 1813, with a great battle near the Saxon city of Leipzig. Historians consider this battle to be the largest battle in Europe before World War I. So many different countries took part that the engagement became know as the Battle of the Nations (German: *Völkerschlacht*). Alliances against Napoleon increased, even during battle, as some member-states of the Confederation, perceiving the French could not last, switched sides. Their defeat the previous year in the futile attempt to invade Russia resurrected resistance to French dominance on the Continent.

A Spessart contingent had suffered grievously in the vainglorious campaign in Russia. One conscript element fought with a French regiment at Smolensk, then fought in the rear guard on the disastrous withdrawal. Of the 1,700 soldiers from the Grand Duchy of Frankfurt, including conscripts from the Spessart, involved in this one foray, 148 made it home, only 40 fit to return to duty.[249]

Leipzig ended the French imperial presence east of the Rhine. The Peace of 1815 revived much of the map of Europe and its dynastic families, but not the previously numerous individual German territories. French governmental practice and political theory also continued. The reforms were welcome; a French dictator was not.

After the battle, there was deep unrest in the Aschaffenburg area. It was a chaotic time. The churches and school buildings were barely able to hold the many wounded and prisoners-of-war. Austrian and Bavarian soldiers were everywhere. The populace had to feed and house everyone. Bavaria coveted the land that had formerly belonged to Mainz as well as that which had belonged to Würzburg, east of the forest. Austria was not contiguous to the area but wanted bargaining chips for land it coveted farther south, land it had lost to Bavaria after Napoleon's invasion. Soldiers from both sides were going to stay put until participants at the Congress of Vienna settled the new boundary lines.[250]

Aschaffenburg and its environs finally were ceded to Bavaria in June of 1814 (some portions in 1816). Würzburg also went to Bavaria. In exchange, Bavaria ceded Tyrol and Vorarlberg to the Austrian Empire.[251] Many in Aschaffenburg cheered. Others, however, were dismayed. Being at the very edge of Bavaria, they feared they would be at great disadvantage. *"Aschaffenburg ist das letzte Haar am Schwanz des bayerischen Löwen."* ("Aschaffenburg is the last hair in the tail of the Bavarian Lion.")[252]

Aschaffenburg had been a city of note and prestige. Famous artists and poets had had significant presence there, including Lucas Cranach the Elder, Grünewald, and the poet Clemens Brentano. It had been the summer residence of the Archbishop of Mainz, boasting a grand castle, palaces, and other fine structures and institutions. It had more recently flourished under the leadership of Dalberg, especially in the areas of art, culture, and science. He had founded a university, with architectural and forestry schools. Now the people feared they would become an unimportant provincial city in the outermost corner of the Bavarian Kingdom.

Maximilian I, the King of Bavaria, well aware of the unrest and resentment, visited Aschaffenburg two months after its annexation. He attempted to spread goodwill but was not truly successful. Two years later, in 1816, he sent his oldest son, Ludwig, to visit. Ludwig loved the city. When he later became Ludwig I, King of Bavaria (reigned 1825-1848), he often visited Aschaffenburg, sometimes for long periods of time, referring to it as "the Bavarian Nice" (after Nice, France). The great Johannisburg Castle was always kept in readiness for him.

His presence did result in some favorable measures for Aschaffenburg. Unfortunately for the city, however, staying at the castle made him familiar with it is wonderful paintings, the valuable books in its library, and also the relics of beloved St. Boniface in the castle chapel. St. Boniface was an English monk who, in the 8th century helped Christianize this part of Germany. Ludwig coveted it all.

Many valuable paintings and other works of art soon found themselves housed in Munich museums, particularly in the then newly-built *Alte Pinakothek* art museum, where they are to this day. Ludwig removed the relics of St. Boniface and then founded St. Boniface Abbey in Munich to house them. To be near the relics in perpetuity, his interment would be in the abbey upon his death. Aschaffenburg's city fathers were able to save the castle's book collection by convincing Ludwig that they were private property, belonging to a former elector.[253]

Serfdom had ended, but peasants who had owed taxes and free labor to their overlords now had to pay equivalent taxes to the state plus a compensatory fee for no longer having to provide labor. If a peasant had land, but could not pay the taxes and fees, the state could take his land. Although now permitted to buy land, most peasants could not and many had to continue working for their old lords under such agreements as they were able to work out between them.[254]

High taxes and little opportunity for advancement, plus a growing population, laid a heavy burden on much of the populace. Revolutionary outbreaks and mass emigrations were right around the corner.

Chapter 12

———···•⌣•···———

Why They Left

W hen did Andreas Wüst first start thinking about emigrating to America? It was 1847. He lived in a crowded household with his siblings, and the wife and children of his oldest brother, Karl. Shoe-making equipment and tailoring materials and tools cramped the small living space. Andreas was already 31 and still single.

He was around the 5th oldest in a family of 12 children.[255] One brother, Josef Wilhelm, had already emigrated to America. He had been a *Schneidergeselle* (*Schneider* = tailor; *Geselle* = journeyman). A journeyman is the second step, after an apprenticeship, in working toward becoming a master in a trade. Karl, the oldest, tended his farm and also worked as a shoemaker. The second oldest son, Johann R., had married and moved out of the home. The second oldest daughter, Magdalena, was no longer in the household. She might also have married or perhaps resided somewhere as a live-in servant.

According to a tax record from around 1845 to 1847, at least seven of the other siblings, including Andreas, were still living in the family home. Except for Karl, all were single. The brothers and sisters worked as day laborers, generally assisting farmers or foresters. Some of the brothers also had a side trade. Josef August was a journeyman shoemaker. Andreas's occupation is listed as farmer and day worker,[256] although we know from an interview he later had in Cincinnati with a trade journal that he also made mattresses, large sacks to be filled with straw.

The Wüst house was a *Doppelhaus* (duplex). At one time, the family had added another house onto the original to accommodate a second family in the growing Wüst clan. In the 1845- 1847 tax record, a Lorenz Adam Wüst lived with his family in one side of the duplex.[257] Lorenz was possibly Andreas's uncle. The house still stands, although mostly rebuilt. More recent owners have converted it to a single-family home. Its current address is #25 Grosskahler Strasse, formerly #30 and #30a Grosskahl.

The house backs to a hill so steep that there is no direct access to the rear yard from the front yard. To reach the back, one goes out the rear door off the second level, crosses a narrow porch, and then walks up some steps to a relatively level area which serves as the back yard.

My great-grandfather Johann K. Fix had decided to emigrate in early 1846, when he was 23. He registered with the authorities in Alzenau for permission to emigrate, but then did not go. His father, Michael, had an inn at #26 Edelbach (current address is #61 Edelbacher Strasse). In tax records for 1848 through 1852, however, Johann is the designated owner of the inn.[258] Since Michael did not die until 1875, Michael must have sold, or in some manner transferred, the farm to Johann. Perhaps he did so to provide his son ownership of a property, enabling him to obtain permission to marry. In any event, Johann stayed and married Anna Maria Pistner, from Grosslaudenbach. (The middle initial K for Johann K. Fix is from his death record; the full name is unknown.)

Originally a half-timbered structure, the inn still stands, although it has undergone a few renovations. Its current name, *Zum Hirschen* (To The Stag), goes back to at least the 1880s and possibly earlier, perhaps back to the time of my great-grandfather. Later owners rebuilt the inn to include a *Pension* (boarding house) with 16 beds.[259]

The Fix house and inn in Edelbach. The photo dates from between 1920 and 1954.

The population was larger than the land could support. The 1755 *Mainz Landrecht* (Mainz Land Law) contributed much to the overpopulation. Increasing density was already endemic in the 18th century. At the time of the 1755 law, however, the Mainz electorate did not want people to leave. It feared losing the workers needed for farm and forestry labor. This was before the industrial revolution had taken firm hold, and farm work was still labor-intensive. Additionally, the more people who had property, the larger was the tax base.

The 1755 decree was actually a binding codification of what had long been a hodgepodge of rules and regulations. All surviving children were to inherit equally from their parents' estate, which included house, land, money, and non-fixed assets. The purpose of the decree, at least in part, was to keep the peasants, workers of the land, from emigrating. With some piece of land ownership, the authorities hoped offspring would choose to stay. And it worked, at first.

After a few generations, inherited lots became too small to support a family, let alone to yield extra produce to sell. In 1783, the Mainz elector decreed that partitioned land parcels could not be less than one-quarter morgen (about 0.15 acre). This was extremely small, even though one household might have several such lots. The land law provided that when it became impossible to divide the land any further, that is, it had reached its minimum size, some heirs would receive assets equivalent in value to what their share of the land would have been. The law specified that all inheritance partners must be satisfied. If not, the property was to be sold to the highest bidder, which could be a family member, with the proceeds divided equally among the inheritors.[260]

Daughters were probably the first who did not share in the partition of the land. Then the younger sons had to accept assets of estimated comparable value. It might be a room in the house. Daughters were more likely to receive non-fixed items such as a piece of furniture or the family bible.[261] Estimates of equivalent value must have been quite fluid. Many inheritors probably accepted what they got, especially if there was little to divide, rather than force a sale.

The house and barns and outbuildings of each family were usually concentrated in a central village. Here too, land was scarce. Most peasants had nowhere to build additional housing for offspring and their families. They might be able to build a small addition, or as in the case of the Wüst home, attach a new house to one side. Or they might be able to reconfigure interior walls to provide some privacy for a new family unit. But eventually, the expanding generations simply crowded together in the living quarters and shared the beds, several to a bed.[262]

Although descendants might share ownership and use of the house and farm buildings, the law decreed that the title went to one person only, usually the oldest son.[263] In the Wüst household, this was Andreas's brother Karl.

Farmers made changes to try to get more yield from the land.

They developed marginal land that they had bypassed before, marshy areas or land on steep terrain. In the early 19th century, Karl Theodor von Dalberg, ruler in Aschaffenburg and its environs, introduced several new farming methods of crop rotation that had been successful elsewhere. It had been tradition to leave one-third of the farming fields fallow each year. Livestock grazed on these fields and their manure enriched the ground, restoring its fertility. Now the farmers kept the livestock in stalls so that they could use all the fields for planting.[264]

Although doing so meant more work, in that the farmers (usually the wives) had to cut fodder and carry it to the animals in the stalls, the manure was much easier to gather and spread on the agricultural fields. Village dwellers also burned the dried dung in their hearths. Since animal stalls were generally close to the house or even attached to it, the dung piles often accumulated right next to the house. So there was a smell people had to get used to, especially when rain leached through the pile. This leached liquid, however, made an especially rich fertilizer.[265]

Dalberg further encouraged the planting of the previously fallow fields with potatoes.[266] Germany first saw potatoes in the late 16th century, when Spanish conquistadores brought them back from the Andean mountains of South America. European farmers, however, distrusted the starchy tuber. They considered potatoes unfit for humans and raised them almost solely for animal feed, particularly for pigs. It took a famine in the early 1770s before people started eating them.[267] Potatoes gradually became an important part of the diet. They had good nutrition and required less land area to provide the same food value as other crops.

These improvements helped, but people were still barely hanging on. And things were to become even more calamitous. In 1846 came the start of several years of extremely bad weather with freezing temperatures, hail that beat down the growing crops, and ruinous rains. The resultant harvests were acutely meager, wreaking havoc on the already desperate people. Grain supplies were down and prices soared.[268]

People were completely depleting their stores of flour and grain. They had to start buying food, but there was little money and little to trade. Someone from the household, usually the father, would go on foot to the nearest sizable town to buy bread or flour. This could mean a good day's journey, and usually there was enough money for just a loaf or two of bread or a pound of flour. Some peasants, completely without funds, would illegally cut down wood in the forest, sneak it out of the forest after dark, and then sell it or trade it to get bread.[269]

People made weak soups from what garden vegetables they still had left, such as cabbage, peas, beans, lentils, or potatoes. Regarding farm animals, the failed harvests meant there was no hay to feed the cows. Most farmers tried to hold onto a few cows for field work. But mostly they had to sell or butcher their cows, which were now in an undernourished state. It seemed things could not get much worse.

Then, in 1846, a potato blight, the same affliction that had already struck Ireland, arrived in Germany. With grain harvests ruined, potatoes had become the main staple. Unlike the Irish case, in which the entire tuber turned to inedible mush, the potatoes in Spessart Forest were often partly salvageable. The edible portions, however, left only meager sustenance as food supply. Pigs, the principal source of income on many farms, could not be sustained and had to be sold off before they were mature.[270]

The populace usually managed to scrape enough food together

somehow to stave off starvation, but was drastically undernourished. Their weakened state made them acutely susceptible to illness and disease. Typhoid epidemics entered the villages, and the mortality rate went up.

Housing conditions often combined with undernourishment to contribute to the illnesses. In some of the poorer areas of Spessart Forest, such as in Rothenbuch and other street villages, the inhabitants felt the poverty sooner than people did in areas where income had been more reliable. Houses in these villages were smaller and of poorer quality, especially where the terrain was mountainous or hilly. Here, people often built their homes directly to the side of a hill such that the rear wall, made of wood planks, backed directly to the hillside. Rainwater and snowmelt accumulated behind the wall and eventually moisture invaded the house. Mildew caked the inner walls of the rear rooms.

In most homes throughout the forest, lack of adequate ventilation often caused inner rooms to be dank and muggy. Further, few homes had chimneys. Smoke billowed from the kitchen through the house to the front door. Even though kitchens were generally toward the front of the house, smoke worked its way throughout the rooms. As a result, many people suffered from a chronic eye sickness known as staphyloma,[271] a weakening of the outer layer of the eye (cornea or sclera), which causes a bulging out or even a protrusion of the cornea or sclera when the underlying tissue pushes through.

Because of the open fireplaces and the need to do most of the family cooking on open flames, there was constant danger of burns from a spitting spark of fire or a piece of clothing getting too close to a flame. My great-great grandmother, Katharina Fix (born Schwarzkopf), died of burns in 1859, five years after her son Johann K. had emigrated to America.

❦ ❦

A major contributor to the increasing poverty was the decline and final closing of the important industries, ones that had sustained the forest inhabitants for centuries. These were primarily the mining and glass industries.

Centuries of mining had brought about a severe depletion of ores by the late 18th century. Many mines were verging on bankruptcy and most were closing. Around 1780, Count Hugo Damian Erwein von Schönborn, in whose territory many of the mines were, bought out the shareholders in those mines. He then infused much of his own money to try to stave off bankruptcy in the mines and prevent mass joblessness.[272] Although his action delayed the inevitable, the mines eventually failed.

Hilfe Gottes, the copper mine near Grosskahl, one of the properties in the Schönborn territory, was still in operation when the territory became part of Bavaria. King Maximilian I of Bavaria had a keen interest in the mineral ores of Spessart Forest and their potential for increased revenue. But, Friedrich Preissler, the first representative the Bavarian government sent in 1818 to run Hilfe Gottes was too inexperienced to turn things around. In 1823, Munich sent Augustin Bezold, who remained for 12 years. Bezold brought new treatment and processing methods, and built a better smelting oven.

Despite these efforts, he too was unable to turn the mine into a profitable enterprise. Munich wanted to prevent mass unemployment, and continued to fund the undertaking, but the deficit only grew. It was costing more to mine and process the ore, while, at the same time, the quality of the raw copper was steadily declining. Hilfe Gottes finally closed in 1837.

Bezold had already left in 1835. He was too sick to continue, most likely due to his living quarters being in the building where the ore washing process took place. He had suffered extensive exposure to the sulfur fumes. His superiors reassigned him to a position in Munich, but he died six years later, at age 47.[273]

Private investors had also bought up closed or bankrupt mines, and tried to resurrect them, but prices for copper and other ores had declined to the point that making a profit was no longer feasible, even with better methods of mining.[274] Some miners were lucky to find mining work in other locations, but many found themselves without work.

Railroad expansion in Germany in the 1840s did little for the Spessart mines. The costs of running lines into the dense forest left the area underserved by this new technology. The industries inside the area could not ship ore and other products economically and suffered accordingly.

Like the mining industry, the glassmaking industry in Spessart Forest was also failing by the late 18th century. Competition, the difficulties of keeping the most-skilled glassworkers, poor management policies at many of the factories, and lower market prices all contributed to its decline.

By 1780, few glass foundries in the forest still survived. The large glassworks by Grosskahl closed and was falling into ruins. But this foundry was to get a reprieve. In 1793, Karl Beck, an investor from Büdingen, in Hesse, leased the works from the Mainz archbishopric-electorate, which had taken over its administration. This is the same Karl Beck who, in 1805, would acquire the leasehold of the glass factory in Emmerichsthal by outbidding the family of my lateral ancestor David Scheinast.

Castle in Lohr, now housing the Spessart Forest museum.

Beck resurrected the Grosskahl factory and greatly enhanced it. Its output included many types of glass products, including fine cut and decorative work. It had 94 full-time employees, housing 24 families in the foundry compound. It also gave employment to many day workers as well as tree cutters and transporters.[275]

For 39 years, under Beck's guidance, the glassworks provided vital employment in the area around Grosskahl. Even in the face of deteriorating economic conditions, Beck kept the foundry going and competitive. With his death in 1832, the absence of his guiding hand soon led to the closing of the factory, putting more than 90 people out of work.[276] Other investors tried to revive the works, but increasing expenses of production and the worsening market value rendered such efforts ineffective.[277] Beck might have kept it going longer, but it probably would ultimately have failed.

168

Even under Beck, the workers were still making glass products by hand and blowing by mouth. The glassworks in Lohr, a premier center of glassmaking in the forest, had converted to modern methods of production. By the mid-19th century, only Lohr still had a viable glass factory in the Spessart region.[278]

Villagers tried to earn income any way they could. They hired out as day workers. They manufactured items at home, usually on consignment. In the Wüst home, in addition to seeking day work, some of the siblings plied trades as shoemakers or as tailors.

It was the businessmen from the cities and larger towns who made possible these cottage industries. City entrepreneurs, desiring to increase their revenue, had long been trying to introduce more efficient procedures in the manufacturing process to increase their output and to reduce costs. However, even after Napoleon's attempt to reform them, the powerful guilds wielded much control over manufacturing and were intent on maintaining the *status quo*, in which they dictated the quantity of goods produced, the production methods, and the prices charged. Doing so prevented competition and kept the income of the guild members equal, ensuring their financial security.

Guilds may have been losing power and control in some of the German states, but that was definitely not always true, especially in southwest Germany. They had extensive authority over all aspects of trade and manufacturing. The guilds licensed selected merchants and manufacturers, thereby making them members of the guilds, but many, even in this coveted position, resented the constraints imposed upon them.

Now, with mass unemployment in rural areas, some businessmen

169

began taking the manufacturing of their products to outlying villages. They took raw materials by wagon to the villagers and then returned to fetch the finished products. Such products could include yarn or thread, lace, ropes, gloves, small metal items such as nails, and woven cloth. The small industries also included making shoes and cutting out or piecing together pre-cut fabric sections for making apparel. Although guilds had much power in the cities, they were unable to control this proliferation of unlicensed workers in the countryside.[279]

The unlicensed workers included journeymen, many of whom the guilds were unlikely to ever accept as members. The guilds kept a tight rein on new entrants in their zeal to limit competition for its existing members. This situation held the journeymen, even with their advanced training, to an existence as wage laborers. As important as help from the city merchants and manufacturers was, it was not enough to turn around the economy. Payments for piecework were low and consignments inconsistent. Guilds in Bavaria had a far-reaching negative effect on economic development, severely retarding the entrance of the industrial revolution into that state. This was also true in many parts of Germany where guilds continued to hold strong influence and power.

It was not just the joblessness and poverty that drove the mass emigrations. Another force—a strong one—driving away the young people was the marriage restrictions. As conditions worsened, local authorities became more and more stringent in granting permission to couples to marry. They wished to curtail the expanding population by ensuring that only men who had the means to support a family married. Town elders, fearful of the expanding poverty and of people becoming wards of the community, often went overboard in turning down marriage applications.

Some illegitimate children were born, of course, but by and large, social mores had a strong influence. The marriage restrictions *did* have a curtailing effect on population growth.

Communities throughout Germany had the authority to deny marriage permission, but town fathers in the southwestern part of the country were particularly severe. Applying for permission to marry was an exacting and extensive process, with little chance of approval, particularly in the time of my great-grandparents, the early- to mid-19th century.

Bavarian law carried forward much of what had been law under Mainz governance, and in 1816, it prescribed that a council made up of local government officials, plus the poor-relief officer, would make a preliminary judgment whether a prospective groom could marry or not. In an effort to stem abuses, it further prescribed that the case, with all supporting documentation, then go to the district court judge for final approval. For my ancestral villages, the district court was in Alzenau. Because the local authorities resented district judges interfering with what they saw as their prerogative, however, the district courts often approved the judgments as forwarded to them.

The applicant had to show economic means of support, list property owned—thoroughly described and documented—and had to meet several other stipulations. A successful applicant usually had property that included land.

The council could take into account the dowry of the intended bride, such as real estate, furniture, or money. If the applicant's intended was bringing cash as part of her dowry, the prospective groom had to show that the money actually belonged to her. The town council also made a determination that what the bride was to receive as her dowry would not be detrimental to or deprive her family.

Other stipulations demanded that the applicant be well-versed in Christianity, be knowledgeable in civic and domestic duties, and that he practiced industry and thrift. The local school inspector provided the applicant's school records. The appropriate church office provided the record of his Christian teaching. The council tested the applicant on his knowledge of civic and domestic duties. The council, with the inclusion of the church council, determined the moral character, diligence, and thrift of the applicant, and if found satisfactory, certified that he met the requirements.

Although the law charged the local council to be unbiased, personal relationships of council members with the applicant did play a role, either to the favor or the detriment of the applicant.[280]

The central authorities in Munich were well aware of local practices of denying most applications. In the early 1860s, they asked the judges in the governing jurisdictions to report their experiences. In April 1863, Judge Vervier, reporting out of his district, wrote of his dismay at the excessive denials to marriage applicants by the local town councils. Based on his review of the cases of 105 applicants who had been turned down, he asserted that only 6 should have been turned down. The other 99 were denied, at least in part because the bride came from a community other than the groom's. The local councils wanted the young men to marry local girls. Instead of bringing another person into the community, they desired that they provide a home for a local girl.

Another judge reported the same abuse. He wrote of an applicant who was well qualified, but his intended bride lived in a different community, on the other side of the Main River in Hesse. The local council, in reporting its denial, said that its own community had many marriageable women, and if the applicant chose one of them, nothing would stand in his way. According to the judge, such meanness should not have legal support. He further stated that not being able to marry was driving many people overseas when, in fact, many of them could live very well in their own homeland. Shortly after these reports, in 1868, Munich finally overturned the marriage restriction laws.[281]

At the time of my great-grandparents, the marriage restrictions were in full force. Andreas was able to marry only after emigrating, at age 31. His bride, Lena, from Grosslaudenbach, was about 10 years younger. Had Andreas possibly cared for someone earlier, only to lose her to someone who was approved? Did he apply for permission, going through the whole procedure, only to be turned down? We will never know.

Ancestors on my mother's side, Johann Valentin Nikolaus and Anna Margaret Schmitt, emigrated from Humprechtshausen, a small village east of Würzburg. They lived under similar restrictions, marrying only after they came to Cincinnati. In this case, both bride and groom were in their early 30s.

The young men were migrating, as well as some young women. But most women did not take that large step even though they had bleak prospects for marriage. Without marriage, it was possible they would not even have a home. Overcrowding in the family home forced many of them out.

Young women and girls as young as 13, looked for live-in positions as servants or maids. Some went to nunneries. If a young woman was an older sister in a large family, she might be of service at home to help with the care of the household and the younger children, and be able to stay.[282] If the family could manage it, and if they had enough room and could stretch the food far enough, younger sisters could stay also.

Some families, however, felt they simply could not continue to feed and house their younger girls. In such cases, they often took them to the closest religious institution that would care for them. Between 1849 and 1854, families took seven such girls to St. Katharina's Church in Schöllkrippen. The pastor, Father Andreas Engert, enlarged one of the auxiliary buildings rimming the church courtyard to house the girls and in 1854 officially founded the *Rettungsanstalt (Rescue Institution)* for girls. He arranged for three nuns to take residence there and care for the girls, whose number quickly grew to 21. The girls attended school in town and, under the tutelage of the nuns, received training for future work such as servants or farm maids.

Poverty continued through the years, and the need for the institution lasted for over a century. When World War II came, the home cared for many boys and girls orphaned during the war. In 1945, there were 50 children there.

By 1967, much of the need for caring for orphaned or abandoned children was gone, and the institution changed its mission to caring for learning-disabled girls. In 1994, its name changed from *Rettungsanstalt* to *Haus Mirjam* (Miriam House).[283]

Today, more than 150 years after its founding, Haus Mirjam houses young unwed mothers and their children, providing care for the children and the young women, plus training and guidance to help the young women become independent.[284]

As the mid-19th century approached, why hadn't people already been leaving in droves? Population density and desperate poverty had long been increasing to untenable levels. Crippling restrictions on people's lives added to the misery.

As seen, there was a large exodus to Hungary in the late 18th and early 19th centuries when Hungary and Russia were looking for settlers. But migrating out was not always easy, whether the destination was another country or another community. Other communities were not likely to accept new residents—individual communities had the right to accept newcomers or not. Much of Germany was experiencing the same problems of overcrowding, poverty, and joblessness. Factories in large cities that could employ large numbers of people were still some time off.

Leaving for another country was daunting. Not knowing where to go or how to get there was a major impediment to migration. Often people left when advertising agents came through the towns lauding the benefits and opportunities of wherever they were advertising for and outlining the means and routes for getting there. It was in trickles at first, and then the momentum built up, especially when letters started coming back from the first adventurous souls.

It was probably a combination of recruitment, letters, and growing intolerable conditions that finally propelled the large waves of emigration. The largest waves were in the 1840s and the 1850s. This was true for Germany as a whole as well as for the Spessart Forest region. Emigration was overwhelmingly to the United States. It was during this time that my four paternal great-grandparents, along with many other emigrants from the Kahlgrund, left for Cincinnati, Ohio.

Simultaneously with this great out-migration, and symptomatic of the times, the simmering pot of frustration was boiling over. For years, the lack of freedoms and the restrictions on people's lives had been generating a smoldering unrest. For many, there was also the overwhelming pressure of poverty. Already, in 1832 and 1833, there had been outbursts and demonstrations. When years of particularly bad weather and ruined crops began in 1846, vexation and anxiety added more fuel to the flames.

The spark that erupted in the revolutions of 1848 actually began in France that February. (There had been revolutionary outbreaks in Italy in January, but not with the impact on the rest of Europe that the uprising in France had.) Street demonstrations of workers and artisans in Paris forced the abdication of King Louis Philippe of France and resulted in the self-proclamation of a democratic republic.

The revolutionary zeal quickly spread throughout Europe. Mass demonstrations and passions run amok were playing out everywhere. Tens of thousands of people were to die. In Berlin, in the state of Prussia, 900 people died in one day, 800 of whom were insurgents.[285]

Demands varied from state to state and within different social groups of a state, but they invariably included calls for more freedom and political rights. Some wanted a unification of German states as a democratic republic. Some wanted constitutional monarchies. The leaders of the demonstrations and speech-makings were usually and initially from the middle class, including university students. But workers and peasants joined them, albeit for different reasons. They resented the restrictions on their lives, the economic laws that made them forever subject to the established order, and the excessive taxation which kept them in perpetual poverty. Uniting all the participants, however, was resentment against the many officials and overlords who wielded their power randomly, often unjustly.

Although there were many bloody clashes between the revolutionaries on the one side and the state soldiers and militia on the other, the bottled-up anger among workers and peasants often erupted into mob violence. Their actions usually stemmed from some current pressing issue.

In Aschaffenburg, the first outbreaks began during *Faschingstagen* (carnival days before lent), March 5 to 7, 1848. Probably fueled by alcohol, a rage grew against the hated *Rechtsrat* (chief councilor), Wilhelm Konrad Bühler. He had recently ordered the arrest of several men of the militia for being absent from exercises, most probably during the carnival days. They felt Bühler's actions were unnecessarily harsh. But he especially drew the ire of the fishermen who lived in the outskirts of the city. His punctilious interpretation of old regulations led to a ban on fishing below the bridge that crossed the Main River, thus cutting into their livelihood. A large throng, mostly of fishermen, marched to the *Rathaus* (city hall), led by one of their number bearing a red flag, the recognized standard of people in revolt. They also carried an axe and a chopping block, shouting all the way that they were going to chop off Bühler's head. Terrified, Bühler hid in a wardrobe. The throng then marched to his residence and executed him in effigy.

The next day, the fishermen again stormed into the town center. This time, the crowd of protestors was even greater. They marched to the landing place for the steamboats that daily plied their trade between Frankfurt and Würzburg. In a rage, they intended to destroy the landing area and the steamships anchored there. They hated the vastly superior competition of the steamboat owners in providing fish to the town. But on sober reflection, cooler heads prevailed as a fear of the probable consequences kept them from carrying out their plans.

Pent-up passions, however, were unleashed. Farmers from the Damm district of Aschaffenburg now marched to the town hall, brandishing pitchforks and scythes, hell-bent on destroying the mortgage records held there. After the Napoleonic wars and after the region came into Bavaria, serfdom had ended, but peasants still carried heavy tax and fee burdens. Many had also gone into deep debt to become owners of the pieces of land they had previously farmed for an overlord. The burden was heavy, and it seemed they would never be free of it. Nevertheless, the bailiff ultimately managed to talk them into disbanding and going home.

Serious violence was averted, but the mayor of Aschaffenburg was badly shaken. He fired Bühler, the most hated official. Also, due to increasing pressure from the populace, the despised commandant of the militia and the similarly hated tax assessor had to leave town. These actions allowed an uneasy peace to settle upon the municipality.[286]

Any peace, even an uneasy one, was yet to settle in Spessart Forest. The forest inhabitants had long suffered under oppressive officials, heavy taxation, and severely restricted freedoms. In the Kahlgrund, the most searing issue was the increasing arrests of game poachers and the punishment of those caught pilfering wood. The population was starving. Crops had failed. The people felt they had no choice but to hunt wild game to supplement their diet or to steal wood which they could use to trade for food. More and more people were chancing it. Munich was sending in more and more soldiers to thwart it.

The first action in the Kahlgrund was on March 14, 1848, in Huckelheim, a short distance northwest of Grosskahl. Foresters had confiscated many of the axes belonging to farmers caught filching wood. A crowd of enraged inhabitants of the surrounding area stormed the *Forsthaus* (foresters' lodge), demanding return of the axes. Their efforts failed, and discontent continued to smolder. Other outbursts took place. Bavarian military forces came in to restore order and housed themselves throughout the region.

The soldiers' presence did not stop the poaching or the wood pilfering, which steadily increased. On Pentecost Sunday, June 10, 1848, inhabitants of Sailauf, south of Schöllkrippen, attacked a group of military there and freed an arrested poacher. A few days later, closer to Schöllkrippen, a mob attacked five soldiers and freed two more captured poachers.

Soldiers started going out in larger patrols, but that did not always help. Probably the worst incident in the Kahlgrund happened on June 29, 1848. A patrol of 14 soldiers caught a poacher, Johann Adam Wissel, outside of Schöllkrippen. They quickly shackled him and promptly started marching him to the district court in Alzenau, hoping to avoid trouble. But word got out immediately and local inhabitants came running. The soldiers tried to escape the crowd with their prisoner.

According to the report of Reitz, the forester who was leading the soldier patrol, the mob caught up with them in about 30 minutes. There were about 30 to 40 peasants in the group, with more arriving. They carried shotguns, pitchforks, axes, and hoes. With threats and curses, they demanded the release of the prisoner. The soldiers issued warnings, but the mob kept pressing in closer, with their weapons at the ready. During the commotion, the prisoner tried to wrest himself free. The soldiers let him succeed, hoping that would appease the crowd. But the soldiers still had the poacher's rifle, which the soldiers intended to hold onto. The crowd was intent on seizing it.

By now, the crowd had become even larger. One of the mob, a farmer named Hock, began waving his pitchfork in the face of one of the soldiers, in the process, thrusting the fork at the soldier's gun, accidentally discharging it. The shot hit Hock in the lower part of his left arm.

The participants scattered. The soldiers took off in fright. A few in the crowd stayed and got Hock to a Dr. Ulrich in Schöllkrippen. But the doctor was unable to prevent Hock's losing his arm.[287]

Luckily, there do not appear to have been any fatal injuries during the incidents in the Kahlgrund. Actually, other than as was the case in much of the rest of Europe, the revolution in Bavaria was mostly non-violent. Ludwig's stepping down helped. In face of the highly charged atmosphere, a few European rulers stepped down. King Ludwig I of Bavaria was one. He had become widely unpopular for his policies, but also and most fervently for his open affair with Lola Montez, a dancer of Irish origin. Obsessed with passion for her, he had made her a countess, fueling speculation that she was wielding undue political influence over him. To try to quell the escalating unrest in Bavaria and to save the monarchy, Ludwig abdicated his throne in favor of his son, Maximilian II, on March 20, 1848.

Reacting to the demands of the citizenry, Bavaria passed a series of reforms in June 1848. However, the political pendulum eventually began to swing the other way again. As fear of more uprisings lessened, there were retractions of many of the reforms, although a few survived. There were a few more assemblies and demonstrations in 1849, but the revolution had basically lost its effect.[288]

Andreas Wüst and his intended bride, Lena, emigrated in 1847, a year before the revolution broke out. Johann Fix was still there and would have been well aware of the events around him. He had stayed, trying to make a go of his inn, but was unable to do so. The people were just too poor to provide a profitable customer base. Johann and his family of five left for the New World in 1854.

Chapter 13

---•••⋮⋮⋮•••---

The Leaving

In the mid-19th century, a German pastor noted: "The name of America has now become as familiar to every peasant and laborer, yea to every child in the street, as that of the nearest neighboring country, whilst to thousands and hundreds of thousands, it is a goal of their warmest wishes and boldest hopes."[289]

With the path to America becoming better known and achievable, many saw a way out of their poverty and futureless existence.

Actually leaving, though, was a difficult and momentous decision, especially the parting from parents. Would they ever see them again? Many hoped to return for visits. But the expense and memory of the arduous trip, and the daily demands of making a living, resulted in a visit back home becoming an elusive dream. (Of my ancestors, Andreas Wüst had already lost his parents, his mother when he was 13 years old and his father in 1838, 9 years before he emigrated to America. Johann Fix's parents were both still living when he left.)

At the time of departure, however, the self-confidence of youth made all things seem possible. So it was with a sense of excitement as well as sadness or misgiving that most people left. After all, the letters arriving from America glowed with reports of opportunity and stories of success.

Whole families might leave together, along with neighbors. Young bachelors left in droves, alone, or in the company of others. Many of the bachelors had girlfriends they would later send for. These young women waited in high anticipation for the word to come to join their fiancés. For most, it was their only hope for a viable future.

❦ ❦

There were many things to attend to before departing. One could not just leave. Where my ancestors lived, the would-be emigrant had to apply to the authorities in the district court in Alzenau for permission to leave. A public notice was then placed in the Aschaffenburg newspaper, alerting possible creditors, to prevent a would-be emigrant from skipping out while owing money. A four-week waiting period followed.[290]

If it turned out that the applicant owed much more than he could reasonably repay, the authorities might still and often did grant permission to leave, in order to get rid of someone who would probably become a burden on the community. By the same token, the authorities might deny emigration permission to someone they deemed could adequately support a family. The goal was to get rid of the poor.[291] The authorities might also deny the petition for other reasons, such as the applicant being subject to military conscription.

If approved, the emigrant had to renounce his citizenship. In the event that he did not succeed in the new country, he would not be able to come back and become a burden to his old community or another community.

The would-be migrant also had to secure funds for the trip. A ticket for the trip over by sailing ship was about 80 gulden for an adult, and 10 to 60 gulden for a child, dependent on the age of the child.[292] One adult's ticket could have been about one third of a year's wages, working steadily. There was also the cost to get to the harbor city: food and lodging on the way to the harbor, food and lodging while waiting for the ship, and buying provisions for the voyage. Further, the emigrant had to pay exit fees to the community he was leaving.

Would-be emigrants saved what they could from their meager

earnings, and sold whatever property they had. Some had little plots of land they could sell. If they owned a room or some part of the family home, they could possibly sell it to a family member. They disposed of possessions such as tools, for cash. Relatives probably helped with funds if they could.

After the final granting of permission and the necessary funds were in hand and the emigrants were ready to depart, friends and family gathered for a farewell party. Music and song were always part of social gatherings, but the songs sung at these farewell parties were particularly poignant. They expressed disappointment and anger at the social and political conditions that forced people to leave, but also hope for a better life. One of the most popular farewell songs was "Jetzt ist die Zeit und Stunde da, wir fahren ins Amerika." (Now has the time and hour arrived, we travel to America.)[293]

The trip to the embarkation port was the first stage of the journey. The port of choice depended on different factors, such as the shipping lines and ports that local agents represented and the ease of means and cost to get there. From the Aschaffenburg area, two primary ports were Bremen, in northwestern Germany, and Le Havre, in northwestern France. After 1850, Bremen became the most popular embarkation point when people could take a train from Frankfurt to the Weser River, and then go by ship to the port at Bremerhaven, just outside of Bremen.[294] But Le Havre was a strong competitor in that, after 1838, France required travelers to have tickets already in hand before they entered the country. This requirement prevented an accumulation of crowds waiting weeks for their ship and the spending of precious funds on food and temporary lodging.[295]

Many emigrants went in groups. In 1840, an assemblage of 166 people out of the Kahlgrund, from in and around the village of Mömbris, formed such a group. It included 22 families and those traveling singly. It also included people who had not properly registered to leave, those leaving on the sly. The group journeyed to Bremen, probably at least part way by wagon or coach, before catching a river boat. They then waited in Bremen before embarking on the sailing ship *Clementine,* headed for Baltimore. The passenger list shows most of them declaring Cincinnati, Ohio, as their final destination. The trip lasted 12 weeks.[296]

Many people left without official permission papers to do so. Some were escaping the law. Previously, there was reference to an 1842 incident in Edelbach in which several young men were roughhousing. One of the men threw a stone at another and accidentally killed him. He paid one of his comrades to take the blame, giving him time to flee to America. After arriving in America, he sent a letter back declaring that he was the one to blame.[297] Not having much time to prepare for the trip, family members may have helped him with the necessary funds, or he may have found odd jobs along the way to the port to pay his way.

Other reasons for leaving without permission included avoiding the stiff exit taxes, skipping out on debts, and avoiding military conscription. It could be someone who did not want to renounce their citizenship, in the event things did not work out in the new country. They did not want to close off an avenue of return. It could also be someone who had applied for permission to leave and had been refused.

Fugitives skirted the main routes as much as possible. There were many checkpoints where a person had to show an emigration permit, especially along the Rhine River, a popular route to several harbors, and there was the probability of imprisonment if caught.[298] Often on foot and hitching rides on wagons, it could take an illegal several weeks to reach a port. It was probably mostly unattached men who took the chance of leaving illegally. It would have been difficult for a family to travel in this fashion, putting the whole family at risk.

Authorities sent arrest warrants and lists of known fugitives to the different ports of departure, but would-be emigrants brought money to these cities, and thus, once they made it to the port city, there was not much diligence in apprehending fugitives.[299]

❧ ❧

The waiting period in a port could be weeks. The emigrants might have tickets in hand, either bought before leaving or purchased at the harbor, but they seldom had a firm date when their ship would leave. They had to await an announcement of their ship's departure. The call for boarding would be just shortly before the ship left, in order to avoid a congestion of passengers assembling on the wharf. People had to be packed and ready to go on short notice.

Meanwhile, people readied themselves for the crossing. They procured the food and cooking utensils they would need on board and exchanged their currency. Unfortunately, there were many swindlers in these ports ready to prey on the innocent arrivals, cheating them in any way they could, charging them too much for goods or too high a rate of exchange. In 1850, the city of Bremen, worried about its reputation as an emigration port and loss of income if it fell out of favor, established an official advice office. It provided information to the travelers and ensured fair prices. It also constructed a vast building to accommodate the crowds of people awaiting their ships.[300]

Passengers prepared for 10 to 12 weeks at sea. Although the average trip was 7 to 9 weeks, it could last several weeks longer, depending on wind and weather. Steamships began traversing the seas after 1839, with a significantly shorter passage of 17 days.[301] However, steamships were much more expensive, and emigrants continued to go mostly by sailing ship until toward the end of the century.[302] Provisions people brought aboard usually consisted of such food items as potatoes, sausage and ham, hard tack, lemons to prevent scurvy, eggs, dried fruit, and coffee and beer. A few ships provided food, but it was not until after 1855 that more than a few ships did so. Even then, the food aboard was meager and advice to people was to bring food with them.[303]

After weeks of waiting, the word would come at last. Their ship was boarding. Full of tense excitement, the emigrants sailing on that ship gathered up their belongings and headed for the wharf. Among the jostling crowd, holding tightly onto their belongings and the hands of small children, the passengers finally made it on board. The crew quickly directed them to steerage (between-decks), keeping the crowd moving.

When the mass emigrations began, shipping lines had hastily begun converting their cargo ships for the transport of passengers. They constructed a deck between the cargo hold and the upper deck, and installed berths. Since, for the return journey, they would be disassembling the berths to store cargo, the berths were temporary. They knocked planks together, making many berths in too small a space. The berths were narrow and usually too short. The passengers provided their own mattresses and bedding.

There was little ventilation, often the only air being that coming through the open hatches. In good weather, the travelers could go up on the upper deck. Otherwise, they were crowded into the poorly-lit between-decks, with little privacy. If there was a storm, the hatches were closed, making it even more stifling. The few toilets were mostly buckets.

In such conditions, there were many illnesses. There were no doctors on board. Sufferers were dependent on each other and on the captain's medical knowledge. Deaths and burials at sea were not uncommon, especially for small children.

If the weather permitted, people cooked their meals on the upper deck. But there were usually only a few galley fires, which sometimes led to quarrels among the passengers. Many simply could not get access to a cooking fire and ended up for days without a hot meal.[304]

Most passengers got seasick, at least during the first part of the voyage. There were many theories on how to combat the problem, and much advice made the rounds. "Hold a peeled raw potato tightly in your hand." "Drink hot coffee with rum and eat some dry bread."[305] Vermin infestation was high. No matter how fastidious a family was, they soon found themselves plagued by lice, fleas, and bedbugs. The relief at finally reaching port must have been immense.

A sailing ship at that time might have carried less than a hundred immigrants to several hundred. On the ship *Clementine*, which carried the 166 passengers from the Mömbris area in 1840, the total number of passengers was 238.[306] The actual number was probably higher, in that ship tallies often counted children as half.

Johann Fix and his wife and three young boys, one an infant, left in 1854, taking the sailing ship *Juventa* from Le Havre.[307] Andreas Wüst had left in 1847. Within the same year, he sent for his intended bride, Lena. It is not known from which port they left, but at least two of Andreas's brothers left from Bremen, Johann Adam in 1846, and Johann (no known middle name) in 1855.

The Juventa, *which carried Johann K. Fix and his family from Le Havre, France, to New York in 1854.*

During the 1820s, an average of fewer than 600 Germans emigrated to America per year. During the 1830s, the number was over 12,000 per year, and continuing to grow. In the early 1840s, the number was 20,000 per year, and it steadily increased until by the end of the decade it was almost 60,000 per year. During the early 1850s, it grew to an average of more than 130,000 per year. The 1840s and the early 1850s were the years of greatest migration. The numbers never again grew to the level they were between 1840 and 1855. The highest rate of emigration was from southwestern Germany where the practices of equal division of property inheritance was most prevalent and stringent measures against marriage were also the highest.[308]

The Wüst home in Grosskahl, 1943–1944. The women in front are from the Jordan family, which eventually owned the house. The man in the group is a French prisoner of war.

Just as rates of emigration varied within the German states, they also varied within different regions. This was true within the Kahlgrund area of Spessart Forest. The populations in some areas of the Kahlgrund hardly changed. But in Oberen Kahlgrund (Upper Kahlgrund), the area where my ancestors lived, which was more remote and less developed, the population was reduced by more than half between 1828 and 1900.[309]

After a presence of 200 years, the Wüst name completely vanished from Grosskahl. All Wüst males left or died. By 1854, the Wüst home (#30a Grosskahl) was in the name of Jordan, and the other side of the duplex (#30 Grosskahl) was in the name of Wagner. Wagner's wife was Margaretha, who could possibly have been Andreas's sister Margaretha.

Wüsts disappeared from Grosskahl, but not all Wüsts disappeared from the forest. During the 200 years after Peter Wüst's migration into Spessart Forest, some of his offspring had migrated to other parts of the forest. It is also possible that Peter had originally come to the Spessart with other family members such as brothers or cousins who settled elsewhere in the forest and had their own children.

In the 1980s, the Wüst name reappeared in Grosskahl, when Alfred Wüst and his wife Theresa (Resel), who was originally from Grosskahl, moved there from another village in the forest. Alfred and Resel, and their son Andreas and his family, have taken firm root in Grosskahl.[310]

In the 1830s, when emigration from Germany to America was increasing, America was not yet a common destination for people of the Kahlgrund area. Recruitment in Kahlgrund at that time included advertising for another part of the world—Greece. Not many answered that call, but one who did was my lateral ancestor Johann Adam Fix, who emigrated to Greece in 1834.

Chapter 14

————————••••┄┄┄••••————————

The Fix Who Went to Greece

Johann Adam Fix, a widower in Edelbach,[311] was a miner. He was 37 years old and in love with Margaretha Naumann, age 24. Margaretha lived in Huckelheim, a village about two miles (three km) west of Edelbach. Fix probably worked in the copper mine "Der Segen Gottes," which was near Huckelheim. He and Margaretha had a small boy, Johann Georg, three years old.[312]

They were not married. Most likely, the couple did not obtain permission to marry. The mining industry was declining, and work as a miner was unsteady. Although Fix did have some farmland, its size was probably insufficient to convince community leaders he could adequately support a family.

Johann Adam Fix was a third cousin, once-removed, of my great-grandfather, Johann K. Fix. (Once-removed implies one generation of difference in descent from their common ancestor.) Johann Adam was a great-great-grandson of Johann (Hans) Fix, through Hans's son Johann Phillipp. Johann K. was a great-great-great-grandson of Hans through his son Johann Michael. Hans was born in 1670 in Heinrichsthal, a village about three miles (five km) south of Edelbach. [313]

Johann Adam and Margaretha were not happy with their situation. They desperately wanted to marry and establish a home together.

Then a daring proposal presented itself. The new king of Greece was seeking settlers from Bavaria to populate the colonial settlement of Heraklion (named after Heracles, the Greek name for Hercules) that the king had founded just north of Athens. Athens had previously been a leading city of Ancient Greece, but at this time was a small town of about 4,000 inhabitants nestled at the foot of the ruins of the Acropolis.[314]

Johann Adam Fix was the first person from the upper Kahlgrund to answer the call, making the daunting move to Greece in 1834. He went alone to establish himself more quickly, after which he would return for Margaretha.[315]

What was to become modern Greece had recently won its independence from the Ottoman Empire. The insurrection began in 1821 and ended with the Battle of Petra in 1829. The Greeks had been under the oppressive rule of the Ottomans for almost 400 years, ever since the Greek Byzantine Empire had fallen to the Ottomans in 1453.

The new nation was half the size it is today. Initially formed by the lands liberated during the revolution, Greece would gradually annex additional areas in which the majority of inhabitants were of Greek ethnicity. The annexations were often the result of territorial reshufflings after major wars; they sometimes resulted from peaceful ceding of land by other countries.

The newly independent country was still unstable, with infighting among various factions of native inhabitants. To prevail against Turkish rule, Greeks had relied on Great Britain, France, and Russia. After the battle for freedom, the Greeks remained economically and militarily weak and continued under the "protection" of their three sponsors, who pursued their own interests, often at the disadvantage of the new republic. With the assassination of the first governor, Ioannis Kapodistria, in 1831, the three protector powers decided to convert the region to a monarchy with a ruler to be supplied from an established European bloodline, and who could impose order and control on the contending factions. Their choice (after a few other European royals had declined) fell upon Prince Frederick Otto, second son of King Ludwig I of Bavaria.[316]

Otto I of Greece (actually his regents, for the new king was only 17) brought with him, besides 3,500 Bavarian soldiers, an entourage of architects and craftsmen for a grand and ambitious building program in Athens, where he established his royal seat. He also brought other professionals such as civil servants, teachers, and doctors. But the colonists he recruited to populate Heraklion were few. As of June 1838, there were only 30 settlers in the village. Of that number, seven had wives, and there were five children.[317]

❦ ❦

My great-grandfather Johann K. Fix was about 12 years old when his distant cousin, Johann Adam Fix, left for Greece. Johann K. would have felt the excitement that must have been emanating throughout the small village. Who could imagine going to that far, ancient land?

The recent revolution of an oppressed people, in the land of origin of much of the West's classical heritage, had stirred many romantic notions. The Greeks' struggle for independence had inflamed the people of the western world. One in particular was Lord George Byron, whose poetry spread visionary ideals of the insurrection. He and others even took up arms to join the revolutionists. (Byron was to die of fever in Greece before seeing action. He was 36.) Otto's father, the king of Bavaria, Ludwig I, was himself a fervent Grecophile. On October 20, 1825, in the midst of the revolution, Ludwig officially and permanently changed the spelling of his kingdom from Baiern to Bayern, using the Greek "*y*" to replace the Roman "*i*," the two letters having equivalent sound.[318]

195

A skilled miner, Johann Adam Fix found immediate employment in Kymi, a coastal town on the island of Euboea, north of Athens. With other miners from Bavaria, he worked there on the restoration of a coal mine. Five years later, at the end of 1839, he felt financially secure enough to go back and marry Margaretha. Margaretha greeted a man much more muscled than the one who had left, for the coal mine Fix worked in was primitive, lacking the labor-saving hoisting equipment then available.

Since Fix was now domiciled out of the country, and had most likely given up his Bavarian citizenship, there was no impediment to his marriage. At the beginning of 1840, shortly after the wedding ceremony, the groom returned to Greece with his new bride. They left their son, now eight years old, in the care of Margaretha's parents, Michel and Katharina Naumann, so he could receive his education in Germany. To compensate the Naumanns for the boy's room and board, Fix transferred over to them his fields and meadows, from which they could derive additional income. In exchange for the land, Margaretha's parents also agreed to pay the boy 200 gulden when he reached 20 years of age. This was roughly equivalent to a little less than a year's wages.

While Johann Adam and Margaretha were building their new life in Greece, economic conditions back in their old homeland were going steadily from bad to worse. In 1848, the year Johann Georg turned 17, Michel Naumann, a miller, was forced to sell his mill. When Johann Adam Fix heard about Naumann's financial difficulties, he tried to get Naumann to pay the 200 gulden to his son that were to be due when the son turned 20. This would enable his son to come to Greece, where the father could see to his future. But Naumann died and his estate was auctioned. The miller's outstanding debts ate up his remaining property, leaving nothing to pay for Fix's passage abroad.

In desperation, the father turned to both the king's ministry in Athens and the foreign affairs office in Munich. King Otto graciously allowed Johann Georg Fix to make the trip on the royal ship, the British frigate HMS *Madagascar*, which was at the Greek king's disposal. The son had to reach one of the ship's ports of call, probably a port in Italy. Apparently enough money was scraped together for that portion of the trip.

But the son's travel pass was for a visit, not to emigrate to Greece. Perhaps he had been unable to get permission to emigrate, or he might have desired to remain in Germany. It appears Johann Georg Fix had learned the beer-making business, very possibly at the suggestion of his father, and probably as an apprentice at one of the breweries in the Aschaffenburg area. The son might have felt he had a future in Germany.

In any event, and finally, the preparation and paper work were in order, and Johann Georg Fix, now 19 years old, was on his way to Greece, arriving in Piraeus, the Athens port, on May 27, 1851. His happy father, with wagon and donkey team, was there to greet him. Joyously, the two began the ride back to Heraklion, where the young man's parents and siblings were now living.

Sadly, the father and son's reunion, after so many years apart, was to come to an abrupt end. As they neared Heraklion Village, robbers suddenly accosted them and blocked their way. They shot and killed the father and took all the pair's possessions. No doubt they had noted the young man in western dress and his traveling bags.

Just before the attack, Johann Adam Fix had indicated the way to Heraklion, where his son, in a state of acute anxiety, fled. He found shelter there with the Amrhein family, the one other family from the Kahlgrund area of Spessart Forest, and whose farmhouse was among the first he came to upon entering the village. The village inhabitants came to where Johann Adam still lay and bore his body to Heraklion. The priest of St. Luke (Heiliger Lukas), the settlement's church, gave the service and the mourners laid him to rest in the cemetery next to the church. He was 54 years old. His wife Margaretha lived another 4 years, dying in 1855, at about 45 years of age.

After the shock of loss and after having reunited with his mother and siblings (his parents had had five more children), Johann Georg would have, in the course of events, returned to Germany. He only had a visitor's pass, and legally could not stay in Greece. But Johann Georg Fix looked around him. He saw many Bavarian soldiers and immigrants—many *thirsty* Bavarian soldiers and immigrants. He was determined to stay.[319]

Although there was already beer brewing in Greece, it had not developed to any significant extent. The soil and climate were better suited to the growing of grapes for wine than cultivating grains. Many colonists brewed beer for themselves and also sold it. But the Bavarians missed their good Bavarian beer.

Staying in Greece, though, was not easy. Johann Georg Fix had lost all his goods during the robbery, including his identification papers, papers that showed his legitimacy. He had been born out of wedlock, but his parents had subsequently married, making him legitimate.[320] This fact was crucial, for at that time there were many restrictions against people of illegitimate status, which affected almost all aspects of their lives, such as inheritance, access to employment, obtaining permission to marry. Further, it complicated getting permission to emigrate from his hometown in the Kahlgrund and gaining acceptance into another Bavarian community, this one in the Kingdom of Greece.

Fix's emigration petition spawned several years of correspondence among the many authorities in Athens, in the region

Johann George Fix, founder of the Fix Beer dynasty in Athens, Greece, and his wife, Eva-Marie Amrhein.

of Unterfranken and in Aschaffenburg, and those in Alzenau—the district court for Fix's hometown in the Kahlgrund. Eventually, the protracted conflict and varied interpretation of regulations between the bureaucrats came to an end. Johann Georg Fix was recognized and registered as a subject of the Athens community on June 9, 1855.

Not waiting for the administrative process to run its course, Fix had married three years earlier, on September 16, 1852. He married Eva-Maria Amrhein, one of the daughters in the Amrheim family that had taken him in after the murderous attack.

Fortuitously, another German colonist, Joseph Peter Scheffler, forged a binding agreement with the couple in which he signed over to them his house and land in return for an annual payment and the right to continue living there. Fix immediately started a small brewery in the house and courtyard, causing Scheffler to bring a lawsuit for breach of the original agreement, which had said nothing about using the property for a commercial enterprise. Scheffler lost the case, and Fix continued with his business on the premises.

"Fix Beer" found an eager market. Not only did the soldiers and colonists become steady customers, but the Greeks tried it and loved it as well. Unlike other home-brewed beer in the town, Fix's consistently had the best taste. Fix brewed his beer according to the Bavarian Purity Law for beer, the only ingredients, besides water, being barley, hops, malt, and yeast. He imported most of the ingredients from Bavaria. Fix was on his way to becoming the beer czar of Greece.

He eventually built a small brewery in Kolonaki, an undeveloped neighborhood on the edge of Athens, (now one of the most opulent parts of Athens), erecting a beer hall next to it, complete with a beer garden and bowling alley. The hall became immensely popular. There was much singing, animated conversation, and drinking, just like in beer halls back home. It became the center of Bavarian social life in Athens. A senior government official from Bavaria, who visited the beer hall after its opening, declared, "Athens has become a suburb of Munich."[321]

There was danger of a setback in 1862 when Otto I was deposed and had to leave the country. His rule had become unpopular and there was open rebellion. Throughout his reign, Otto had faced political challenges stemming from Greece's financial weakness and continued dependence on Great Britain, France, and Russia. The countries granted loans at high interest, contributing to high taxes imposed on the Greek population. The three countries, particularly Great Britain, used their purse strings and military might to bend Greece to their will, interfering with the country's politics, always in furtherance of their own interests. They were impervious to the impact on Greece or the impact on Otto's standing with the Greeks.

Three times between 1841 and 1853, the British Royal Navy blockaded Piraeus, the port of Athens. Great Britain generally interfered whenever Otto and the Greek nation contemplated taking any action that would be detrimental to the Ottoman Empire. Britain depended on the Ottomans to keep Russia landlocked in the east. Even after they had helped the Greeks to win their independence from the Ottomans, England had sought to keep the Ottomans pacified by insisting that Greece take out a loan from England to compensate Turkey for losses incurred during the war.

On King Otto's part, although he loved Greece and considered it his home even after his deposition, he was often insensitive to the results of his actions. When he married, for example, he married in Germany instead of in Greece, dismaying his Greek subjects. He reigned as an absolutist ruler, almost completely barring Greeks from any inclusion in their governance. In 1844, a popular rising had forced Otto to accept a constitution limiting his powers.[322]

The Greek National Assembly, still favoring a monarchy rather than a return to a republican form of government, chose a Danish prince as king. George I of Greece ruled for 50 years, carefully avoiding his predecessor's missteps.

Under Otto's rule, farmer-settlers were given a certain amount of land, clothing, farm tools, seeds, and some cash, which engendered resentment and envy on the part of the native Greeks in the area, resulting in an attack on Heraklion when a chance finally presented itself.[323]

When Otto left, and most of his Bavarian subjects—soldiers, servants, civil service workers—went with him, local Greeks, anger unleashed, beset Heraklion Village, plundering and setting fires to all the homes, including that of the Johann Georg Fix family, which now included three children. Although his brewing enterprise was in the Athens section of Kolonaki, Fix and his family had continued to live in the walled village of Heraklion. The ravagers were able to gain entry through a gate that was either undergoing repair or had been left unlocked.

The Fix family salvaged what belongings they could and moved to Kolonaki, a safer area, in a district where native Greek citizens also lived. Fix bought two more parcels of land there. He built the new family home on one parcel, and by 1864, completed two new breweries on the second parcel. He ran one brewery himself. The other he transferred to his oldest son, Ludwig. Presumably, this was when Ludwig came of age. Ludwig, born in 1853, was only 11 years old in 1864 when the brewery was completed. Later, Johann Georg Fix transferred his own brewery, the one he had been running, to his son Karolos, born in 1865, after Karolos had completed his management studies.[324]

There was another son, Gulielmos, born in 1860, between Ludwig and Karolos. He died young, 31 years old.[325] I found no indication that Gulielmos participated in the brewery business. He may have been sickly or otherwise not suited to the business. Or his participation in the beer business may not have made the annals or family memory.

Karolos, the youngest son, was an especially effective businessman. He led his brewery with skill and a strong hand. He modernized the cooling system so that it now cooled the entire cellar, permitting increased storage capacity of the beer and thus more output. He acquired competing breweries north and west of Athens.

The father, Johann Georg, also continued to expand his enterprises. In 1880, he bought a large parcel of land in another part of Athens, which Syngrou Avenue runs through today. On this land, he built a large brewery and two houses. Together, the Fix family held the beer monopoly in Greece.

But not all was well within the family. According to stories handed down by Ludwig's descendants, Johann Georg favored Ludwig, either from traditional favoring of the oldest son, or because of a personal bonding.

On February 22, 1880, Johann Georg and Eva-Maria transferred to Ludwig a grand home they had built, Ludwig having married the year before. (Villa Fix, called the *Stone House* by the local populace, still stands, just south of St. Luke Church.) Ludwig and his parents signed a bestowal agreement. But we'll never know for sure what they verbally agreed to. At least two of the signees, Johann Georg and Ludwig, signed something other than what they believed they were signing.

The document was in Greek, which father and son, and perhaps Eva-Maria, could not read, especially the ornate Greek script in which the document was written. Later, as events unfolded, many in the family came to suspect Eva-Maria of having manipulated the document and knowing its actual contents. According to family tradition, Eva-Maria favored the youngest son and by extension, might have resented Ludwig.

Ludwig, in exchange for the villa, had unknowingly renounced all rights to any inheritance from his father. Ludwig already possessed the brewery in Kolonaki, which his father had earlier transferred to him. But the villa and the brewery were of much less value than the total of the father's extensive assets at the time of signing—estates, breweries, vast landholdings, and a large vineyard.

It is not known how much the younger brother, Karolos, previously knew of the contents of the agreement, but according to Ludwig's grandson Rodolfos Fix, strife between the two brothers was no secret.

Johann Georg Fix, founder of the Fix beer dynasty, died 15 years later, on October 26, 1895, at 64 years. Within a short time after his burial, the family, including the unsuspecting Ludwig, attended the reading of the will. It is not clear what the widow Eva-Maria and the two daughters received. The two surviving sons, Ludwig and Karolos, would receive extensive property, including the large parcel of land on Syngrou Avenue containing Johann Georg's major brewery and two houses.

But now, the agreement between Ludwig and his parents, signed 15 years previously, came into play. As the document whereby Ludwig renounced all rights to any inheritance from his father was read, Ludwig gradually began to realize what evil play had been wrought on him. Stunned into shock, he tried to jump out of a window, but others stopped him.[326]

Ludwig left the brewery business in 1906, turning to agriculture and wine-grape-growing. He died in Athens in 1929 at 76 years. He and his wife, Johanna nee Wagner, had seven children: three sons and four daughters.

In 1890, 25-year old Karolos had married 14-year-old Iakinthi Skassi, from the island of Syros. Renowned for her beauty, she became known as the "Rose of Athens."[327]

Staying within one's faith was still generally a prerequisite for marriage. Even in 1890, finding a suitable partner in Greece for a Roman Catholic was difficult, as Catholics were in a definite minority. When the settlement of Heraklion was first founded, the shortage of Catholic women was an acute problem, as most of the immigrants, including Otto's soldiers who elected to stay in Greece after they mustered out, were Bavarian Catholic bachelors. Although the Catholic priests in Greece might have been tolerant of mixed marriages out of necessity, the priests of the Greek Orthodox Church were not. Then one Catholic priest had an idea.

Syros, about 73 miles (117 km) southeast of Athens, was a Roman Catholic enclave. Catholic men in Athens could have willing marriageable girls shipped over.

After the overthrow in 1204 of Constantinople and the Byzantines during the Fourth Crusade, in which the Venetians participated, Syros came under the rule of Venice, a Catholic state. The Greeks on the island became Catholic. Later, under the Ottomans, they had religious freedom, with most of the inhabitants remaining Catholic. During the Greek Revolution of the 1820s, Syros was a shelter for Greek refugees, and at the end of the revolution, it was part of the new modern state of Greece. The island became a long-standing source of brides for the Catholic men of Heraklion.[328]

Karolos and Iakinthi Fix had two sons and five daughters. Karolos died in 1922, having just turned 57. He died while at a health spa in the Austrian town of Baden, near Vienna. His family had his body transported back to Athens, where he is buried.

Eva-Maria, the family matriarch, outlived her husband, Johann Georg, by six years, dying in 1901, at age 73.

After the death of Karolos Fix, his two sons, Johann and Anton, now 29 and 24, took over the family enterprise. Together, they continued to expand, building several new factories, with additional products including wine and soft drinks. The number of workers grew to 500 and production of beer grew to 26,000 gallons (1000 hectoliters) per day. It was one of the most important industries in Greece.

Not only did the popularity of Fix beer extend into other Mediterranean countries, it was prized throughout numerous parts of Europe, winning medals from Brussels to Rome.

Unable to produce enough to meet demand, the Fix firm began renovating, greatly enlarging, and modernizing the brewery on Syngrou Avenue in Athens, basically constructing a new building, designed by the famous Athens architect Takis Zenetos. Construction took place between 1957 and 1963. The beautiful building became a city landmark. But the outlay of funds had been great.

In 1962, before completion of the building, Karolos Fix, grandson of the first Karolos, took over the firm, at a point when it was seriously overextended. The new brewery opened in 1965, and failed almost immediately. Although it probably would have eventually recouped its construction costs, the firm met a new and overwhelming challenge. Foreign breweries had been making inroads into Greece: Amstel out of Holland, Heineken out of Switzerland, Henninger out of Germany, and Carlsberg from Denmark. With extensive use of advertising campaigns and price wars, they gathered forces to push the Fix Brewery out of its great monopoly of the Greek beer business. Depleted of reserves and unable to meet the new competition, the Fix brewing industry finally folded. Henninger and Carlsberg, the smaller of the new companies, also fell by the wayside during the campaigns. In 1968, the Fix enterprise was abandoned.

There was a revival in 1972 when Heineken took over the firm, with Karolos Fix maintaining a share of the business.[329] The owners took a close look at the two land parcels with the largest factories of the Fix Enterprise, the one on Syngrou Avenue and the other on Patission Street. Both parcels, being near the center of Athens, were increasing tremendously in value. The Patission Street property consisted of 2.6 acres (1.0 hectare) and the Syngrou Avenue property was almost as large. To attain better financial footing, the firm decided, in 1976, to transfer the brewing of Fix beer to the outskirts of the city, and to restructure and rebuild the buildings on the downtown properties for more appropriate use, capitalizing on their locational value.

On the Syngrou Avenue parcel, they planned to build an office and shopping complex. A group of investors was ready and willing to invest funds in developing the property. In 1979, the firm obtained the building permit and in 1980 contracted with a construction company.[330]

But the timing was bad. Socialist sentiments in Greece were rapidly gaining momentum. In 1981, a leading socialist party, the Panhellenic Socialist Movement (PASOK), finally won a majority in parliament. Andreas Papandreou, the party founder, became the prime minister of Greece. In the anti-capitalist atmosphere, resentment against major privately owned industries came to the forefront. The vulnerable ones were those industries with large debts. This included the Fix brewery. And the mayor of Athens coveted its land.

In 1980, before Fix Brewery could begin its building program on the Syngrou Avenue property, the Municipal Council of Athens, without obtaining the required approval of the relevant authorities, had designated the firm's two downtown properties for public parks and a youth center. The brewery and its waiting investors immediately protested. They wrote to the appropriate ministers in an attempt to get the property seizure overturned, but were unsuccessful. Fix Brewery offered to hand over to the city, free of charge, part of the land and part of the planned building space for city use, but to no avail.

The beer company then filed a lawsuit against Greece, the city of Athens, and the mayor personally, who had already started planting trees and installing park benches on the brewery's land. The company lost its case, and on November 8, 1982, the Minister for Economic Affairs ordered liquidation of the firm. Because of their high debt and the freeze imposed on use of their Athens properties, the Fix Brewery shareholders decided on August 30, 1983, to shut down the entire company.

Karolos Fix subsequently got out of the beer business, moving with his family to Switzerland, where he opened an investment firm.

Remaining shareholders in the Fix enterprise continued fighting to regain the company. Years of appeals and legal struggles followed, culminating in an appeal to the European Court of Human Rights in Strasbourg in 1994. This too ended in defeat. The Greek government expropriated the buildings and land. All remaining assets, movable and immovable, went to the National Bank of Greece, the major holder of the company's debt. One of the largest assets of the company, the "Fix Beer" trade name, also went to the bank.[331]

In 1994, the year Athens finally acquired the large Fix Brewery building on Syngrou Avenue, the city demolished part of the building for a subway station and underground parking. The rest of the building, too, was slated for demolition. But the citizens and preservationists of the city raised a large protest against further destruction of the beautiful building. Yielding to the protests, the city retained the remaining 295 feet (90 meters), linear measurement, of the structure to house two national museums, one for architecture and one for modern art.[332]

There was a similar protest to keep the Fix structure on Patission Avenue, an early 20th century building, from demolition, but that effort failed. The city demolished the building in 2002, and the mayor got his park.

There are many visual and tangible reminders of the Fix enterprise throughout Athens. Fix Quarter is a district of Athens. There is a Fix Street, and Syngrou-Fix is a streetcar stop. Several old buildings of the firm, which survived dismantling and now serve other uses, still have the name *Fix* visible on their exteriors. There have been ongoing efforts to preserve some of the old Fix brewery buildings as memorials.

A museum in Bavaria houses many artifacts from the golden days of Fix Brewery. The Otto König von Griechenland Museum (King Otto of Greece Museum), located southeast of Munich in Ottobrunn, displays many items containing the Fix name, including beer steins, jugs, bottles, coasters, and labels.[333]

❦ ❦

For all of its recent turbulent history, Fix beer is still very much alive. Its resurgence has its own history. Because of the legacy of the Fix name, many companies have tried to obtain use of the company's trademark, beginning shortly after it went bankrupt. Some firms tried to use the brand name surreptitiously. Others acquired the trademark legitimately from the National Bank of Greece, but failed to make a sustained go of brewing Fix beer. In 1995, the D. Kourtakis wineries bought the Fix trademark for a large sum from the National Bank of Greece. Kourtakis formed Olympic Brewery in Greece, but it was not financially successful.[334]

Meanwhile, as efforts were underway to resurrect Fix beer in Greece, an importer in the United States came into the picture. During the time of the Fix brewery's financial difficulties in the 1970s and 1980s, Importers Wine and Spirits, owned by Aris A. Zissis and headquartered in Washington, D.C., had been importing Fix beer from the Greek brewery for distribution in the United States. But the imports dried up in August 1983, when the Greek government shut down the brewery.[335]

Zissis, who immigrated to the United States from Greece in 1955, grew up knowing about Fix beer and its popularity in the land of his birth. In the 1990s, Zissis set events into motion to again sell Fix beer in the U.S. In June 1994, he filed an application with the United States Patent and Trademark Office to register the Fix trademark for beer.[336] Zissis acquired the exclusive right to sell and brew Fix beer in the United States. In 1995, he was again distributing the beer, and as of 2005, brewing the beer in the United States, now under the name "Fix 1864 Special." Brewing and bottling is by Fix U.S.A., Wilkes-Barre, Pennsylvania.[337]

And now Fix beer appears to also be making a flourishing

rebound in Greece. In 2009, the Athens firm Hitos AVEE bought the floundering Olympic Brewery and, in 2010, brought Fix beer once more to the Greek market.[338] This time, an aggressive advertising campaign, emphasizing the strong historic legacy of Fix beer in Greek society, has led to a robust comeback. The company touts it as an original Greek beer owned by Greeks. (There is less emphasis on its originally being brewed by a German immigrant.) The beer's popularity in the Mediterranean countries, as well as in many European cities, has helped significantly with its resurgence.

Chapter 15

---·•·:•:·•·---

Life in Cincinnati

There was no Fix beer in Cincinnati, where many immigrants from the Kahlgrund made their home, but there was plenty of beer—in Over-the-Rhine, that is. The German enclave bordered the north side of the Miami and Erie Canal, which ran through Cincinnati. Residents soon dubbed the canal "The Rhine" and the area of German settlement became known as Over-the-Rhine. The Germans themselves called it Über'm Rhein. Today, the district is in the National Register of Historic Places.

Until 1849, the incorporated part of Cincinnati only went as far as the street called Northern Row, which ran east and west, bisecting Over-the-Rhine. On the north side of the street was the section of Over-the-Rhine known as The Northern Liberties, which was not subject to municipal law. It soon became a haven for bootleggers, saloons, gambling houses, dance halls, brothels—and breweries. Northern Row was later renamed Liberty Street, the name not deriving from patriotic sentiment.

In the 19th century, Over-the-Rhine was one of the most densely populated places in America. It was hemmed in on all sides by hills or other portions of Cincinnati, the city itself bounded by rivers and hills. An average of nine people lived in each dwelling unit, the size of the units generally quite small. Many of the tenement buildings had no yard, only a small courtyard for the communal outhouse. Amid the residential buildings, in addition to the brewing and bottling plants and saloons, were slaughterhouses, lumberyards, and carpentry shops. There were tanneries, foundries, and stables. Merchants and residents alike dumped trash into gutters and water courses. The city's canal itself became a giant open sewer choked with rubbish.[339]

One can imagine the stench and noise and smoky air. The poor sanitation system, with insufficient access to fresh water, no doubt contributed to the high consumption of beer. There were epidemics of cholera, smallpox, and typhoid fever. Andrew's youngest son, my grandfather Joseph, born in 1864, suffered smallpox as a child.

At the time of my great-grandparents' arrival to the district in the mid-19th century, about two-thirds of Over-the-Rhine's population consisted of immigrants from German lands, growing to an estimated 75 percent of the population by the end of the 19th century. The newcomers came from states throughout Germany, including Prussia, Saxony, and Bavaria. As a result, among the German-descent population, there was a variety of customs, dialects, and religions.[340]

Predictably, the predominant language in the area's schools, churches, and newspapers was German. As late as 1917, half of Cincinnati's population could speak German, many only that language.[341] By this time, a large percentage of Over-the-Rhine's population had moved out of the area into other parts of the city, contributing to the spread of the German language in Cincinnati as a whole. Two of the community's churches, St. Mary Catholic Church and Concordia Lutheran Church, still conduct services in German.[342]

The old German neighborhood has retained its Over-the-Rhine moniker, but the "Rhine River" disappeared, as transportation by canal became obsolete. The city abandoned the Miami and Erie Canal by the late-19th century, drained it in 1920, and began construction of a subway system in the canal bed, although that system never materialized. Central Parkway now runs over the top of the completed and partly-completed tunnels.

Three breweries situated in the downtown area of Cincinnati on and near Hamer Street. The sketch is from the Robinson Cincinnati Atlas *for 1883–1884.*

In 1880, Cincinnati was recognized as the "Beer Capital of the World," with the northern portion of Over-the Rhine, The Northern Liberties, being its center of brewing. One of the busiest centers of brewing was on and to the west of Hamer Street. A large network of tunnels ran underground, including under Hamer Street. The excavations were for beer storage, and they connected different buildings of the brewing complexes. Brewing and bottling, for example, were usually in different buildings.[343]

In the mid-19th century, a new type of beer, lager, of German origin, was coming into production. Lager beer requires a longer brewing process and cool temperatures while brewing, the cooler temperatures provided by the underground caverns and tunnels.

Lager comes from the German word *lagern* (to store).

Hamer, a short street of little over one-tenth of a mile, is where both sets of my paternal great-grandparents moved shortly after their arrival in Cincinnati in the mid-19th century.

Andrew Wuest would move to 16 Hamer Street, while John Fix would move into an apartment building at 12 Hamer Street. It is likely that 200 years before, the Wuest and Fix families lived near each other in Alsace, before members of both families emigrated to Spessart Forest in the mid-17th century, possibly in the same caravan. They then lived in villages close to each other in the Spessart, and now, in the mid-19th century, in Cincinnati, Ohio, members of the two families were still neighbors.

"On a spring morning in the late 1840s, a steam packet," going from Pittsburgh to New Orleans, "pulled up to the Ohio River docks" of Cincinnati. My great-grandparents, Andrew and Lena Wuest, newly married, had reached their destination and new home. (This is from a 1964 journal article on the mattress company founded by Andrew.)[344]

The couple appears to have rented lodgings at various locations the first years after their arrival, but by 1859, they lived at 16 Hamer Street. The address later changed to 1632 Hamer Street. Although most residents in Over-the-Rhine moved out of the district when they attained financial security, Andrew and Lena remained in the German enclave the rest of their lives, living in the same building until they died. They owned the apartment building they lived in, which is probably why they remained. Although the deed of purchase was not found in archived land records, the deed of sale at auction shows the property to be part of Andrew's estate. Andrew probably

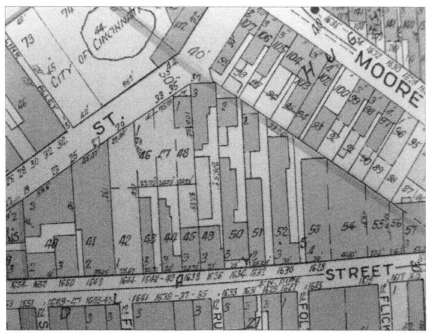

Andrew Wuest's property shown at 1632 Hamer Street [plat 51] in the 1922 Sanborn Insurance *map of Cincinnati.*

bought the property at the time he moved in, around 1859. The 1860 census states that Andrew owned $1,500 worth of real estate.

The original structure appears to have been added to over time, probably starting with two units and reaching about seven by 1890. This assumption is based on the number of families living at the address in the various censuses. The Sanborn Insurance map for Cincinnati for 1922 depicts the building as having three sections, two two-story brick sections fore and aft, with a narrower frame section in between, connecting the two outer sections. The lot was 25.2 feet wide, with the fore and aft sections of the three-part structure extending the entire width of the lot. The complete building, which ran from the front of the property line to the rear property line, was approximately 180 feet long. A five-foot wide alley ran along the

215

right side of the structure.[345]

Andrew and Lena do not appear to have minded their home being amid brewing companies, or perhaps the breweries came later. One, the John Kauffman Brewing Company, completed its first building, between Hamer Street and Vine Street, in 1860, within about a year of Andrew and his family moving in. The 1883-1884 Robinson Cincinnati Atlas shows Andrew's building virtually surrounded by breweries. Just one narrow property to the right was the John Kauffman Brewing Company. Two or three narrow properties to the left was another major brewery. A short distance diagonally from the rear of his property was yet another large brewery.[346]

The Wuest property sold at auction within a year of Andrew's and Lena's deaths, both deaths occurring in November 1903. Their children inherited the property as tenants in common, and opted to sell it. Shortly before the auction, the property's appraised value was $3,500, and at the auction, it sold to the highest bidder, George T. Dinser, for $3,250. The building appears to have been razed before 1930; it is taped over in the Sanborn insurance map of Cincinnati for that year.

Several of Andrew's brothers had also come to Cincinnati. Andrew seems to have been especially close to his younger brother George. Before Andrew moved to Hamer Street, he and George lived, for several years, in the same apartment building on Vine Street. Andrew named his first son George, and Andrew's brother George named his first son Andrew. The older George, who was a shoemaker, moved to Indiana around 1857, where he worked as a shoemaker the rest of his career.

Sadly, Andrew's son George did not live to adulthood, dying by the time of the 1860 census when he would have been 12. Andrew and Lena had seven children who survived childhood. The children received an education normal for the times. At age 15, my

Three Generations: Andrew Wuest [center], his son Adam [right], and his grandson Adam.

grandfather Joseph was no longer going to school, but was apprenticed as a tinsmith, the occupation he undertook his entire working years. Joseph would retire when he was 89.

During his first few years in Cincinnati, Andrew worked as a laborer. By 1850, he had saved enough to start his mattress business, which gradually grew. He first opened shop in a modest storeroom in the downtown area of Cincinnati. Although there was public transportation, namely omnibuses (large carriages) pulled by horses, Andrew probably walked to work, since the distance between home and the shop was only a little over half a mile.

For about the first 15 years, he moved his business to several different locations, but then, around 1869, he settled in for many years at 157 West Fifth Street. He appears to have bought the property, for the 1870 census states that Andrew owned $10,000

Andrew Wuest & Son, 157 West Fifth Street, in 1884.

worth of real estate, a figure that would have included his house as well. After 1877, his business was at various locations on East Third Street. Information in city directories indicates that, around 1891, when Andrew was 75, he turned the business over to his oldest surviving son, Adam, for then the business appears under Adam's name.

At first, most of Andrew's mattresses were made from excelsior (fine curved softwood shavings) stuffed into canvas-like material. Cotton later replaced the excelsior, although moss and corn husks were also sometimes used. During the Civil War, when cotton was in short supply, Andrew used hair, such as horse hair.[347]

Like many immigrants to the German community, as he became more prosperous, Andrew began to contribute to local causes. He contributed especially generously to the Saint Aloysius Orphan Asylum for German Catholics, founded in 1837.[348]

"Orphans" included children with parents who were unable to support them, a situation that often occurred when parents arrived in the city almost penniless and were unable to find employment, or a parent got sick or lost a job. In the first half of the 19th century, cholera epidemics left many children homeless and in need. The asylums strove to find homes for the children, or they kept them until the parents or other relatives could take over their care. If the children were still under the care of an asylum by their mid- or late-teens, the asylum administrators would arrange an apprenticeship for them.

By 1865, there were eight orphan asylums in Cincinnati. As the end of the 19th century approached, the asylums had taken in tens of thousands of Cincinnati children. There was an asylum for Irish Catholics and asylums for Protestant children. Entry rules, however, were not always that strict between the Catholic and Protestant institutions. Determining factors were generally the language spoken and the location. Until 1917, only children who spoke German were admitted to Saint Aloysius.

Originally only for boys, the Saint Aloysius Orphan Asylum began accepting girls in 1850. At first, the boys were housed in private homes, and then in buildings that the orphanage administrators procured. As the institutions grew and became more crowded, and local unsanitary conditions continued unabated, some of the institutions moved farther out from the city.

In 1856, Saint Aloysius was moved to a new location, on Reading Road in Bond Hill, a neighborhood north of Over-the-Rhine. It had 71 acres of farmland with grazing for livestock, and, with the growing of fruits and vegetables, it was self-sustaining. The main building, erected in 1861, is still in use today.[349]

Nuns from Germany, from the order of the Sisters of Notre Dame, took over the day-to-day running of the orphanage in 1877, at a time when it was caring for over 200 orphans, and still run it. Its mission now is to serve troubled children and their families.[350]

Andrew's granddaughter Mathilda Clear (nee Wuest) recalled that because of his generous support to the Saint Aloysius Orphan Asylum, at his death, the children of the orphanage took part in his funeral procession.

Ten years old when Andrew and Lena died, within days of each other, Mathilda had many memories of them. Mathilda, the daughter of Andrew's oldest son Adam, died in 1989, but I had had a chance to interview her in 1987, when she was 94. Mathilda related, "Grandmother was stricter than Grandfather and on the bossy side." She kept an immaculate place. The children could "never play" on the outside steps to the cellar because the steps were always "just washed."

The grandparents spoke German and the grandchildren spoke mostly English. The generation in between could speak both, and Mathilda said they often interpreted between the grandparents and grandchildren.[351] Still, some of the grandchildren could speak German. My father's older siblings spoke mainly German in their home, although by the time my father, the youngest, was born in 1908, there was a mixture of the two languages in the home. His oldest siblings had only known German when they started school and had to learn English quickly. Although classes were in English, the school was in a German neighborhood, and my father remembered that their song books were in German.

Mathilda said that her older male cousins, Andrew's grandsons, were "dandies" and carried walking sticks with silver handles which held whiskey. Canes were popular fashion accessories at the time. On his 70th birthday, Andrew's sons gave him a cane with a gold handle. This would have been before Mathilda was born, but she knew about it, as did I. Since by tradition, most property was inherited by the oldest son, the sons requested that this time the tradition be reversed and that the walking stick go to Andrew's youngest son, and then to that son's youngest, in perpetuity. Andrew agreed. Thus the cane went to my grandfather Joseph, then to my father, John Howard Wuest. My youngest brother now has the cane, which will eventually go to his son. (In case one might wonder, the gold handle does not screw off for storing whiskey.)

The inscription on the handle reads:

The author's brother and nephew with the gold-headed cane inherited from Andrew Wuest.

1816 to 1886
Andrew Wuest
from
his sons
on his
71st birthday
January 7

According to the then-custom, the 71st birthday was when a person turned 70, for a person's first birthday was the day he was born.

My ancestors apparently had their prejudices, at least as remembered by Mathilda. Even though they lived on a street surrounded by breweries, they drank wine and disdained beer drinkers. They disparaged Germans who spoke *Plattdeutsch*, a dialect spoken in northern Germany.

The Irish did not fare much better in my ancestors' estimation. There was a great commotion when Mathilda fell in love with an Irish-American, Doctor James T. Clear.[352] Even though he was educated— possessing a degree in medicine—this was not sufficient to overcome his deficiency in being Irish. But strong-willed Mathilda finally won out.

Perhaps Andrew himself was not quite as strict as some of his offsprings' families. His second surviving son, John Adam, married Francis (Fannie), who came from Bohemia, a region formerly part of the Austrian Empire and today in the western part of the Czech Republic. My Bavarian ancestors considered Bohemia to be inferior. According to my father's older sisters, Fannie was well liked by the family, but even so, her in-laws habitually referred to her as "the Bohemian."

Mathilda described Andrew's apartment building as having two stories in the front and three stories in the rear (probably including the cellar). There were some trees on the property, for Andrew had to plant staves around the trees to keep the horses from damaging them. She also remembered that Andrew had his son Joe, my grandfather, install a hiding place below the wardrobe for money.

On New Year's Day, all of Andrew and Lena's children and grandchildren would come to visit them. The grandchildren were taught to say "Glückliches Neujahr!" ("Happy New Year!"), which they dutifully did, after which they received cookies and a glass of wine.

In 1903, Lena contracted pneumonia and became bedridden for some time. Mathilda said she had beautiful long hair which had to be cut when she became ill. Then Andrew came down with pneumonia, and was bed-ridden just three hours before he died.[353] Andrew died on November 11, 1903, at age 87. Lena died two days later, age 78. Andrew and Lena lie side by side in one grave at St. John's cemetery in Cincinnati.

Every family has its tragedies. About two and a half years after Andrew and Lena died, their second son, John Adam, killed himself, in 1906, at age 50. He had taken carbolic acid (phenol) and died on the way to the hospital. Carbolic acid was a common form of suicide at the time. What drove John to such a desperate state? Mathilda could not shed much light on it, but stated that he was a wonderful man and had deeply loved his wife, Fannie. He had also been close to his father. Census records and city directories show that John was a mattress maker; and as such, he might have worked for Andrew.

John Adam's wife died around the end of 1899 or the beginning of 1900. At some point John moved back into his father's apartment building, and was living in one of the units when his parents died in 1903. His son George John was living with him in 1904, but then married shortly after that. John Adam had one other child, a daughter Ida, who was already married and out of the home. There was a lot of loss to deal with in a short time, but we can never know entirely what pressures and forces were bearing on him.

Like Andrew, my other paternal great-grandfather, John Fix, and his family, moved to Hamer Street soon after their arrival in Cincinnati. Other Fix families also lived on Hamer Street as well as in other parts of Cincinnati, so it is likely that close relatives of my Fix great-grandfather came to Cincinnati, just as the Wuests followed each other. Pistner families, too, lived on Hamer Street and in other parts of Cincinnati. Pistner was the maiden name of John's wife, Mary Ann.

John Fix rented an apartment on Hamer Street. By 1871, his family moved into their own home, a stone house which they bought or had built, at 1382 Harrison Avenue, outside of Over-the-Rhine.

Although John lived to age 74, he was never completely healthy. My aunts said that he worked as a rag-picker, someone who scrounged for used items and then sold them on the street. My aunts were quick to add that it was considered a respectable occupation. Later, John rolled cigars for his oldest son Alois (Al) who owned a cigar store.[354]

A major unhappy event for the Fix family was when their second son, Paul, who was four when the family emigrated from Germany, deserted the army in 1871, and again in 1873, this time changing his name and eventually moving out west.

As was the case during the Civil War, there were many desertions from the military during the years that followed the War, even though the punishment could be severe if one were caught. Execution, generally by hanging, was a frequent punishment. Lesser punishments included prison terms averaging one to two years, corporal punishment such as branding or flogging, or other punishments designed to humiliate.

For the post-war years 1865 to 1891, estimates of the rate of desertion vary from 14 percent to almost one-third of the military population. Apprehension was difficult and not always pursued, although spurts of concerted effort and offers of cash awards for capturing deserters often bore fruit.

Life in the service was demoralizing, consisting of hard labor, poor food and living conditions, and poor pay. Time passed between boredom and the terror of battle. Scurvy was common, due to the lack of vegetables, and disease was rampant. The soldiers experienced petty tyranny and abusive treatment from superiors. Poor conditions, fear of battle—desertion was more common just before an anticipated battle—and problems of one's own making, such as gambling debts, were all motivators to desert.[355]

A star symbol

By age 18, Paul Fix was a cigar maker, working in Cincinnati alongside his two brothers. But when Paul was about 21, he appears to have craved more excitement, or at least a more rewarding job. He moved to St. Louis, Missouri, and shortly after arriving, enlisted in the army, on June 29, 1871.[356] Jefferson Barracks, located in St. Louis, was the starting point for many of the actions taken against Indians.[357] This may have been the excitement Paul craved.

Whatever adventures Paul hoped to participate in, he did not fight Indians. His orders took him to Jackson Barracks, in New Orleans, Louisiana, where he was assigned to Company D, 19th Infantry Regiment.[358] In the post-Civil War Reconstruction era, there was a lot of unrest and violence in the South. In Louisiana, times were particularly tumultuous during virtually all the national and local elections held between 1868 and 1876.

Jackson Barracks, current headquarters of the Louisiana National Guard, sited on the Mississippi River, is down river from the French Quarter. Paul's Company D had its share of desertions, if not quite as bad as elsewhere. For a 20-month period between the end of October 1870 and the end of June 1872, the rate of desertion for enlisted men in Company D averaged five to six percent of its enlisted men per month. The company maintained its average strength of 55 enlisted men through new enlistments, transfers in, and returned deserters. Paul arrived at Jackson Barracks on August 5, 1871, and deserted on September 11, 1871, about a month after arriving.[358]

In 1873, he was back in Cincinnati, again rolling cigars. Toward the end of that year, he surrendered to the military authorities, and was sent to Newport Barracks in Kentucky. Whatever military proceedings were conducted against him, there does not appear to have been much punishment. Paul was to serve time remaining on his enlistment. The standard term of enlistment then was five years.[359] Thus, Paul would have been obliged to serve until June, 1876. But Paul did not stick around. After 11 days, he deserted again, from Newport Barracks.[360]

This time, he changed his name to Paul J. Edwards. His whereabouts during the next 22 years are unknown, but, as of 1895, he was in Colestin, Oregon, just north of the California border. He had married Emilia (Emma) in 1879 or 1880, when he was about 30 and she was about 27. They had no known children.

Colestin was a mineral springs and summer resort town, where Paul was a watchman at the station for the Southern Pacific Railroad. In 1914, he bought 160 acres of land north of Colestin, but by 1921, was living in Seattle, Washington. When I visited Colestin in the early 1980s, there was no longer a town, just the deserted resort hotel and a shack.

Paul's family missed him terribly. My aunts said his parents and siblings consoled themselves, ever saying: "Someday Paul will come home." Over the years, Paul had kept in touch with his older brother Al, who notified him when their mother died in 1894.

Devastated, Paul finally wrote a letter to his family home. Written from Colestin on February 28, 1895, the penmanship is good, but there are spelling and grammatical errors which I have left in.

Dear sister Katie I is the hardest thing for me to write a letter but after not writing for so many years I am duty bound to write a few lines. dear sister it seems the hardest blow that came to me when I got brother Al's letter last week and told me of our good Mother had died. as I spoke to Emma my Wife a good deal of Mother and father and all of you. and that I should like to see the old home once more. and if God spare me I shall come back some day and visit our father and the rest of you. Dear sister you must tell Father that I cannot write in German els I would write to him but tell him that I am very sorry for his lonely home. Katie if you have on of mother Picture to spare pleas sent one to me and if you only halve one pleas have it copied and sent one to me sent me sister Lizzis addres. So Closing with our bst regards to you all ever from your brother Paul and my wife.

Paul's family read his letter over and over again, attested to by the worn creases where it was repeatedly folded and unfolded. When Paul's sister Katie died, the letter passed to their younger sister Lizzie, my grandmother. It then went to her oldest daughters who kept it for years, subsequently giving me the letter.

According to my aunts, Paul did come home for a visit shortly after he wrote the letter and saw his father, John, who was to die just two years after his wife. Paul had brought his wife, Emma, with him and had asked the family to agree to his story that he was a stepson, because his wife did not know his real name or that he was a deserter.

And so my ancestors began their lives in their new country. As in all families everywhere, they had their triumphs and struggles. They had happy times and times of sorrow. But at all times, their Spessart roots were firmly planting themselves in a new homeland.

Chapter 16

————•••⫶⫶⫶•••————

Deep Ancestry

About 46,000 years ago, a man,[361] probably in present-day Armenia or eastern Turkey, had a genetic mutation. Many millennia later, one of his male descendents entered Europe. And thus began the origin of my Wuest ancestral line.

During the time I was researching and writing *Spessart Roots*, DNA analysis was becoming popular as a genealogical tool, both for trying to find "close matches" with other participants and thereby establishing family linkages, as well as for exploring ancestral origins, or "deep ancestry." Where did our ancestors originate and what migratory paths did they take?

As more and more people have their DNA analyzed, and with the extensive ongoing research and analysis of the data, knowledge of our deep past is ever increasing.

Intrigued as to what DNA could tell us about our ancient ancestry, I decided to have DNA analysis conducted for both my Wuest and Fix bloodlines. For the genealogical studies of the type I was interested in, testing is done on the Y-chromosome. The Y-chromosome remains basically intact over time, but there are occasional changes— mutations—many of which are permanent, passing down from father to son, continuing down that particular male line. With the test results, analyzers are able to place individuals into different groups and subgroups, the members of which share the same historical mutation, or set of mutations, and thus a common ancestor, even though that ancestor might be from tens of thousands of years back.

Continual testing for and discovery of new mutations facilitates the founding of subgroups, and further subgroups. When subgroups divide, members of a new subgroup share an even more recent ancestor.

Studies based on known factors about a subgroup, such as locational concentrations of its members, present and past; variations in DNA compared to other subgroups; known rates of mutation; linguistic evidence; and archaeological finds, all add to the growing knowledge of our deep ancestry.

Since only men have the Y-chromosome, DNA samples from a male Wuest relative and a male Fix relative were needed. One of my brothers volunteered for testing of the Wuest line; for the Fix line, a third cousin graciously agreed to donate his DNA, which is collected through a cheek swab. (Our testing was through Family Tree DNA, which sends a kit to each participant.)

Our Wuest line belongs to Y-DNA's major group: G.[362] Members of the G-group are relatively uncommon, found mainly in Europe and Southwest Asia, typically representing 5 to 10 percent of the total population in those areas, a greater percentage in Southwest Asia than in Europe. Significantly high proportions of G-people exist in a few locations in and around the Caucasus mountains. The Caucasus is a region situated between the Black and the Caspian Seas. The northern part lies mostly in Russia; the southern part includes small nations such as Georgia and portions of larger nations such as Turkey.

Europe averages about five percent G-people, with a higher percentage (about 10 percent) in southern Europe. The farther north one goes in Europe, the smaller the percentage, until, in Scandinavia, it is less than one percent.

As noted, the G-group had its origin about 46,000 years ago. The dwelling place of the man who had the mutation that founded the G-group was probably in the area of present-day Armenia and eastern Turkey.

People in the G-group are of non-Indo-European ancestry. In generations past, they spoke non-Indo-European languages, which are now largely extinct. Remnants of those languages spoken by early G-people exist today in only a few isolated regions, such as in the northwest Caucasus and in the nation of Georgia.

G-people were the majority population in Europe as of an estimated 5,000 to 7,000 years ago. The migratory paths most likely included Mediterranean Sea routes, with the migrants entering southern Europe through Italy and Sardinia, whose coasts were easily accessible. Contact with the people of Italy and Sardinia already existed through trade and commerce.

For several thousand years, G-people seem to have made up a much higher proportion of the European population than they do today. But their numbers were to drastically diminish. Many different incoming groups were contributing to the populating of Europe. At first there would have been plenty of room for the different tribes to carve out their own areas. But then, approximately 4,000 to 6,000 years ago, droves of Indo-European-speaking people began entering Europe, vastly increasing their numbers there. These waves of new tribal groups mainly came from the steppes north of the Black and Caspian Seas. Eventually, the different tribes in Europe began pushing up against each other. G-persons did not assimilate well with the Indo-European people—their language and culture were too different. Battles and skirmishes ensued. The numerically stronger Indo-Europeans gradually drove out large numbers of the G-people, as well as other non-Indo-European populations. By 2,000 BC, Europe had become mostly Indo-European.[363]

Attesting to the earlier predominance of G-persons is a spate of skeletons found throughout much of Europe, in Italy, France, Spain, and Germany, dating from 5,000 to 7,000 years ago. The testable sample size was small–a little over two dozen of the skeletons–but the samples represent all the aforementioned countries and are almost all of the G-group.

DNA samples from Ötzi, the mummified remains of a man found in the Italian Alps in 1991, and who lived about 5,300 years ago, show that he belonged to the G-group. People today who have DNA most similar to Ötzi's live in Sardinia. Perhaps during those ancient migrations, a group separated themselves, traveling to and remaining on the island. Or perhaps some escaped to Sardinia when Indo-European tribes were forcing G-tribes out of Europe.[364]

Members of one non-Indo-European culture in Europe lasted in significant numbers longer than the others—the Etruscans of northwest Italy. They had much mineral wealth and a strong military tradition. Ultimately, however, the Romans conquered the Etruscans, and surviving Etruscans assimilated into the Roman culture. There is a relatively high incidence of G-people in the area of historical Etruscan occupation, indicating there may have been many members of the G-population among the Etruscans.

G-people in Europe today are believed to be descended both from those earlier arrivals who weathered the force of incoming Indo-European tribal groups and from more recent migrants, those who came in after about 2,000 to 1,000 BC.[365]

Our Wuest line belongs to a small subgroup, identified as the G-U1 subgroup.[366] G-U1 exists in its heaviest concentration in the Caucasus, most significantly in the northwest area of the Caucasus, where it is found among the Adyghe people domiciled there. They are an ethnic group of people within Russia, who still today speak a non-Indo-European language. About half the Adyghe men in the northwest Caucasus probably belong to our subgroup.[367] We clearly share a common ancestor with them. Based on average rates of mutation on the Y-chromosome, estimates are that our common ancestor lived about 12,000 years ago.[368]

We can't be sure where our G-U1-ancestor lived. Perhaps he lived in or near eastern Turkey, in the ancestral region of the G-population. Later, a party of people, including a high percentage of his descendents, could have migrated north to the northwestern Caucasus.

When the hordes of Indo-European tribes in areas north of the Black and Caspian Seas started making their long treks outward, some went south through the Caucasus and then westward through Turkey. They would have pushed before them many people of the Caucasus, as well as of Turkey, people trying to escape the marauding invaders. The G-U1-ancestor of the eventual Wuest line could have been one of these people coming down from the Caucasus, or, may have come from the G-U1-population still in the Turkey region.

Although being pushed forward by the great numbers of Indo-Europeans migrating toward Europe, the G-U1-people might have hidden out somewhere, such as in the mountain ranges of Turkey or in Greece, for an interim period, keeping out of the way of enemy tribes. G-U1-people entered western Europe an estimated 2,000 to 4,000 years ago, during the heights of the Bronze and Iron Ages. There was on-going migration, as well as trade and cultural interaction with Europe during that time.[369]

Y-chromosome DNA testing shows that our Fix line belongs to the R-group.[370] It is the most frequently occurring group in Europe—45 percent of the European population—and exists in high percentages in many other world locations. It comprises about 40 percent of the population in South Asia and about 31 percent of the population in Central Asia. It is of Indo-European origin.[371]

The R-group is believed to have arisen around 35,000 to 40,000 years ago, in West-Central Asia.[372] A subgroup, identified as R1b, entered Europe sometime after that, forming the ancient Celtic tribes. Almost all Celts were R1b.

My Fix ancestry belongs to a subgroup of R1b called U-152, which comprises about 20 percent of the population in the Alpine region of Switzerland, northern Italy, and eastern France.[373] This finding fits with the evidence, presented in the chapter on the Thirty Years War, that our most distant known Fix ancestor, Peter Fix, came from Alsace, France, from where he emigrated to Germany in the mid-17th century. The man who had the U-152 mutation lived somewhere in the Alpine region, an estimated 5,000 years ago.[374]

The science of identifying mutations on the Y-chromosome is growing by leaps and bounds. It is becoming faster, cheaper, and more extensive. Current estimates of time frames will become tighter and more accurate. As new subgroups are established, we come closer and closer to our migratory history, as well as to a better determination of occurrence times.

Our deep ancestry is from long before the general use of

surnames. Most common people did not have surnames until the 14th century. Although the first family surnames in much of Europe started developing in the early 12th century, it was a long time before family names became widespread.

Along with studies of DNA groups, there are surname projects, with the goal of tracing the origins of a surname, plus getting a handle on the historical migration patterns of people who eventually acquired that surname. Many people who have submitted their DNA for testing join surname projects, providing their own known generational history, and thereby contributing to the store of knowledge for these studies.

The Fix surname is generally associated with the Rhine River—it occurs up and down and on either side of the river. The name appears to have originated in a relatively small geographic area along the Rhine, that portion of the Rhine running from the Alps and along the eastern border of France.[375] This portion of the river would have been a natural settlement location for migrants spreading out from the Alpine region. It includes the French Alsace Region, the area where my most distant known Fix ancestor, Peter Fix, most likely originated.

The Fix name is patronymic—it derives from a son's father's or grandfather's first name. The first name in this case was Vitus. Saint Vitus was a particularly popular saint in the Rhineland. Vitus, born in Sicily, was legendary. At age 12, he died a martyr's death, supposedly in AD 303, during the time of Roman persecution of Christians. His name was once given to many boys, particularly in the Rhineland. Fix (or Vix) was the nickname for Vitus, and eventually became a surname in several families. There are other variations of the name, including Fixx, Fitz, and Vitz. In German, "v" is pronounced as "f", and as a result, most variations of the name have both a "v" version and an "f" version.[376]

❦ ❦

There is as yet no Wuest surname project, although there is some knowledge of the name's origin. The word "wüst" is an adjective or adverb, but the surname may have come from the dwelling place or nearby area of our first ancestor who acquired that name.

According to Brian Barr Wiest, author of *History & Genealogy of the Wiest Family*, "wüst" derives from the meaning of an uncultivated area, and that the man to take on the name was a dweller on or near uncultivated land or on wasteland. Wiest also states that in a typical feudal manor, "wasteland" was the name given to a section of the farm that was cleared land, but had gone to meadow, or was being left fallow.[377]

It is certainly preferable to think of this as the origin of the surname rather than its being based on some of its other meanings. The numerous shades of meanings for the word "wüst" include: uncultivated (not only referring to land), desolate, deserted, fallow, confused, wild, disorderly, wasteful, dissolute, and chaotic. In some dialects, it goes even farther. It can mean filthy, ugly, vulgar, or rakish.[378]

The word "Wüste," which obviously derived from the same origin as "wüst," is the noun form, with the meanings: desert, wasteland, or wilderness.[379]

Although it is certainly possible more than one man adopted Wüst as his surname, there are indications that the origin of the Wüst line I descend from was in the area of Zurich, Switzerland.

All the earliest known records of the Wüst name are in and around Zurich. The first found written record of a Wüst is for a Heinrich Wüsto in 1330. The record appears in the Zurich archives for the town of Zollikon, which today is a municipality on the southern edge of Zurich. Wiest states that Wüsto was an old form of the name, although there appears to be only the one record where it is written in that form. Heinrich was listed along with 11 other men as being one of the 12 overseers of the town's forests.

Coat of arms [left] for the Wüst/Wuest family, Zollikon, Switzerland, dating to 1250. This painting was completed in Zürich in 1933, based on records held by the Zürich Heralds. At right, the family's canting arms.

The name goes even farther back, however, than 1330. There was a coat of arms for the family "Wuest von Zollikon," (using the Latinized version of Wüst) going back to 1250. The Guild of the Zurich Heralds maintained a description of the coat of arms at least into the 1930s. In 1933, the gild master, Emil Huber, of the "Zurich Heralds," made a painting of the coat of arms based on the archived description.

Prior to the coat of arms, there was a Wüst "canting arms" (or clan arms), likely going back to the 12th century. The display of personal or family heraldic emblems began in the days of the Crusades, when knights used them on their shields and surcoats, for identification during the course of battle. It was the job of heralds to record the conduct of battle and the deeds and fates of the knights. The identifying insignia also became a distinguishing mark for a family. (We don't know if or what battles our Wüst ancestors participated in, or if indeed, any were knights.)

The heralds designed the canting arms, also called a shield, in accordance with heraldic standards, with a simple design incorporating some aspect of the family surname. The Wüst shield was a simple tulip shape, representing the initial "W." Later, as was typical, a crest was added, effecting a coat of arms. Initially, the Wüst crest incorporated the head and torso of a Moor, with his arms extended and positioned in the shape of a "W." The Moor was an allusion to the Crusades.

Different branches of families having the same shield and coat of arms often had variations made to differentiate between the branches. To differentiate from the Zurich Wüsts, the Zollikon branch had the tulip of their shield "quilted" with diamond-shapes.

Around 1250, the Moor in the crest was replaced with a figure denoting a man of legal authority, a magistrate. This figure, positioned similarly to that of the Moor, also represents the shape of a "W," albeit with a little imagination.

Up to the mid-14th century, other Wüst individuals appear in records in and close to Zurich and Zollikon, and then gradually, by the late-14th century, the name appears in other Swiss towns. By the early-15th century, the name begins to appear in nearby states such as Austria and down the Rhine River into Alsace. With this apparent gradual movement outward, it appears that Zollikon/Zurich could well be the cradle of our Wüst line.

The first Wüst of record in Alsace appears in 1409 in Erlenbach, in what is now Bas Rhin, the district covering the northern half of Alsace. Brian Wiest's ancestors came from Dierbach, about 12 miles northeast of Erlenbach. By the 17th century, the majority of Wüsts in Alsace were in Dierbach. There was a long-held tradition in Wiest's family that they were originally from Switzerland.[380]

In the chapter on the Thirty Years War (1618-1648), I related that my first known Wuest ancestor was Peter Wüst, who as of 1650, was living in Grosskahl, in what is now Bavaria. I also discussed the evidence that strongly indicates that he, like my Peter Fix ancestor, most probably was born in Alsace. My Wüst ancestors, like my Fix ancestors, could have originally migrated into Alsace from Switzerland, as seems to have been a pattern.

If, indeed, my Wüst ancestors originated in Zurich or Zollikon, which seems highly probable, we could be of the Alemanni tribes. Zurich and the surrounding area were in a definite homeland territory of Alemanni. The Alemanni, who had absorbed other smaller tribes in southern Europe, had been the predominant population in northern Switzerland since the early 5th century AD, even during the time of Frankish occupation for several centuries beginning around AD 500.

Our understanding of our past is ever-evolving, never static. DNA research for genealogy is still in its infancy—much more is to come. In studying and researching my Spessart roots, I did not anticipate also learning about the long history of my ancestors before their coming into Spessart Forest. For both my deep ancestry and my more recent heritage, I am ever grateful to the many others who also share a fascination with our pasts and whose efforts I was able to draw upon.

Genealogy

*Because of intermarriage in the families reflected here,
the names of Lucas Schwarzkoph and Catherina Gessner
appear in the following charts as ancestors of
both Anna Maria Pistner and Johann K. Fix.*

Pedigree Chart for
Andrew Wuest

Johannes Adam Wüst

b: 1716 in Schöllkrippen
m: 27 Jan 1738 in
Schöllkrippen
d: 05 Oct 1748 in
Blankenbach

Johann Adam Wüst

b: 15 Aug 1745 in
Blankenbach
m: 17 Sep 1770 in Jakobsthal
d: 07 Feb 1825 in Grosskahl

Eva Peter

b: 15 Aug 1712 in
Blankenbach
d: 29 Jan 1777 in Kahl

Johann Adam Wüst

b: 13 Jun 1776 in Grosskahl
m: 09 Feb 1806 in
Schöllkrippen
d: 26 Apr 1838 in Grosskahl

Katharina Pistner

b: 1746
d: 15 Feb 1817 in Grosskahl

Adam Pistner

Andrew Wuest

b: 08 Jan 1816 in Grosskahl
m: Abt. 1847 in USA
d: 11 Nov 1903 in Cincinnati

Johann Adam Stenger

b: Schneppenbach
m: 05 Nov 1742 in Krombach
d: Bef. 14 Feb 1779

Johann Stenger

b: Oberwestern
m: 14 Feb 1779 in
Schöllkrippen

Anna Maria Rosenberger

Eva Stenger

b: 27 Jan 1785 in Western
d: 13 Jun 1829 in Grosskahl

Johann Michael Hornick

b: Western
m: 26 Apr 1735 in
Schöllkrippen
d: Bef. 14 Feb 1779

Margaretha Hornick

b: 13 Jan 1752 in Western

Katharina Ries

	Wiegand Wüst	Peter Wüst
Konrad Wüst	b: 1645 in Kahl	d: 20 Mar 1676 in Kahl
b: 1684 in Grosskahl	m: 26 Apr 1667 in Schöllkrippen	Margaretha
m: 13 Apr 1706 in Schöllkrippen	d: 02 Feb 1686 in Grosskahl	d: 05 Mar 1676 in Kahl
d: 27 Jan 1728 in Kahl		Andreas Völker
	Eva Völker	b: Rodenbach
	b: Rodenbach	
	d: 30 Dec 1727 in Kahl	

	Johann Weis
Anna Maria Weis	b: Edelbach
b: 18 Oct 1682 in Edelbach	d: Bef. 13 Apr 1706
d: 05 Sep 1755 in Edelbach	Margaretha Schwarz

Johann Adam Peter

b: Blankenbach
d: Bef. 27 Jan 1738

Elisabetha Fleckenstein

Johann Stenger

b: Krombach
d: Bef. 05 Nov 1742

**Johann Adam
Rosenberger**

Andreas Hornick

b: Schöllkrippen

Johann Ries

b: Western

Pedigree Chart for
Maria Magdalena Gessner

Johann Bartholomäus
Gessner

b: 27 Jul 1720 in Forstmühle
m: 29 Jan 1747 in
Schöllkrippen
d: 24 Feb 1772 in
Schöllkrippen

Heinrich Gessner

b: 28 May 1756 in
Forstmühle
m: 17 Jan 1779 in
Schöllkrippen
d: 15 Mar 1814 in Forstmühle

Anna Maria Vormwald

b: 05 May 1724 in
Schöllkrippen

Johann Jakob Gessner

b: 07 Feb 1801 in Forstmühle
m: 10 Feb 1824 in
Schöllkrippen
d: 08 Feb 1843 in
Grosslaudenbach

Kaspar Scheinast

b: Kahl
m: 01 May 1752 in
Schöllkrippen

Anna Maria Scheinast

b: 08 May 1755 in Grosskahl
d: 02 Mar 1837 in Forstmühle

Dorothea Hubert

b: Kahl

Maria Magdalena Gessner

b: 07 Sep 1825 in
Grosslaudenbach
m: Abt. 1847 in USA
d: 13 Nov 1903 in Cincinnati,
Ohio

Johann Adam Fleckenstein

m: 15 Feb 1795 in
Schöllkrippen
d: 30 Nov 1832 in
Grosslaudenbach

Katherina Fleckenstein

b: 01 Aug 1800 in
Grosslaudenbach

Konrad Rosenberger

Katherina Rosenberger

Johann Paul Gessner

b: 20 Jun 1695 in Forstmühle
m: 30 Oct 1719 in
Schöllkrippen
d: 29 Mar 1753 in Forstmühle

Johann Adam Gessner

b: 13 Dec 1665 in Edelbach
m: 23 Nov 1683 in Edelbach
d: 30 Oct 1719 in Reuschberg

Adam Gessner

b: Edelbach
d: 23 Feb 1683 in Reuschberg

Barbara

d: 15 Feb 1699 in Edelbach

Katharina Weis

b: Laudenbach
d: 15 Feb 1699 in Edelbach

Anna Katharina Wagner

b: 27 Sep 1700 in
Schöllkrippen
d: 07 Feb 1736 in Forstmühle

Balthaser Wagner

b: Schöllkrippen

**Johann Wilhelm
Vormwald**

Elisabetha Neff

David Scheinast

Johann Adam Hubert

**Pedigree Chart for
Anna Maria Pistner**

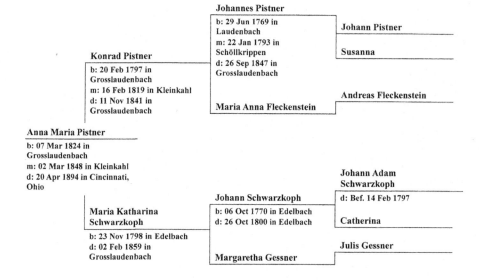

Johannes Pistner

b: 29 Jun 1769 in
Laudenbach
m: 22 Jan 1793 in
Schöllkrippen
d: 26 Sep 1847 in
Grosslaudenbach

Johann Pistner

Susanna

Konrad Pistner

b: 20 Feb 1797 in
Grosslaudenbach
m: 16 Feb 1819 in Kleinkahl
d: 11 Nov 1841 in
Grosslaudenbach

Andreas Fleckenstein

Maria Anna Fleckenstein

Anna Maria Pistner

b: 07 Mar 1824 in
Grosslaudenbach
m: 02 Mar 1848 in Kleinkahl
d: 20 Apr 1894 in Cincinnati,
Ohio

Johann Adam
Schwarzkoph

d: Bef. 14 Feb 1797

Johann Schwarzkoph

b: 06 Oct 1770 in Edelbach
d: 26 Oct 1800 in Edelbach

Catherina

Maria Katharina
Schwarzkoph

b: 23 Nov 1798 in Edelbach
d: 02 Feb 1859 in
Grosslaudenbach

Julis Gessner

Margaretha Gessner

Lucas Schwarzkoph

Catherina Gessner

**Pedigree Chart for
Johann K. Fix**

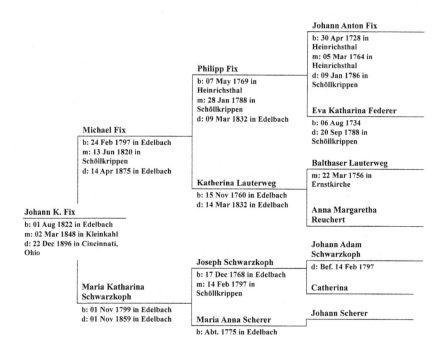

Johann Anton Fix
b: 30 Apr 1728 in
Heinrichsthal
m: 05 Mar 1764 in
Heinrichsthal
d: 09 Jan 1786 in
Schöllkrippen

Philipp Fix
b: 07 May 1769 in
Heinrichsthal
m: 28 Jan 1788 in
Schöllkrippen
d: 09 Mar 1832 in Edelbach

Eva Katharina Federer
b: 06 Aug 1734
d: 20 Sep 1788 in
Schöllkrippen

Michael Fix
b: 24 Feb 1797 in Edelbach
m: 13 Jun 1820 in
Schöllkrippen
d: 14 Apr 1875 in Edelbach

Balthaser Lauterweg
m: 22 Mar 1756 in
Ernstkirche

Katherina Lauterweg
b: 15 Nov 1760 in Edelbach
d: 14 Mar 1832 in Edelbach

Anna Margaretha
Reuchert

Johann K. Fix
b: 01 Aug 1822 in Edelbach
m: 02 Mar 1848 in Kleinkahl
d: 22 Dec 1896 in Cincinnati,
Ohio

Johann Adam
Schwarzkoph
d: Bef. 14 Feb 1797

Joseph Schwarzkoph
b: 17 Dec 1768 in Edelbach
m: 14 Feb 1797 in
Schöllkrippen

Catherina

Maria Katharina
Schwarzkoph
b: 01 Nov 1799 in Edelbach
d: 01 Nov 1859 in Edelbach

Johann Scherer

Maria Anna Scherer
b: Abt. 1775 in Edelbach

Christoph Fix

b: Heinrichsthal
m: 18 Nov 1668 in Wiesthal;
Heinrichsthal

Hans (Johann) Fix

b: 05 Apr 1670 in
Heinrichsthal
m: 09 Oct 1690 in Wiesthal

Anna Scheider

b: Heinrichshütte

Johann Michael Fix

b: Heinrichsthal
m: 11 Sep 1724 in
Heinrichsthal

Adam Weigand

b: Framersbach

Eva Weigand

b: Frammersbach

Maria Barbara Brünner   **Laurentius Brünner**

b: Heinrichsthal

Jakob Federer

d: Bef. 05 Mar 1764

Johann Lauterweg

Johann Reuchert

Lucas Schwarzkoph

Catherina Gessner

Peter Fix

Johann Scheider
b: Henrichshütten

A descendant chart for Hans {Johann] Fix follows.

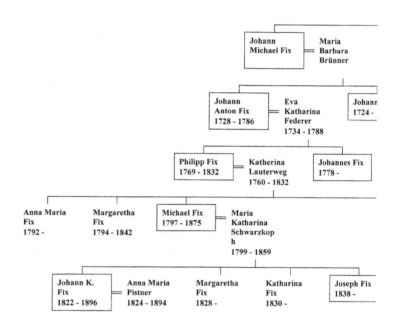

Descendant Chart for
Hans (Johann) Fix

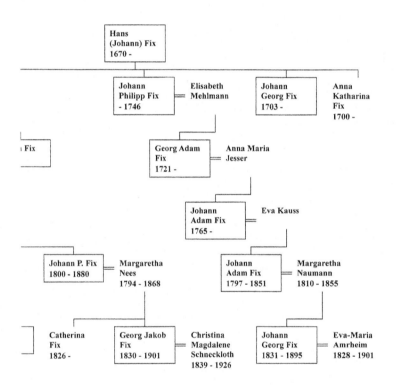

Acknowledgments

I am grateful to all who helped me along the way in the writing of this book, in small ways and large, freely giving of their knowledge and time, sitting down with me, answering e-mail queries, or directing me to additional research materials.

There are some particularly special people I wish to acknowledge:

Members of The [Washington Area] Historical Fiction and Non-fiction Writers Small Group, for all their help and advice during the writing process.

Johanna Willner—writer, translator, German instructor, and good friend. A large portion of my research was in German-language sources. Johanna translated many of the difficult passages which often occurred in the older writings. She helped with my understanding of many of the old customs and regulations.

Heather Covault Dunn, niece and copy editor, who helped during the beginning stages—correcting grammatical errors and providing explanations so that I avoided repeating errors, and patiently answering my myriad questions pertaining to correctness and style.

Ed Jaffee, writer and copy editor, who did the final inclusive editing of the book. His accuracy and skill, plus his approach always from the reader's point of view, ferreting out misleading wording, or spotting where content begged further explanation, rendered a more readable work.

Alfred M. Beck, professional historian and publisher. Fred helped immeasurably with the style editing, formatting, and cover design, not to mention myriad details, such as the index. He enhanced the quality of the images I wanted to include, and expertly inserted them in the accompanying text. Fred's generous and proficient support greatly facilitated the end-stage process of getting *Spessart Roots* to the market.

Debra L. Bonsel, niece and graphics artist, who, answering an urgent call, quickly and competently got the cover in the correct format for printing, and selected just the right colors for enhancing the cover design.

Hans Rosenberger and Lothar Schultes, local historians residing in the area of my ancestors. Some of the richest information and stories about my ancestors are from these two gentlemen. They generously shared from their own collections of historical materials and pointed me to obscure sources I would never have found on my own. Each gave me tours of sites pertaining to my ancestors; and Hans located the long-sought homes of my two great-grandfathers based on old addresses I had.

Gerhild Wehl, chairman of the Archaeological Society in Schöllkrippen and curator of the history museum in Schöllkrippen. Frau Wehl met with me at the museum after hours and shared her extensive knowledge of local history, followed by explanatory tours of the museum's exhibits on everyday life in the local region.

Roswitha Brandes and Elke Bahnemann, professional tour guides in Aschaffenburg and Lohr, respectively, who sat with me one-on-one, helping me to further my understanding of many different aspects of the regional history.

Reinhard Hofer, professional genealogist, who over the years has so competently researched the many branches of my family, and conducted related searches, particularly in finding the connection between my Fix ancestry and Johann Adam Fix, the emigrant who went to Greece.

Alfred Diel and Herbert Speckner. I owe them special thanks for the story on the Fix father and son who emigrated to Greece. Herr Diel researched and wrote an article on the subject, published in the 2004 edition of *Unser Kahlgrund,* from which I drew much information. He also helped me by e-mail with additional questions I had. Dr. Speckner, a historian residing near Munich, provided me with much material for the chapter, including copies of his own research papers and his translations of selected Greek papers.

Lastly, with fond memories, I wish to thank my aunts: my father's older sisters—Clara, Florence, and Corinne Wuest, and by extension, their cousin Mathilda Wuest Clear. They are all deceased now, but the stories they told about my great-grandparents added life to the material gleaned from archived records.

Illustration/Map Acknowledgments

Wüst Ancestral House in Grosskahl: courtesy of Hans Rosen-berger.

Map of Germany with Spessart Forest, source: Karte Naturparks Deutschland by Lencer, courtesy of Lencer.

Map of Spessart Forest: Bowring Cartographic, Arlington, VA.

European Black Woodpecker: Wild Wonders of Europe/ Zacek/ Naturepl.Com/ National Geographic Stock.

The following are reprinted by permission of Arbeitsgemeinschaft für Heimatforschung und Heimatpflege, Kahlgrund e.V. Sitz Alzenau, publishers of the Unser Kahlgrund Heimatjahrbuch series: (1) Bildstock in Sommerkahl (*Unser Kahlgrund 1982*, p. 134); (2) Map of the Kahlgrund (*Unser Kahlgrund 1987*, p. 170); (3) Witch Execution Site in the Kahlgrund (*Unser Kahlgrund 1985*, p. 64); (4) Fix Ancestral House and Inn (*Unser Kahlgrund 1987*, p. 116); (5) Johann Georg Fix and his wife Eva-Maria Amrhein (*Unser Kahlgrund 2004*, p. 169).

Liturgical Toys: photo by author of items from the collection at the Schöllkrippen museum.

The following are reprinted from *Kleinkahler Heimatbuch*, 2001, by permission of Gemeinde Kleinkahl, Kleinkahl, Germany: (1) Heilig-Kreuz Kapelle (Holy Cross Chapel); (2) St. Josef Church; (3) First School Building in Kleinkahl.

The 1696 Bell, in grotto in Edelbach: courtesy of Bill Wuest.

The *Juventa*: courtesy of LaVell Johnson.

Other illustrations and photos are by the author or are in the public domain.

Notes

[1] "Nation's Oldest Family-Held Bedding Firm: Adam Wuest, Inc.," *National Association of Bedding Manufacturers*, March 1964 issue, pp. 2–3.

[2] Adam's sons Herbert and Elmer led the company from the early 1930s until 1908. Herbert's daughter Marion's husband, James R. Fanning, joined the firm in the early 1960s. From 1980 until 1999, when the company was sold, it was led, consecutively, by Marion Wuest Fanning, Mary Jane Wuest Deye (Elmer's daughter), and David Wuest Deye (Mary Jane's son).

[3] Herbert Wuest served as its chairman in the 1950s and David Wuest Deye served as its vice-chairman in the 1990s.

[4] Wilhelm Hauff, *Das Wirtshaus im Spessart*, 1827; SWAN Buch – Vertrieb GmbH (1999); selected lines from beginning of first chapter.

[5] Sky Phillips Beaven, resident of Alexandria, VA, telephone interview by the author, 1/4/2009.

[6] Rudolf Virchow, *Die Noth im Spessart*, pub. Orbenstein Edmund Acker, 63619 Bad Orb im Spessart, reprint 1998, pp. 8–9.

[7] Roswitha Brandes, professional tour guide, Aschaffenburg, Germany, in-person interview by the author, Aschaffenburg, 7/30/2009.

[8] Karl Becker/ Elisabeth Becker, "Hallstatt- und Latènezeit [La Tène is a European Iron Age culture] in Kahl: Weitere Besiedlung in der Kahlaue Gefunden," *Unser Kahlgrund 2009*, pp. 18–20.

[9] Roswitha Brandes, in-person interview, 7/30/2009.

[10] Hellmuth Wolff, *Der Spessart - Sein Wirtschaftsleben*: Aschaffenburg, Germany, C. Krebschen Buchhandlung, 1905, p. 123.

[11] Heinz Staudinger, *Des Spessarts Erzwilddieb Johann Adam Hasenstab*: Naturpark Spessart, Germany, 1999, p. 13.

[12] Dave Sherry, Fleckenstein Family Origins, access through http://lists.rootsweb.com/index/intl/DEU/DEU-ALZENAU-KAHLGRUND.html, select "Browse the "Deu-Alzenau-Kahlgrund archives," stroll to May 2008, select the second message for Fleckenstien Family Origins," accessed 3/31/2011.

[13] Dr. Udo P. Krauthausen, "Dateline of Germanic History," *The Palatine Immigrant*, Vol. XX, No. 4, Sep 1995, p. 180.

[14] http://www.strasbourg.com/strasbourg/us/visitor/monuments/453.html., p.1, accessed 3/31/2011.

[15] Dave Sherry, Fleckenstein Family Origins.

[16] Heinz Staudinger, pp. 13, 32–33. This is the source for the foregoing six paragraphs on the difficulty of life for residents of the street villages.

[17] Karl Becker/ Elisabeth Becker, *Unser Kahlgrund 2009*, pp. 18–20.

[18] Roswitha Brandes, interview by the author, 7/30/2009.

[19] Albrecht Sylla/ Martin Hahn/ Roland Ebert, *Blickwinkel Aschaffenburg: Ein Gang durch die Stadt und ihre Geschichte*: Aschaffenburg, Germany, Alibri Verlag, 1996, p. 16.

[20] Gerhild Wehl, Chairman of the Archaeological Society in Schöllkrippen; curator of the local history museum in Schöllkrippen; in-person interview by the author in Schöllkrippen, Sep 2007.

[21] The eighth elector was added to the Electoral College in 1623; the ninth was added in 1708. The Electoral College was formally established in 1356 by the decree known as the Golden Bull.

[22] At its peak, the Holy Roman Empire encompassed much of present-day central Europe and parts of Eastern Europe. It included at least present-day Germany, Austria, Switzerland, Belgium, the Netherlands, Liechtenstein, Luxembourg, the Czech Republic, and Slovenia; and large parts of present-day France, Italy, and Poland. (It is believed that of the 300-plus territories, only Liechtenstein remains in its former configuration.)

[23] Udo P. Krauthausen, "Dateline of Germanic History," *The Palatine Immigrant*, periodical, Vol. XX, No. 4, Sep 1995, p. 180.

[24] Robert A. Selig, "And Give us this Day our Daily Bread: Food and Agriculture in 18th Century Germany," *German Life*, periodical, April/May 2002, p. 37.

[25] Teva J. Scheer, *Our Daily Bread: German Village Life, 1500–1850*; North Saanich, British Columbia, Adventis Press, 2010, p. 23.

[26] Ernst Pfahler, "Feldkahl im Spiegel der Einwohnerzahlen und Familiennamen bis zum Ende des 18. Jahrhunderts," *Unser Kahlgrund 1987*, pp. 45–46.

[27] Robert A. Selig, "Underpaid and Overworked: The Plight of Servants in Eighteenth Century Franconia," in Proceedings of the Twelfth European Studies Conference held at the University of Nebraska at Omaha, 1987, *European Studies Journal*, University of Northern Iowa, Cedar Falls, p. 259.

[28] Edmund Rücker, "Die Kahlgründer Auswanderer nach Ungarn im 18. Jahrhundert," *Unser Kahlgrund 1981*, pp. 53–58.

[29] Robert A. Selig, author, college professor in German studies, and German historian, telephone interview by the author, 5/25/09.

[30] Teva J. Scheer, p. 16.

[31] Robert A. Selig, telephone interview, 5/25/09.

[32] Gerd-Peter Lux, "Die Wirtschafts- und Bevölkerungs-struktur des Kahlgrundes im 19. Jahrhundert," *Unser Kahlgrund 1995*, p. 146.

[33] Anna Maria Kilgenstein, resident of Schöllkrippen, in-person interview by the author, in Schöllkrippen, Sep 2007.

[34] Robert A. Selig, "From Wertheim to Sainte Lucie and San Juan: *Löwensteiner Jäger* in the Caribbean, 1795 to 1797, ", *German Life*, April/May 2009, pp. 46–49. This is the source for the section on Prince Dominik Constantin's conscripted soldiers.

260

[35] L. Schöppner, "Weistum der Landsiedeln," *Unser Kahlgrund 1959*, pp. 90–93. This is the source for all the passages from the 1541 proclamation by the Counts Ulner von Dieburg.

[36] Elke Bahnemann, interview by the author, 7/16/2009.

[37] Johanna Willner, instructor in and translator of German, and writer of historical fiction of German events, in-person interview by the author, Arlington, VA, Sep 2010.

[38] L. Schöppner, pp. 90–93.

[39] Johanna Willner, interview, Sep 2010.

[40] L. Schöppner, pp. 90–93.

[41] Teva J. Scheer, p. 26.

[42] Gerhild Wehl, interview by the author, Sep 2007.

[43] Gerhild Wehl, e-mail to author dtd 4/29/2014; Heinz Staudinger, p. 55.

[44] Heinz Staudinger, pp. 55–56.

[45] Heinz Staudinger, pp. 104–105.

[46] Tourist Bureau, Rothenbuch, Germany, www.rothenbuch.de/rothenbuch/ sofing allesan, p. 1, accessed 3/31/2011.

[47] Heinz Staudinger, pp. 71–73, 104.

[48] Heinz Staudinger, pp. 47–48.

[49] Robert A. Selig, "Hunting in Germany," *German Life*, Dec/Jan 2010, p. 44.

[50] Heinz Staudinger, p. 47.

[51] Heinz Staudinger, p. 36.

[52] Gerhild Wehl, interview, Sep 2007.

[53] Heinz Staudinger, pp. 30–31, 37, 47–48.

[54] Herbert Bald and Rüdiger Kuhn, *Die Spessarträuber Legende und Wirklichkeit*: Würzburg, Königshausen & Neumann, 2nd ed. 1991, p. 27.

[55] Heinz Staudinger, pp. 60, 64, 68–70, 86–91.

[56] Heinz Staudinger, pp. 95-96; also "Der Wildschütz Johann Adam Hasenstab," http://www.1447-aschaffenburg.de/Uber_uns/Chronik/Scheiben/hasenstab.html, p.1, accessed 3/31/2011.

[57] Heinz Staudinger, pp. 97, 100, 103–108.

[58] Gerhild Wehl, interview, Sep 2007.

[59] Hans Friedel, "Woher die Bamberger Mühle ihren Namen hat," *Unser Kahlgrund 2008*, p. 20.

[60] Karlheinz Markert, owner of Bamberger Mühle, Kleinkahl, Germany, in-person interview by the author, Kleinkahl, 7/20/2009.

[61] Gerhild Wehl, e-mail to author, dtd, 4/29/2014.

[62] Frieda Reising, "Heimbach, ein Ortsteil von Mömbris," *Unser Kahlgrund 2003*, p. 31.

[63] "Bildstöcke" *Kleinkahler Heimatbuch*: Horb am Neckar, Germany, Geigerdruck GmbH, 2001, p. 44.

[64] Hans Rosenberger, interview, Sep 2003.

[65] Hans Rosenberger, interview, Sep 2003.

[66] Günther Pistner, resident of Edelbach, Germany, in-person interview by the author, Edelbach, Sep 2003.

[67] Georg Hubert, "Vom Backen im Kahlgrund," *Unser Kahlgrund 1982*, p. 87.

[68] Günther Pistner, in-person interview, Sep 2003.

[69] Georg Hubert, "Vom Backen im Kahlgrund," *Unser Kahlgrund 1982*, pp. 84–86.

[70] Günther Pistner, interview, Sep 2003.

[71] Lothar Schultes, local historian, Schöllkrippen, Germany, in-person interview, Schöllkrippen, Sep 2007.

[72] Georg Hubert, "Glaube – Aberglaube, Sitten und Bräuche," *Unser Kahlgrund 1993*, pp. 86–88; comment re Johann Adam Hasenstab is from Heinz Staudinger, p. 44.

[73] Gerhild Wehl, interview, Sep 2007.

[74] Georg Hubert, "Glaube – Aberglaube, Sitten und Bräuche," *Unser Kahlgrund 1993*, pp. 79-80.

[75] Georg Hubert, "Glaube – Aberglaube, Sitten und Bräuche," *Unser Kahlgrund 1993*, pp. 79–81. The details of the mother's blessing is from Teva J. Scheer, p. 120.

[76] "Der Spessart als Menschlicher Lebensraum," *Mensch und Wald* series (Abteilung: Not im Spessart), brochure issued by Spessart Museum, Lohr, Germany, p.1.

[77] Gerhild Wehl, Sep 2007.

[78] "Der Spessart als Menschlicher Lebensraum," *Mensch und Wald* series (Abteilung: Not im Spessart), brochure issued by Spessart Museum, Lohr, Germany, p. 1.

[79] Gerhild Wehl, interview, Sep 2007.

[80] "Alte Maße, Gewichte und Münzen," *Kleinkahler Heimatbuch*: p.44.

[81] Robert A. Selig, "*Malter, Klafter, Morgen, Schuh*: How much is that in *Schoppen* – or Gallons, as the case may be?, " *German Life*, periodical, June/July 2009 issue, pp.30–31.

[82] Gerhard Kampfmann/Stefan Krimm, *Die mittelalterlichen und frühneuzeitlichen Glashütten im Spessart*, pub. Geschichts- und Kulturvereins Aschaffenburg, 1982, Band 1, p. 123. This is the source for the account of the glass foundry established by Hans Adam Hubert and his sons-in-law, except as otherwise noted.

[83] Johann Kugler, "Der Bergbau bei Grosskahl (1 Teil)," *Unser Kahlgrund 1991*, pp. 158–159.

[84] Edmund Rücker, "Ein Plan von der Kupfer-, Blei- und Kobaltzeche Segen Gottes bei Huckelheim," *Unser Kahlgrund 1985*, pp. 100–102.

[85] Johann Kugler, "Der Bergbau bei Grosskahl (2 Teil)," *Unser Kahlgrund 1993*, pp. 129–134.

[86] "Zechstein and Mining in the Spessart," http:/www.pcl-eu.de/virt_ex/detail.php?entry=zechstein, p. 2 of 3, article taken from Stefan Huck/Jürgen Jung, "Diversitätswandel kleinräumiger Landschaftsausschnitte, Zechstein-Dolomit-Standorte im Spessart," Natur und Museum 132, 2002, 63-76, accessed 11/4/2007.

[87] "Die Andreas-Kapelle (vorgängerkirche)," http://www.vg-partenstein.de/Sites/gensite.asp?SID=cms260620140334558690759&Art=0232, accessed 6/25/2014.

[88] "Geschichte der Glasherstellung," *Mensch und Wald* series: brochure issued by Spessart Museum, Lohr, Germany, p.3.

[89] gbv-partenstein.de/wp-content/uploads/2011/10/glasmacher.pdf. Accessed 5/2/2014.

[90] Gerhard Wenzel,Fr., former resident of Spessart Forest and hobbyist historian, e-mail to the author, dtd 12/13/2010.

[91] Lorenz Schöppner, "Der Glashüttenhof oberhalb Grosskahl," *Unser Kahlgrund 1964*, pp. 98–99.

[92] Konrad Weigel, "Notizen aus der Kahler Glashütte," *Unser Kahlgrund 2002*, pp. 78–80.

[93] Gerhard Kampfmann/Stefan Krimm, *Die mittelalterlichen und frühneuzeitlichen Glashütten im Spessart*, pub. Geschichts- und Kulturvereins Aschaffenburg, 1982, Band 1, pp. 119–123. Source for the home village of Hubert and his sons-in-law: Lothar Schultes, local historian, Schöllkrippen, Germany, in-person interview by the author in Schöllkrippen on 8/28/07.

[94] H. P. Göbel, *Glashütten und Glasmacher im Sinntal*, pub. 6466 Gründau-Breitenborn, Germany, Jan 1980, p. 16.

[95] Kampfmann/Krimm, *Die mittelalterlichen und frühneuzeitlichen Glashütten im Spessart*, Band 1, pp. 119–123

[96] Elke Bahnemann, interview with the author, 7/16/2009.

[97] Kampfmann/Krimm, *Die mittelalterlichen und frühneuzeitlichen Glashütten im Spessart*, Band 1, pp.120–123.

[98] Lothar Schultes, interview with the author, 8/28/07.

[99] Lothar Schultes, interview with the author, 8/28/07.

[100] H.P. Göbel, *Glashütten und Glasmacher im Sinntal,* p. 49–50.

[101] Lothar Schultes, interview with the author, 8/28/07.

[102] Kampfmann/Krimm, *Die mittelalterlichen und frühneuzeitlichen Glashütten im Spessart*, Band 1, pp. 123–124.

[103] H.P. Göbel, *Glashütten und Glasmacher im Sinntal,* pp. 18–20.

[104] Kampfmann/Krimm, *Die mittelalterlichen und frühneuzeitlichen Glashütten im Spessart*, Band 1, pp. 123–124.

[105] Historical sign at glassworks remains, Grosskahl, Germany, Sep 2009.

[106] Gerhild Wehl, interview with the author, 8/28/2007.

[107] Elke Bahnemann, interview with the author, 7/16/2009.

[108] "Geschichte Spiegelkabinett," *Mensch und Wald* series: brochure issued by Spessart Museum, Lohr, Germany, p.3.

[109] "Kurmainzische Spiegelmanufaktur," *Mensch und Wald* series: brochure issued by Spessart Museum, Lohr, Germany, p.2.

[110] "Kurmainzische Spiegelmanufaktur," *Mensch und Wald* series: brochure issued by Spessart Museum, Lohr, Germany, p.2.

[111] Kampfmann/Krimm, *Die mittelalterlichen und frühneuzeitlichen Glashütten im Spessart*, Band 1, pp. 124–125.

[112] Oskar Oberle, "Die Mühlen in Schöllkrippen Teil 1," *Unser Kahlgrund 1990*, p. 136.

[113] Oskar Oberle, "Die Mühlen in Schöllkrippen Teil 1," *Unser Kahlgrund 1990*, p. 136.

[114] Hans Rosenberger, interview with the author, 8/29/2007.

[115] Oskar Oberle, "Die Mühlen in Schöllkrippen Teil 1," *Unser Kahlgrund 1990*, p. 135.

[116] Oskar Oberle, "Die Mühlen in Schöllkrippen Teil 2," *Unser Kahlgrund 1992*, p. 102.

[117] Michael Hughes, *Early Modern Germany, 1477-1806*; University of Pennsylvania Press, Philadelphia, 1992, p. 15.

[118] Hans Friedel, "Von Burgen, Raubrittern und Unterirdischen Gängen in und um Mömbris," *Unser Kahlgrund 2004*, pp. 18–21. This is the source for the account of the robber knights in the Kahlgrund, except as otherwise noted.

[119] Johanna Willner, in-person interview, Aug 2011.

[120] Hans Friedel, " *Unser Kahlgrund 2004*, pp. 18–21. The information that the Kolling men were hung is from: *Verwaltungsgemeinschaft Schöllkrippen*, information brochure obtained at the town administrative office in Schöllkrippen, pp. 7–8.

[121] Helmut Winter, "Der Dettinger Raubüberfall am 4. Februar 1807 und seine Folgen," *Unser Kahlgrund 2001*, pp. 31–33.

[122] Herbert Bald and Rüdiger Kuhn, pp. 73–75.

[123] Helmut Winter, "Der Dettinger Raubüberfall am 4. Februar 1807 und seine Folgen," *Unser Kahlgrund 2001*, pp. 31–33. The story about Peter Eichler is from Herbert Bald and Rüdiger, p. 73–75.

[124] Herbert Bald and Rüdiger Kuhn, pp. 73–74, 78, 80–82.

[125] Karin Stegmann Steinhoff, "Spuren der Stauferzeit im Schloss Schöllkrippen?," *Unser Kahlgrund 2004*, pp. 89–91.

[126] Ludwig A. Mayer, "Forsthube, Kirche und Schloss in Schöllkrippen," *Unser Kahlgrund 2009*, p. 44.

[127] "The Spessartsmuseum", 1-page handout at Spessart Museum, Lohr, Germany, obtained Jul 2009.

[128] Handout provided at the entrance to Mespelbrunn Castle, Sep 2007.

[129] Karlheinz Bartels, *Schneewittchen: Zur Fabulologie des Spessarts*: Lohr am Main, Buchhandlung von Töme, 1986, pp. 53–55.

[130] "Alfeld (Leine) Didn't put Snow White but Tourists to Sleep," www.mygerman city.com/alfeld, accessed 9/5/2011.

[131] "New Stories About Snow White," 1-page (double-sided) handout at Spessart Museum, Lohr, Germany, obtained Jul 2009. Detailed information about mirrors is from Karlheinz Bartels, pp. 57–58. This is the source for the description connecting the story of Snow White with Spessart Forest.

[132] Wolfgang Behringer, *Witches and Witch-Hunts*, Malden, MA, Polity Press, 2004, pp 149–150.

[133] Albrecht Sylla/ Martin Hahn/ Roland Ebert, p. 41.

[134] Alfred Diel, "Grausame Folter – schrecklicher Tod," *Unser Kahlgrund 2007*, p 27.

[135] Arthur Heinl, "Albstädter Opfer der Hexenverfolgung im 17. Jahrhundert," *Unser Kahlgrund 1985*, pp 62–64.

[136] Albrecht Sylla/ Martin Hahn/ Roland Ebert, p. 44.

[137] Arthur Heinl, "Albstädter Opfer der Hexenverfolgung im 17. Jahrhundert," *Unser Kahlgrund 1985*, p. 63.

[138] Behringer, *Witches and Witch-Hunts,* p 129.

[139] Albrecht Sylla/ Martin Hahn/ Roland Ebert, pp 43–46.

[140] Albrecht Sylla/ Martin Hahn/ Roland Ebert, pp 43–46.

[141] Wolfgang Behringer, *Shaman of Oberstdorf: Chonrad Stoeckhlin and the Phantoms of the Night*, Charlottesville, Univ. Press of Virginia, 1998, pp 112–113.

[142] Behringer, *Witches and Witch-Hunts*, pp 30–31, 34.

[143] Behringer, *Witches and Witch-Hunts*, p 34.

[144] "Die Hexenprozesse," publication issued by Frauenzentrum [a women's group], Gelnhausen, Germany, 1999, p. 10.

[145] Christine Raedler, abridged and adapted by Horst Gunkel, "Terror Gegen Frauen und Juden in Gelnhausen," http://www.kommundsieh.de/judenhex.html, p. 1 of 9, accessed 12/20/2009.

[146] Behringer, *Witches and Witch-Hunts*, p. 57.

[147] Behringer, *Witches and Witch-Hunts*, pp. 72–73, 76–77.

[148] Susan R. Brodo & Leslie Heywood, *Unbearable Weight: Feminism, Western Culture, and the Body*, Berkeley, Univ. of California Press, 2004, p. 161.

[149] Behringer, *Witches and Witch-Hunts*, pp 72-73, 76-77.

[150] Robin Briggs, *Witches and Neighbors: The Social and Cultural Context of European Witchcraft*, New York, NY, Penguin Books, 1996, p 330.

[151] Behringer, *Witches and Witch-Hunts*, pp 169–170.

[152] Robin Briggs, p. 331.

[153] "The Burning Times: the Time Line: the Dark Ages to now," http://www.religioustolerance.org/wic_burn2.htm, p. 2 of 4, accessed 11/10/2009.

[154] Behringer, *Witches and Witch-Hunts*, p. 75.

[155] Robin Briggs, p. 107.

[156] "Die Hexenprozesse," pp. 13–14.

[157] Albrecht Sylla/ Martin Hahn/ Roland Ebert, p. 41.

[158] Arthur Heinl, "Albstädter Opfer der Hexenverfolgung im 17. Jahrhundert," *Unser Kahlgrund 1985*, p. 63.

[159] Albrecht Sylla/ Martin Hahn/ Roland Ebert, pp. 42–43.

[160] Gerhild Wehl, interview by the author, Sep 2007.

[161] Albrecht Sylla/ Martin Hahn/ Roland Ebert, p. 46.

[162] Gerhild Wehl, interview by the author, Sep 2009.

[163] Behringer, *Witches and Witch-Hunts*, pp 88, 104, 113–114.

[164] Scott A. Mandia, "The Little Ice Age in Europe," http://www2.sunysuffolk.edu/mandias/lia/little_ice_age.html, updated 6/4/2009, p 1, accessed 9/7/2011.

[165] Behringer, *Witches and Witch-Hunts*, p. 88.

[166] Robin Briggs, p. 408.

[167] Sylla/ Hahn/ Ebert, pp 43, 46. The figure of seven percent is based on an estimated population figure of 3,300, from Roswitha Brandes, e-mail to the author, dtd 2/26/2010.

[168] Jim Lambert, retired fireman, description of physical process during burning provided during telephone interview by the author, 2011.

[169] Burning Witches," http://www.shanmonster.com/witch/torture/burning.html, p. 1 of 2, accessed 11/10/2009.

[170] Tour guide, witch tour, Gelnhausen, Germany, 7/26/2009.

[171] "Die Hexenprozesse," pp. 1–2, 18, 20, 22.

[172] George L. Burr, *The Witch Persecutions*, Philadelphia, Univ. of Pennsylvania Press, 1897, p 12.

[173] Behringer, *Witches and Witch-Hunts*, p 109.

[174] Robert A. Selig, historian and author of German events, e-mail to the author, 2/28/2010.

[175] George L. Burr, p. 29.

[176] Charles Mackay, "Extraordinary Popular Delusions and the Madness of Crowds," Barnes & Noble Publishing, Inc., 2009 reprint of 1852 second edition, p.431.

[177] Behringer, *Witches and Witch-Hunts*, pp 109–110.

[178] Behringer, *Witches and Witch-Hunts,* pp 120–121.

[179] Thomas J. Schoeneman, "The Witch Hunt as a Culture Change Phenomenon," http://legacy.lclark.edu/~schoen/culturetext.html, accessed 9/7/2011.

[180] Patricia Schlager, "Julius Echter von Mespelbrunn," *Catholic Encyclopedia 1913*, Vol 5, New York: Rupert Appleton Co. 1909, http://www.newadvent. org/cathen/05271a.htm. 1, accessed 9/7/2011.

[181] Behringer, *Witches and Witch-Hunts*, pp 95, 108–109, 135, 177, 179.

[182] Behringer, *Witches and Witch-Hunts*, p. 89.

[183] Behringer. *Witches and Witch-Hunts*, pp 89, 120, 173.

[184] Burr, p 31.

[185] Albrecht Sylla/ Martin Hahn/ Roland Ebert, pp. 46–47.

[186] Behringer, *Witches and Witch-Hunts*, pp 117, 179–180.

[187] For a background feel of the times during the Thirty Years War, I included fictional novels as part of my research. They formed the basis for some of my background imagery in this chapter. I am particularly indebted to Doris Riedel, author of the historical fiction/romance novel: *Julie: Roman aus dem Dreißigjärigen Krieg*, and its sequel: *Julies Heimkehr: Historischer Roman*, pub. TRIGA Verlag,, Gelnhausen, Germany, 1999 and 2000. Riedel is from Spessart Forest, where her romance novels take place.

[188] Norman Davies, *Europe: A History,* Oxford, Oxford University Press, 1966, p. 698.

[189] James C. Johnston Jr., "Coins of the Thirty Years War, The Wonderful World of Coins," *The Journal of Antiques & Collectibles*, Jan 2004 issue.

[190] Gerhild Wehl, interview by the author, 8/28/ 2007.

[191] Robert A. Selig, "The Defenestration of Prague, 23 May 1618, and the Origins of the Thirty Years War," *German Life*, April/May 2008 issue, p. 28. Information regarding the arrest of the burghers, Vienna's sharp rebuke to the Protestants, and the action in Hradschin Castle is from: Peter H. Wilson, *The Thirty Years War: Europe's Tragedy*, Cambridge, The Belknap Press of Harvard University Press, 2009, pp. 3-4, 270-271.

[192] C. V. Wedgwood, *The Thirty Years War*, London, Jonathan Cape, Ltd, 1938, pp. 114-115.

[193] Teva J. Scheer, p. 60.

[194] C. V. Wedgwood, p. 205.

[195] Albrecht Sylla/ Martin Hahn/ Roland Ebert, pp. 48–49.

[196] Christian Grebner, "Der Dreissigjährige Krieg und seine Auswirkung im Freigericht Alzenau," *Unser Kahlgrund 1999*, p. 56.

[197] Helmut Winter, "Der Dreißigjährige Krieg im Freigericht und Untermain nach 1634," *Unser Kahlgrund 2004*, pp. 42,45.

[198] Rudolf Virchow, pp 26–27.

[199] Anna Maria Kilgenstein, interview by the author, Sep 2003

[200] Christian Grebner, "Der Dreißigjährige Krieg und seine Auswirkungen im Freigericht Alzenau," *Unser Kahlgrund 1999*, p. 57.

[201] Albrecht Sylla/ Martin Hahn/ Roland Ebert, pp. 48–52.

[202] Michael Hughes, p. 95.

[203] Edmund Rücker, "Dörfer des oberen Kahlgrundes in der "Cent vorm Spessart" im 30Jahrigen Krieg," *Unser Kahlgrund 1983*, p. 25.

[204] Rudolf Virchow, p. 14.

[205] Gerhild Wehl, interview by the author, 8/28/ 2007.

[206] Handout from an evening course on local history held in the fall of 1985 in Kleinkahl, Germany, based on material from a 1651 Mainz document; photo copy of handout in possession of author; Hans Rosenberger, local historian, provided the copy. Also, see Edmund Rücker, "Dörfer des oberen Kahlgrundes in der 'Cent vorm Spessart' im 30 jährigen Krieg", *Unser Kahlgrund 1983*, p. 26.

[207] Theo Büttner, *Pfarrkirche St. Katharina der Pfarrei Ernstkirchen in Schöllkrippen*: Heimatbote-Druckerei, Schöllkrippen, Germany, pp. 1, 3.

[208] Curator, St. Katharina Church, Ernstkirche-Schöllkrippen, Germany, in-person conversation with author, Schöllkrippen, 9/24/ 2003.

[209] Theo Büttner, "Die Reichsritterschaft zwischen Kahl und Westerbach," *Unser Kahlgrund 1985*, p. 32.

[210] "Die Heilig-Kreuz-Kapelle," Kleinkahler Heimatbuch, p. 72.

[211] Roswitha Brandes, interview with the author, 7/30/2009.

[212] On-site historical sign, Holy Cross Chapel, Grosskahl, Germany.

[213] "Die Edelbacher Glocke," Kleinkahler Heimatbuch, p. 97.

[214] Michael Rosenberger, resident of Kleinkahl, Germany community, in-person interview with author, Grosslaudenbach, Germany, July 2009.

[215] "Die Heilig-Kreuz-Kapelle," Kleinkahler Heimatbuch, p. 72.

[216] "Die Edelbacher Glocke," Kleinkahler Heimatbuch, p. 97.

[217] A photo in the archives of the museum in Schöllkrippen purports to be a photo of the bell, and 1697 is clearly engraved on the bell. The photo in the museum was seen by the author July 2009.

[218] "Die Edelbacher Glocke," Kleinkahler Heimatbuch, p. 97.

[219] Gerhild Wehl, interview with the author, 8/28/2007.

[220] "Der Notwendige Kirchenbau in Kleinkahl," Kleinkahler Heimatbuch, pp. 72–74.

[221] "Der Notwendige Kirchenbau in Kleinkahl," Kleinkahler Heimatbuch, p. 74.

[222] Edmund Rücker, "Die Schulorganisation im Bereich des Kahlgrundes im Jahre 1834," *Unser Kahlgrund 1982*, p.77.

[223] Gerhild Wehl, interview by the author, 7/20/2009.

[224] Karin Thoma, "In der Nachbarshaft mit Juden: Vom Zusammenleben mit der jüdischen Gemeinde in Schöllkrippen," *Unser Kahlgrund 2007*, p. 138.

[225] Albrecht Sylla/ Martin Hahn/ Roland Ebert, p. 157.

[226] Karin Thoma, "In der Nachbarshaft mit Juden: Vom Zusammenleben mit der jüdischen Gemeinde in Schöllkrippen," *Unser Kahlgrund 2007*, p. 138.

[227] Gerhild Wehl, interview by the author, 7/20/2009.

[228] Franz Niehoff, Museum, Landshut 5, Maria Allerorten, Ausstellungskatalog, Landshut2000, p. 282., Artikel zu Schluckbildchen, www.bilderlernen.at/anekdoten/schluckbilder.html, accessed 3/28/ 2011.

[229] Gerhild Wehl, interview by the author, 7/20/2009.

[230] Roswitha Brandes, interview by the author, 7/30/2009.

[231] Roswitha Brandes, interview by the author, 7/30/2009.

[232] Wolfgang Behringer, *Witches and Witch-Hunts*, p. 110.

[233] Gerhild Wehl, interview by the author, 7/20/2009.

[234] Theo Büttner, *Pfarrkirche St. Katharina der Pfarrei Ernstkirchen in Schöllkrippen*, p. 42.

[235] Gerhild Wehl, interview by the author, 7/20/2009. The family lineage for Dorothy is archived at the history museum in Schöllkrippen.

[236] Edmund Rücker, "Kahler Schulhäuser in 3 Jahrhunderten,", *Unser Kahlgrund 1981*, p. 110.

[237] "Ortsansichten," *Kleinkahler Heimatbuch*, p.18.

[238] Artur Heinl, "87 Schulkinder in Einem Raum," *Unser Kahlgrund 1982*, p. 81.

[239] "Entwicklung des Schulwesens in Kleinkahl," *Kleinkahler Heimatbuch*, pp. 55–56.

[240] Edmund Rücker, "Die Schulorganisation im Bereich des Kahlgrundes im Jahre 1834," *Unser Kahlgrund 1982*, pp.76–77.

[241] Artur Heinl, "87 Schulkinder in Einem Raum," *Unser Kahlgrund 1982*, p. 82.

[242] "Entwicklung des Schulwesens in Kleinkahl," *Kleinkahler Heimatbuch*, pp. 55–56.

[243] "Censurbuch der Schule in Kleinkahl," book for years 1823 to 1825; book for years 1831 to 1839; written notes from selected pages held by the author.

[244] Hans Rosenberger, interview by the author, Jul 2009.

[245] " Censurbuch der Schule in Kleinkahl," book for years 1823 to 1825; book for years 1831 to 1839; written notes from selected pages held by the author.

[246] "Censurbuch der Schule in Kleinkahl," book for years 1823 to 1825; book for years 1827 to 1829; written notes from selected pages held by the author.

[247] Michael Hughes, pp. 179–80, 183.

[248] Theo Büttner, "Übersicht über die politischen Ereignisse im Kahlgrund von 1802 bis 1816," *Unser Kahlgrund 1991*, p. 22.

[249] Albrecht Sylla/ Martin Hahn/ Roland Ebert, p. 60

[250] Albrecht Sylla/ Martin Hahn/ Roland Ebert, p. 67.

[251] Theo Büttner, "Übersicht über die politischen Ereignisse im Kahlgrund von 1802 bis 1816," *Unser Kahlgrund 1991*, p. 23.

[252] Albrecht Sylla/ Martin Hahn/ Roland Ebert, pp. 67–71

[253] Albrecht Sylla/ Martin Hahn/ Roland Ebert, pp. 68–71. The notes on St. Boniface Abbey are from: "St. Bonifaz in München. 150 Jahre Benediktinerabtei und Pfarrei," Eine Ausstellung der Benediktinerabtei St. Bonifaz München und Andechs und des Bayerischen Hauptstaatsarchivs zum 150. Jubiläum der Gründung durch König Ludwig I. München 2000 (Ausstellungskataloge der Staatlichen Archive Bayerns; 42) [*exhibition catalogue produced by the Bavarian State Archives for the 150th anniversary of the abbey's foundation*].

[254] Dr. Robert A. Selig, telephone interview by the author, 5/25/09.

[255] Ten of the children, known from baptism records and in order of birth, are Karl (b. 1807), Maria Elisabetha (b. 1809), Johann R. (b. 1811), Magdalena (b. 1813), Andreas (b. 1816), Johann (probably Johann Wilhelm, since there is a Johann Wilhelm living in the house, but no Johann without a middle name) (b. 1818), Margaretha (b. 1820), Johann Adam (b. 1822), and twins Katharina and Johann Georg (b. 1825). There are indications from a tax record from around 1847 that there were an additional two sons named Josef Wilhelm and Josef August. There are a few baptism records too smudged for legibility but appear to be for a Wüst family in Grosskahl; the baptism records for these two sons probably are among the damaged records. In addition, my father's older sisters often mentioned a Joe, a brother of Andrew, who settled in Iowa.

[256] Grundsteuerkataster von Grosskahl Eigentümer von Hausnummer 30 (before 1848), Vermessungsamt (surveyor's office) Aschaffenburger.

[257] Grundsteuerkataster von Grosskahl Eigentümer von Hausnummer 30 (1848-1850).

[258] Grund- und Renten Besitzer in der Steuergemeinde Edelbach: Grundsteuerkataster der Steuergemeinde Edelbach, 1848–1852, Band I., p. 5, Staatsarchiv [state archives] Würzburg.

[259] Theo Büttner, "Wirtshäuser in der Gemeinde Kleinkahl," *Unser Kahlgrund 1987*, pp. 115–116.

[260] "Zum Mainzer Landrecht von 1755," *Unser Kahlgrund 1959*, p. 39.

[261] Roswitha Brandes, interview by the author, 7/30/2009.

[262] Rudolf Virchow, p. 12.

[263] Johanna Willner, interview by the author, Sep 2010.

[264] Gerd-Peter Lux, "Die Wirtschafts- und Bevölkerungsstruktur des Kahlgrundes im 19. Jahrhundert," *Unser Kahlgrund 1995*, p. 146.

[265] Teva J. Scheer, pp. 135–136.

[266] Gerd-Peter Lux, "Zur Wirtschaftlichen Entwicklung des Kahlgrundes im 19. Jahrhundert," *Unser Kahlgrund 1991*, p. 139.

[267] Teva J. Scheer, pp. 136–137.

[268] Rudolf Virchow, pp. 21–23.

[269] Johann Theodor Fleckenstein, "Aus Harten Tagen," *Unser Kahlgrund 1994*, pp. 87–88.

[270] Rudolf Virchow, pp. 21–23.

[271] Rudolf Virchow, pp. 12–15, 21–23, 32.

[272] Johann Kugler, "Der Bergbau bei Grosskahl (1. Teil)," *Unser Kahlgrund 1991*, p 162.

[273] Johann Kugler, "Der Bergbau bei Grosskahl (2. Teil)," *Unser Kahlgrund 1993*, pp. 129-131.

[274] Johann Kugler, "Der Bergbau bei Grosskahl (2. Teil)," *Unser Kahlgrund 1993*, p. 131.

[275] "Der Glashüttenhof oberhalb Grosskahl" *Kleinkahler Heimatbuch*, p.33.

[276] Theo Büttner, "Die Reichsritterschaft zwischen Kahl und Westerbach," *Unser Kahlgrund 1985*, p. 39.

[277] Konrad Weigel, "Notizen aus der Kahler Glashütte," *Unser Kahlgrund 2002*, p. 79.

[278] Gerhild Wehl, interview by the author, Sep 2007.

[279] Teva J. Scheer, p. 138.

[280] E. Rücker, "Heiratserlaubnis mit Schwierigkeiten," *Unser Kahlgrund 1963*, pp. 51–53.

[281] E. Rücker, "Heiratserlaubnis mit Schwierigkeiten," *Unser Kahlgrund 1963*, pp. 51–53.

[282] Elke Bahnemann, interview by the author, 7/16/2009. The age of girls (age 13) when hiring themselves out is from Ewald Lang, "Anna und Margarete Höfling aus Grossostheim," *Spessart: Monatszeitschrift für die Kulturlandschaft Spessart*, pub: Main-Echo GmbH & Co. KG, Aschaffenburg, Germany (www.spessart-online.de), p. 21.

[283] Gerhild Wehl and Debora Schneider, "150 Jahre "Rettungsanstalt" für Mädchen in Schöllkrippen-Ernstkirchen," *Unser Kahlgrund 2004*, pp. 150–151.

[284] Stiftung Haus Mirjam, "Unser Leitbild," http://www.haus-mirjam.de/bwo/dcms/ sites/bistum/extern/haus_mirjam/Leitbild.html.

[285] Mike Rapport, *1848 Year of Revolution*, pub: New York, Basic Books, 2009, p. 77.

[286] Albrecht Sylla/ Martin Hahn/ Roland Ebert, "Rote Fahnen, ein Hackklotz und ein Scharfes Beil," *Blickwinkel Aschaffenburg: Ein Gang durch die Stadt und ihre Geschichte*, pp. 79–81. This is the source for events that took place in Aschaffenburg during the 1848 Revolution.

[287] Theodor Rückert, "Im Frühjahr 1848 wurde der Kahlgrund von der Bürgerlichen Revolution Erfasst," *Unser Kahlgrund 1990*, pp 36–38. This is the source for events that took place in the Kahlgrund during the 1848 Revolution.

[288] James E. Harris, 2004, "Bavaria," *Encyclopedia of 1848 Revolution*, http://www.ohio.edu/chastain/ac/bavaria.htm, accessed 5/16/2011.

[289] Teva J. Scheer, p. 163, taken from Levine, *The Spirit of 1848*, p. 53. (The pastor was unnamed in the Levine source.)

[290] Matthias Klotz, archivist at Stadt- und Stiftsarchiv Aschaffenburg, Germany, in article titled *Emigrations to America in the 19th Century – part 1*, undated, 1st page.

[291] Robert A. Selig, e-mail to the author, dtd 7/10/09.

[292] Matthias Klotz, article titled *Emigrations to America in the 19th Century – part 2*, undated, 1st page.

[293] *Good bye Bayern Grüssgott America: Auswanderung aus Bayern nach Amerika seit 1683*, booklet pub. Bayerisches Staatsministerium für Wissenschaft, Forschung und Kunst Haus der Bayerischen Geschichte, Augsburg, Germany (www.hdbg.de), p. 17.

[294] Matthias Klotz, article titled *Emigrations to America in the 19th Century – part 1*, undated, 2nd & 3rd pages.

[295] Teva J. Scheer, p. 158.

[296] Hans Friedel, "Nachkommen der USA-Auswanderer im Forschungsfieber," *Unser Kahlgrund 2002*, pp. 26–27. [This source states that the ship Clementine was a steamship, but it was a sailing ship.]

[297] Hans Rosenberger, interview by the author, Sep 2003.

[298] Teva J. Scheer, p. 155.

[299] David Whitfield, Genealogist-Historian, from his handout at a presentation to the Fairfax Genealogical Society (Virginia) German Special Interest Group, Burke, VA, 2010.

[300] *Good bye Bayern Grüssgott America: Auswanderung aus Bayern nach Amerika seit 1683*, p. 19.

[301] Shirley J. Riemer, *The German Research Companion*, Lorelei Press, Sacramento, 1997, p. 46.

[302] Matthias Klotz, article titled *Emigrations to America in the 19th Century – part 2*, undated, 1st page.

[303] Teva J. Scheer, p. 158.

[304] Shirley J. Riemer, pp. 45–46.

[305] Adam Druschel, *Am Schwarzen Stein: Geschichte einer Auswanderung*, pub. Rhön Verlag, Hünfeld, Germany, undtd, p. 46. [This is a fictional book but based on historical researach.]

[306] Hans Friedel, "Nachkommen der USA-Auswanderer im Forschungsfieber," *Unser Kahlgrund 2002*, pp. 26–27.

[307] LaVell Johnson, www.clegghistory.org; and e-mail to the author, 1/17/2012: The *Juventa* was a 1,186-ton ship built in 1853 at Thomaston, Maine, and was owned by the Eastern Star Line and the Black Diamond Line.

[308] Teva J. Scheer, pp. 109, 162.

[309] Gerd-Peter Lux, "Zur Wirtschaftlichen Entwicklung des Kahlgrundes im 19. Jahrhundert, " *Unser Kahlgrund 1991*, p. 144.

[310] Jutta Wüst, resident of Grosskahl, Germany, and Alfred Wüst's daughter-in-law, e-mails to the author, 6/8/2011 and 6/9/2011.

[311] Church archives for Geiselbach, Diözesanarchiv Würzburg, Germany.

[312] Alfred Diel, "Johann Georg Fix: Griechenland 1854 mit bayerischem Bier erobert," *Unser Kahlgrund 2004*, pp 169, 177.

[313] Church archives, Wiesthal and Ernstkirche parishes; Diözesanarchiv Würzburg, Germany.

[314] Robert A. Selig, "Otto von Wittelsbach, King of Greece: 1 June 1835 – 10 October 1862," *German Life,* periodical, June/July 2011, p 30.

[315] Alfred Diel, pp 169–170.

[316] Robert A. Selig, "Otto von Wittelsbach, King of Greece: 1 June 1835 – 10 October 1862," *German Life,* periodical, June/July 2011, p 29.

[317] Herbert Speckner, in e-mail to author on 2/7/2012. Speckner obtained the information regarding the number of settlers from *Irakleio Attikis*, by Antoni A. Theodoropoulo, pub. Athens 1977, pp 146, 155, 178-181. The number of Bavarian soldiers that came with Otto is from Robert A. Selig, "Otto von Wittelsbach, King of Greece: 1 June 1835–10 October 1862," *German Life*, periodical, June/July 2011, p. 29.

[318] Robert A. Selig, "Otto von Wittelsbach, King of Greece: 1 June 1835 – 10 October 1862," *German Life,* periodical, June/July 2011, p 29.

[319] Alfred Diel, pp 170–171, 177–178. This is the source for the account of Johann Adam Fix and his offspring, and the founding of Fix Beer, except as otherwise noted. (One handed-down story of the murder states that there was a scuffle between Johann Adam Fix and the robbers and that Fix was stabbed—Karl Fix, "Kahlgründer zogen nach Griechenland", *Unser Kahlgrund 1957*, p 160. Karl Fix is not related.)

[320] Alfred Diel, p 171.

[321] Alfred Diel, pp 169, 171–172, 178. The information about other beer in Heraklion is from Herbert Speckner's paper: "Bayerisches Bier und griechischer Wein: Die abenteuerliche Geschichte der Getränkedynastien Fix und Clauss," p 5. Regarding the contract between Johann Georg Fix and Scheffler, Rodolfos Fix (grandson of Ludwig Fix) states, in his family history, that the annual payment to Scheffler was to be paid in the event Scheffler did not live in the house with Fix: Herbert Speckner's notes and translation of: *Rodolfos Fix: Die Geschichte der Familie Fix aus Iraklion*, a copy of which was provided to the author by Speckner.

[322] Robert A. Selig, "Otto von Wittelsbach, King of Greece: 1 June 1835 – 10 October 1862," *German Life,* periodical, June/July 2011, pp 28–31.

[323] Herbert Speckner, "Bayerisches Bier und griechischer Wein: Die abenteuerliche Geschichte der Getränkedynastien Fix und Clauss," lecture/paper prepared by Speckner for the University of Munich sometime in 2000-2010, p. 3.

[324] Alfred Diel, pp 172–174, 178.

[325] Herbert Speckner, notes and translation: *Rodolfos Fix: Die Geschichte der Familie Fix aus Iraklion*, a copy of which is held by the author.

[326] Alfred Diel, pp 172–174, 178; also, Rodolfos Fix: Die Geschichte der Familie Fix aus Iraklion; and Herbert Speckner, "Bayerisches Bier und griechischer Wein: Die abenteuerliche Geschichte der Getränkedynastien Fix und Clauss," lecture/paper prepared by Speckner for the University of Munich sometime in 2000-2010, p. 3. Note: In the Rodolfos Fix source, it states that J. Georg Fix died without a will. Rodolfos Fix later amended this to J. Georg having a will in his article: "The True History of the Fix Family and its Factory in Greece," as reported by Herbert Speckner, in an e-mail to the author, dtd 9/28/2013.

[327] Alfred Diel, p. 174.

[328] Herbert Speckner, copy of research notes held by the author.

[329] Alfred Diel, pp 175–176, 178–179. The information about the Syros Island becoming a source for brides is from Herbert Speckner, "Bayerisches Bier und griechischer Wein: Die abenteuerliche Geschichte der Getränkedynastien Fix und Clauss," lecture/paper prepared by Speckner for the University of Munich sometime in 2000-2010, p. 4.

[330] "In the case of Agrotexim and Others v. Greece (1)," http://www.javier-leon-diaz.com/property/Agrotexim%20and%20others.pdf, accessed 1/3/2012, p 3. ["Agrotexim and Others" were the stockholding companies of Fix Brewery, representing 51% of the stock shares.]

[331] "In the case of Agrotexim and Others v. Greece (1)," pp 1–9.

[332] Alfred Diel, p 176.

[333] Alfred Diel, p 176.

[334] Disposition, United States Patent and Trademark Office, Trademark Trial and Appeal Board, hearing: 9/26/2000, Paper No. 50, dtd 1/19/01, pp 2,4, http://www.oblon.com/sites/default/files/ttab/2001/23470.pdf, accessed 12/9/2011.

[335] Aris A. Zissis, owner of *Importers Wine and Spirits*, telephone interview by the author, 12/8/2012.

[336] Disposition, United States Patent and Trademark Office, Trademark Trial and Appeal Board, hearing: 9/26/2000, Paper No. 50, dtd 1/19/01, pp. 2,4, http://www.oblon.com/sites/default/files/ttab/2001/23470.pdf, accessed 12/9/2011.

[337] Aris A. Zissis, telephone interviews by the author, 12/8/2011 and 1/23/2012.

[338] "A Beer to FIX all Woes," http://neoskosmos.com/news/en/a-beer-to-fix-all-woes, dtd Apr 30, 2012, accessed on Oct 29, 2012.

[339] Michael D. Morgan, *Over-The-Rhine: When Beer was King*: The History Press, Charleston, South Carolina, 2010, pp. 112-113.

[340] "History of the Brewery District," www.otrbrewerydistrict.org/history_district.php, website for Over-The-Rhine Community Urban Redevelopment Corp., accessed 10/29/2012.

[341] Edward Behr, "Prohibition: Thirteen Years That Changed America," Arcade Publishing, 1996, p. 64.

[342] Gert Niers, "Tracing Cincinnati's German Heritage," *German Life,* periodical, Dec 2006/Jan 2007, p. 52.

[343] Michael D. Morgan, p. 20.

[344] "Nation's Oldest Family-Held Bedding Firm: Adam Wuest, Inc.," *National Association of Bedding Manufacturers*, March 1964 issue, p. 1.

[345] *Insurance Maps Cincinnati, Ohio*, pub: Sanborn Map Co., New York, 1922, volume 2, sheet 55.

[346] Elisha Robinson and R. H. Pidgeon, *Atlas of the City of Cincinnati, Ohio: from official records, private plans & actual surveys*, pub. by E. Robinson, New York, 1883–84, plate 11.

[347] "Nation's Oldest Family-Held Bedding Firm: Adam Wuest, Inc.," *National Association of Bedding Manufacturers*, March 1964 issue, pp. 1-2.

[348] Mathilda Clear nee Wuest, granddaughter of Andrew Wuest, in-person interview by the author, Cincinnati, Ohio, Sep 1987.

[349] Deb Cyprych, "Cincinnati Orphan Asylums and Their Records, Part One: Founded Before the Civil War," *Tracer*, periodic publication by the Hamilton County (Ohio) Genealogical Society, www.hcgsohio.org, issue 32:1 (Feb 2011), pp. 16-18.

[350] "St. Aloysius Orphanage," published by St. Aloysius Orphanage, Cincinnati, Ohio, on the occasion of their sesquicentennial (1837-1987) celebration, p. 7.

[351] Mathilda Clear, Sep 1987.

[352] Mathilda Clear, Sep 1987.

[353] Mathilda Clear, Sep 1987.

[354] My father's oldest sisters (Clara, Florence, and Corrine, born in the years 1889 to 1892): from stories they told throughout the years, in the author's hearing, during visits to Cincinnati, Ohio.

[355] John D. McDermott, "Were They Really Rogues? Desertion in the Nineteenth-Century U.S. Army," *Nebraska History* – Winter 78 (1997), pp. 165-171, www.nebraskahistory.org/publish/publicat/.../NH1997Desertion.pdf.

[356] Enlistment record and company muster rolls: Roll Call Box No. 561, Regular Army Muster Rolls, Jackson Barracks, La., 19th regular infantry, company D, Dec 25, 1861 – Jun 30, 1898; held at National Archives, Washington D.C.

[357] Alfred M. Beck, retired career researcher and historian at the U.S. Army Center of Military History, Washington, D.C., e-mail to the author, 6/4/2012.

[358] Enlistment record and company muster rolls, National Archives, Washington, D.C.

[358] Enlistment record and company muster rolls, National Archives, Washington, D.C.

[359] Robert M. Utley, author and historian, and former chief historian of the National Park Service, e-mail to the author, 9/19/2012.

[360] Enlistment record and company muster rolls: Roll Call Box No. 561, Regular Army Muster Rolls, Jackson Barracks, La., 19th regular infantry, company D, Dec 25, 1861 – Jun 30, 1898; held at National Archives, Washington D.C.,

[361] Ray Banks, adminstrator of the Haplogroup G Project, in annual e-mail to Haplogroup G Project members, dtd5/18/2013.

[362] Our Wuest line belongs to the subgroup: G2a3b1a1. Each letter and number represents a particular permanent Y-DNA mutation, in order of their occurrence. The last numeral "1" refers to the last known mutation. The letter "G" refers to the first mutation, the one that established the major group (haplogroup) G. For easier identification, the subgroup is generally referred to as the G-U1 subgroup.

[363] Rolf Langland, G-Project Co-Administrator, in e-mails to author dtd Aug 4, 2012 and Aug 16, 2012. (The Haplogroup G Project is the collaborative effort for organizing and assimilating test results and historical information, contributing to the knowledge of deep ancestry within the G Haplogroup.) The estimate that G-people were in the majority in Europe 5,000 to 7,000 years ago is updated information from Ray Banks, administrator of the Haplogroup G Project, in annual e-mail to Haplogroup G Project members, date 5/18/2013.

[364] "The G Skeletons," 2012 G News Site, https://sites.google.com/site/2012g newssite/home, p 1 of 2, accessed 7/30/2012. (This is the news site for the Haplogroup-G Project.)

[365] Rolf Langland, e-mail to the author, 8/4/2012.

[366] The Wuest line belongs to the YDNA-G-subgroup G2a3b1a1, identified as the G-U1 subgroup.

[367] Ray Banks, "Important New Subgourp under U1," Haplogroup G Newsletter for 7 August 2012, http://tech.groups.yahoo.com/group/HaploGNewsGrp/message/80, accessed Aug 15, 2012. (Ray Banks is the G-Project administrator.)

[368] Ray Banks, administrator of the Haplogroup G Project, in annual e-mail to Haplogroup G Project members, dtd 5/18/2013.

[369] Rolf Langland, e-mails to the author, 8/4/2012 and 8/16/2012.

[370] Our Fix line belongs to the subgroup is R1b1a2a1a1b3.

[371] Website for Family Tree DNA, www.familytreedna.com,, accessed 7/30/2012.

[372] "Learn about Y-DNA Haplogroup R," http://www.genebase.com/learning/article/11, updated 8/29/2012, accessed 10/29/2012.

[373] "U152 Overview," Dec, 2010, under paragraph heading: Geographical Distribution; www.U152.org: website for administrators of the U152 subclade of the R1b haplogroup; accessed 8/27/2012.

[374] Steve Gilbert, administrator for the U152 subclade project, in e-mail to author, 8/23/2012.

[375] Steve Fix, Fix DNA Surname Project administrator, http://www.familytreedna .com/public/fixdnaproject/, "Background," under tab: About This Group, accessed 8/1/2012.

[376] Karen Fix Curry, "Origin of the Fix Surname," post on Genealogy.com, http://boards.ancestry.ca/thread.aspx?mv=flat&m=93&p=surnames.fix, 7/9/2001, accessed 8/1/2012. The information about the popularity of The Fourteen Helpers (includes Saint Vicus) in the Rhineland is from: Benjamin Straley, "In the Beauty of Holiness: Earthly Terror and Heavenly Music, http://www.yale. edu/ism/events/StudyTourStraley.html, accessed 10/29/2012.

[377] Brian Barr Wiest, *History & Genealogy of the Wiest Family*; Studio City, Calif; Hollywood Theatre & Realty Corp., 1975, pp. 29–31. This is the source for the account of the origins of the Wüst name, the name's spread from Switzerland to Alsace, and the early family canting arms and crest. Note: Wiest was a consummate researcher who spoke several languages and traveled extensively throughout the areas of his European homeland (including Switzerland, Austria, and Alsace, France), doing exhaustive research in their archives and utilizing other available sources. For the origin of the Wüst surname, Wiest culled information from researchers in the history of surnames.

[378] "The New Cassell's German Dictionary: German-English, English-German," editor: Harold T. Betteridge; copyright © 1962 by Cassel & Co., Ltd.; pub: Funk & Wagnalls Co., New York

[379] German-Dictionary, www.dict.cc/Wüste.

[380] Brian Barr Wiest, pp. 13, 31–34, 37–45.

Selected Bibliography

Bahnemann, Elke. Professional tour guide in Lohr, Germany. In-person interview by the author in Lohr, 7/16/2009.

Bald, Herbert and Rüdiger Kuhn. *Die Spessarträuber Legende und Wirklichkeit.* Würzburg, Königshausen & Neumann, 2nd ed. 1991.

Banks, Ray. "Important New Subgourp under U1." Haplogroup G Newsletter for 8/7/2012, http://tech.groups.yahoo.com/group/HaploGNewsGrp/message/80, accessed 8/15/2012.

Bartels, Karlheinz. *Schneewittchen: Zur Fabulologie des Spessarts.* Lohr am Main, Buchhandlung von Töme, 1986.

Beaven, Sky Phillips. Resident of Alexandria, VA. Telephone interview by the author, 1/4/2009.

Beck, Alfred M. Retired career researcher and historian at the U.S. Army Center of Military History, Washington, D.C. E-mail to author, dtd 6/4/2012.

Becker, Karl and Elisabeth Becker. "Hallstatt- und Latènezeit [La Tène is a European Iron Age culture] in Kahl: Weitere Besiedlung in der Kahlaue Gefunden." *Unser Kahlgrund 2009.*

Behr, Edward. "Prohibition: Thirteen Years That Changed America." Arcade Publishing, 1996.

Behringer, Wolfgang. *Witches and Witch-Hunts.* Malden, MA, Polity Press, 2004.

_____. *Shaman of Oberstdorf: Chonrad Stoeckhlin and the Phantoms of the Night.* Charlottesville, Univ. Press of Virginia, 1998.

Brandes, Roswitha. Professional tour guide in Aschaffenburg, Germany. In-person interview by the author in Aschaffenburg, 7/30/2009.

Brodo, Susan R. and Leslie Heywood. *Unbearable Weight: Feminism, Western Culture, and the Body.* Berkeley, Univ. of California Press, 2004.

Burr, George L. *The Witch Persecutions.* Philadelphia, Univ. of Pennsylvania Press, 1897.

Büttner, Theo. "Die Reichsritterschaft zwischen Kahl und Westerbach." *Unser Kahlgrund 1985.*

_____. Pfarrkirche St. Katharina der Pfarrei Ernstkirchen in Schöllkrippen. Heimatbote-Druckerei, Schöllkrippen, Germany.

_____. *Pfarrkirche St. Katharina der Pfarrei Ernstkirchen in Schöllkrippen.* Heimatbote-Druckerei, Schöllkrippen, Germany.

_____. "Übersicht über die politischen Ereignisse im Kahlgrund von 1802 bis 1816." *Unser Kahlgrund 1991.*

_____. "Wirtshäuser in der Gemeinde Kleinkahl." *Unser Kahlgrund 1987.*

Clear, Mathilda, granddaughter of Andrew Wuest. In-person interview by the author, Cincinnati, Ohio, Sep 1987.

Curry, Karen Fix, "Origin of the Fix Surname." Post on Genealogy.com, http://boards.ancestry.ca/thread.aspx?mv=flat&m=93&p=surnames.fix, dtd 7/9/2001, accessed 8/1/2012.

Cyprych, Deb, "Cincinnati Orphan Asylums and Their Records, Part One: Founded Before the Civil War," *Tracer*, periodic publication by the Hamilton County (Ohio) Genealogical Society, www.hcgsohio.org, issue 32:1 (Feb 2011).

Davies, Norman, *Europe: A History.* Oxford, Oxford University Press, 1966.

"Die Hexenprozesse." Publication issued by Frauenzentrum [a women's group]. Gelnhausen, Germany, 1999.

Diel, Alfred. "Grausame Folter – schrecklicher Tod." *Unser Kahlgrund 2007.*

_____. "Johann Georg Fix: Griechenland 1854 mit bayerischem Bier erobert." *Unser Kahlgrund 2004.*

Druschel, Adam. Am Schwarzen Stein: Geschichte einer Auswanderung. Pub: Rhön Verlag, Hünfeld, Germany, undtd, p. 46. [This is a fictional book but based on historical research.]

Fix, Karl. "Kahlgründer zogen nach Griechenland." *Unser Kahlgrund1957.* [Karl Fix is not related.]

Fix, Steve. Fix DNA Surname Project administrator. Http://www.familytreedna. com/public/fixdnaproject/, "Background," under tab: About This Group, accessed 8/1/2012.

Fleckenstein, Johann Theodor. "Aus Harten Tagen." *Unser Kahlgrund 1994.*

Friedel, Hans. "Nachkommen der USA-Auswanderer im Forschungsfieber." *Unser Kahlgrund 2002.*

_____. "Von Burgen, Raubrittern und Unterirdischen Gängen in und um Mömbris." *Unser Kahlgrund 2004.*

_____. "Woher die Bamberger Mühle ihren Namen hat." *Unser Kahlgrund 2008.*

Gilbert, Steve. Administrator for the U152 subclade project. E-mail to the author, Aug 23, 2012.

Göbel, H. P. *Glashütten und Glasmacher im Sinntal.* Pub. 6466 Gründau-Breitenborn, Germany, Jan 1980.

Good bye Bayern Grüssgott America: Auswanderung aus Bayern nach Amerika seit 1683. Booklet pub. Bayerisches Staatsministerium für Wissenschaft, Forschung und Kunst Haus der Bayerischen Geschichte, Augsburg, Germany (www.hdbg.de).

Grebner, Christian. "Der Dreißigjährige Krieg und seine Auswirkungen im Freigericht Alzenau." *Unser Kahlgrund 1999.*

Harris, James E., 2004, "Bavaria," *Encyclopedia of 1848 Revolution,* http://www.ohio.edu/chastain/ac/bavaria.htm, accessed 5/16/2011.

Hauff, Wilhelm, *Das Wirtshaus im Spessart,* 1827; SWAN Buch –VertriebGmbH (1999).

Heinl, Arthur. "Albstädter Opfer der Hexenverfolgung im 17. Jahrhundert." *Unser Kahlgrund 1985.*

_____. "87 Schulkinder in Einem Raum." *Unser Kahlgrund 1982.*

Hubert, Georg. "Glaube – Aberglaube, Sitten und Bräuche." *Unser Kahlgrund 1993.*

_____. "Vom Backen im Kahlgrund." *Unser Kahlgrund 1982.*

Hughes, Michael. *Early Modern Germany, 1477-1806.* University of Pennsylvania Press, Philadelphia, 1992.

Johnson, LaVell, www.clegghistory.org, and by e-mail correspondence to the author , Jan 17, 2012.

Johnston, James C., Jr. "Coins of the Thirty Years War, The Wonderful World of Coins." *The Journal of Antiques & Collectibles,* Jan 2004 issue.

Kampfmann, Gerhard and Stefan Krimm. *Die mittelalterlichen und frühneuzeitlichen Glashütten im Spessart.* Pub. Geschichts- und Kulturvereins Aschaffenburg, 1982, Band 1.

Kilgenstein, Anna Maria. Resident in Schöllkrippen, Germany. In-person interview by the author in Scöllkrippen, Sep 2003 and Sep 2007.

Kleinkahler Heimatbuch. Pub. Horb am Neckar, Germany, Geigerdruck GmbH, 2001.

Klotz, Matthias. Archivist at Stadt- und Stiftsarchiv Aschaffenburg, Germany. Article titled *Emigrations to America in the 19th Century – part 1,* undated.

_____. Article titled *Emigrations to America in the 19th Century – part 2,* undated.

Krauthausen, Dr. Udo P. "Dateline of Germanic History." *The Palatine Immigrant,* Vol. XX, No. 4, Sep 1995.

Kugler, Johann. "Der Bergbau bei Grosskahl (1 Teil)." *Unser Kahlgrund 1991.*

_____. "Der Bergbau bei Grosskahl (2 Teil)." *Unser Kahlgrund 1993.*

Lambert, Jim. Retired fireman. Telephone interview by the author, 2011.

Lang, Ewald. "Anna und Margarete Höfling aus Grossostheim." *Spessart: Monatszeitschrift für die Kulturlandschaft Spessart.* Pub:Main-Echo GmbH

& Co. KG, Aschaffenburg, Germany www.spessart-online.de), p. 21.

Langland, Rolf. G-Project Co-Administrator. E-mails to author dtd 8/42012 and 8/16/2012.

Lux, Gerd-Peter. "Die Wirtschafts- und Bevölkerungsstruktur des Kahlgrundes im 19. Jahrhundert." *Unser Kahlgrund 1995.*

_____. "Zur Wirtschaftlichen Entwicklung des Kahlgrundes im 19. Jahrhundert." *Unser Kahlgrund 1991.*

Mackay, Charles. "Extraordinary Popular Delusions and the Madness of Crowds." Barnes & Noble Publishing, Inc., 2009 reprint of 1852 second edition.

Mandia, Scott A. "The Little Ice Age in Europe." Http://www2.sunysuffolk. edu/mandias/lia/little_ice_age.html, updated 6/4/2009, p 1, accessed 9/7/2011.

Markert, Karlheinz. Owner of Bamberger Mühle, Kleinkahl, Germany. In-person interview by the author, Kleinkahl, 7/20/2009.

Mayer, Ludwig A. "Forsthube, Kirche und Schloss in Schöllkrippen." *UnserKahlgrund 2009.*

McDermott, John D. "Were They Really Rogues? Desertion in the Nineteenth-Century U.S. Army." *Nebraska History* – Winter 78 (1997), pp. 165–171, www.nebraskahistory.org/publish/publicat/.../NH1997Desertion.pdf.

Morgan, Michael D. *Over-The-Rhine: When Beer was King.* The History Press, Charleston, South Carolina, 2010.

"Nation's Oldest Family-Held Bedding Firm: Adam Wuest, Inc." *NationalAssociation of Bedding Manufacturers*, March 1964 issue.

Niehoff, Franz. Museum, Landshut 5, Maria Allerorten, Ausstellungskatalog, Landshut2000, p. 282., Artikel zu Schluckbildchen, www.bilderlernen.at/anekdoten/schluckbilder.html, accessed 3/28/ 2011.

Niers, Gert. "Tracing Cincinnati's German Heritage." *German Life,* periodical,Dec 2006/Jan 2007.

Oberle, Oskar. "Die Mühlen in Schöllkrippen Teil 1." *Unser Kahlgrund 1990.*

_____. "Die Mühlen in Schöllkrippen Teil 1." *Unser Kahlgrund 1990.*

Pfahler, Ernst. "Feldkahl im Spiegel der Einwohnerzahlen und Familiennamen zum Ende des 18. Jahrhunderts." *Unser Kahlgrund 1987.*

Pistner, Günther. Resident of Edelbach, Germany. In-person interview by the author in Edelbach, Sep 2003.

Raedler, Christine, abridged and adapted by Horst Gunkel. "Terror Gegen Frauen und Juden in Gelnhausen," http://www.kommundsieh.de/judenhex.html, p. 1 of 9, accessed 12/20/2009.

Rapport, Mike. *1848 Year of Revolution.* Pub: New York, Basic Books, 2009.

Reising, Frieda. "Heimbach, ein Ortsteil von Mömbris." *Unser Kahlgrund 2003.*

Riemer, Shirley J. *The German Research Companion.* Lorelei Press, Sacramento, 1997.

Rosenberger, Hans. Local historian in Grosslaudenbach, Germany. In-person interview by the author in Grosslaudenbach, Jul 2009.

Rosenberger, Michael. Son of Hans Rosenberger, resident of Kleinkahl, Germany. In-person interview with the author, Grosslaudenbach, Germany, July 2009.

Rücker, Edmund. "Die Kahlgründer Auswanderer nach Ungarn im 18. Jahrhundert." *Unser Kahlgrund 1981.*

_____. "Die Schulorganisation im Bereich des Kahlgrundes im Jahre 1834." *Unser Kahlgrund 1982.*

_____. "Dörfer des oberen Kahlgrundes in der "Cent vorm Spessart" im 30Jahrigen Krieg." *Unser Kahlgrund 1983.*

_____. "Ein Plan von der Kupfer-, Blei- und Kobaltzeche Segen Gottes bei Huckelheim." *Unser Kahlgrund 1985.*

_____. "Heiratserlaubnis mit Schwierigkeiten." *Unser Kahlgrund 1963.*

_____. "Kahler Schulhäuser in 3 Jahrhunderten." *Unser Kahlgrund 1981.*

Rückert, Theodor. "Im Frühjahr 1848 wurde der Kahlgrund von der Bürgerlichen Revolution Erfasst." *Unser Kahlgrund 1990.*

Scheer, Teva J. *Our Daily Bread: German Village Life, 1500-1850.* North Saanich, British Columbia, Adventis Press, 2010.

Schlager, Patricia. "Julius Echter von Mespelbrunn." *Catholic Encyclopedia1913*, Vol 5. New York, Rupert Appleton Co. 1909, http://www.newadvent. org/cathen/05271a.htm. 1, accessed 9/7/2011.

Schoeneman, Thomas J. "The Witch Hunt as a Culture Change Phenomenon, "http://legacy.lclark.edu/~schoen/culturetext.html, accessed 9/7/2011.

Schöppner, Lorenz. "Weistum der Landsiedeln." *Unser Kahlgrund 1959.*

_____. "Der Glashüttenhof oberhalb Grosskahl." *Unser Kahlgrund 1964.*

Schultes, Lothar. Local historian in Schöllkrippen, Germany. In-person interview by the author in Schöllkrippen, Sep 2007.

Selig, Robert A. "And Give us this Day our Daily Bread: Food and Agriculture in 18th Century Germany." *German Life*, April/May 2002.

_____. "The Defenestration of Prague, 23 May 1618, and the Origins of the

Thirty Years War." *German Life*, April/May 2008.

_____. "From Wertheim to Sainte Lucie and San Juan: *LöwensteinerJäger* in the Caribbean, 1795 to 1797. " *German Life*, April/May 2009.

_____. "*Malter, Klafter, Morgen, Schuh*: How much is that in *Schoppen* – or Gallons, as the case may be?" *German Life*, June/July 2009.

_____. "Otto von Wittelsbach, King of Greece: 1 June 1835 – 10 October 1862." *German Life,* June/July 2011,

_____. "Underpaid and Overworked: The Plight of Servants in Eighteenth Century Franconia." Proceedings of the Twelfth European Studies Conference, held at University of Nebraska at Omaha, 1987. *European Studies Journal* , University of Northern Iowa Cedar Falls.

_____. E-mails to the author, dtd 7/10/2009 and 2/28/2010, and telephone interview by the author, 5/25/2009.

Sherry, Dave. "Fleckenstein Family Origins," access through http://lists.rootsweb. com/index/intl/DEU/DEU-ALZENAU-KAHLGRUND.html, Select: Browse the "Deu-Alzenau-Kahlgrund archives," stroll to May 2008, select: the second message for "Fleckenstien Family Origins."

Speckner, Herbert. Researcher and historian in Munich, Germany. Copy of paper prepared by Speckner for Univ. of Munich, "Bayerisches Bier undgriechischer Wein: Die abenteuerliche Geschichte der Getränkedynastien Fix und Clauss;" translated copies of (1) *Irakleio Attikis*, by Antoni A.Theodoropoulo, pub. Athens 1977, and (2) *Rodolfos Fix: Die Geschichte der Familie Fix aus Iraklion*.

Staudinger, Heinz. *Des Spessarts Erzwilddieb Johann Adam Hasenstab.* Naturpark Spessart, Germany, 1999.

Steinhoff, Karin Stegmann, "Spuren der Stauferzeit im Schloss Schöllkrippen?"*Unser Kahlgrund 2004.*

Straley, Benjamin. "In the Beauty of Holiness: Earthly Terror and Heavenly Music," http://www.yale.edu/ism/events/StudyTourStraley.html, accessed Oct 29, 2012.

Sylla, Albrecht/ Martin Hahn/ Roland Ebert. *Blickwinkel Aschaffenburg: Ein Gang durch die Stadt und ihre Geschichte.* Aschaffenburg, Germany, Alibri Verlag, 1996.

Thoma, Karin. "In der Nachbarshaft mit Juden: Vom Zusammenleben mit der jüdischen Gemeinde in Schöllkrippen." *Unser Kahlgrund 2007.*

Utley, Robert M. Author and historian, and former chief historian of the

National Park Service. E-mail to author, dtd Sep 19, 2012.

Virchow, Rudolf. *Die Noth im Spessart.* Pub. Orbenstein Edmund Acker, 63619 Bad Orb im Spessart, reprint 1998.

Wedgwood, C. V. *The Thirty Years War.* London, Jonathan Cape, Ltd, 1938.

Wehl, Gerhild. Chairman of the Archaeological Society in Schöllkrippen; curator of the history museum in Schöllkrippen. In-person interview by the author in Schöllkrippen, Sep 2007 and Jul 2009.

Wehl, Gerhild and Debora Schneider. "150 Jahre "Rettungsanstalt" für Mädchen in Schöllkrippen-Ernstkirchen." *Unser Kahlgrund 2004.*

Weigel, Konrad. "Notizen aus der Kahler Glashütte." *Unser Kahlgrund 2002.*

Wenzel, Gerhard, Fr. Former resident of Spessart Forest and hobbyist historian. E-mail to the author, 12/13/2010.

Whitfield, David. Genealogist-Historian. Handout at his presentation to the Fairfax Genealogical Society (Virginia) German Special Interest Group, Burke, VA, 2010.

Wiest, Brian Barr. *History & Genealogy of the Wiest Family.* Studio City, Calif; Hollywood Theatre & Realty Corp., copyright 1975.

Willner, Johanna. Instructor in and translator of German; writer of historical fiction of German events. In-person interview by the author in Arlington, VA, Sep 2010 and Aug 2011.

Winter, Helmut. "Der Dettinger Raubüberfall am 4. Februar 1807 und seine Folgen." *Unser Kahlgrund 2001.*

_____. "Der Dreißigjährige Krieg im Freigericht und Untermain nach 1634." *Unser Kahlgrund 2004.*

Wolff, Hellmuth. Der Spessart - Sein Wirtschaftsleben. Aschaffenburg, Germany,C. Krebschen Buchhandlung, 1905.

Wüst, Jutta. Resident of Grosskahl, Germany, and Alfred Wüst's daughter-in-law. E-mails to the author on 6/8/2011 and 6/9/2011.

Zissis, Aris A. Owner of Importers Wine and Spirits. Telephone interviews by the author, 12/8/2011 and 1/23/2012.

"Zum Mainzer Landrecht von 1755." *Unser Kahlgrund 1959.*

❦ ❦

In addition to the sources listed above, the following also served as reference material:

Brochures and handouts from: (1) Spessart Museum, Lohr, Germany (Sep

2009); (2) administrative office, Schöllkrippen, Germany (Sep 2009); and (3) Mespelbrunn Castle, Mespelbrunn, Germany (Sep 2007).

"Censurbuch der Schule in Kleinkahl." School record books for the Kleinkahl school, 1823 to 1839. The author took notes from these books, Jul 2009. The books are privately held.

The curator at St. Katharina Church in Schöllkrippen. In-person interview by the author, 9/24/2003.

Enlistment record and company muster rolls. National Archives, Washington D.C.

Exhibits and archived collections at the local history museum in Schöllkrippen, Germany.

Grundsteuerkataster von Grosskahl Eigentümer, Vermessungsamt [surveyor's office] Aschaffenburger.

Grund- und Renten Besitzer in der Steuergemeinde Edelbach: Grundsteuerkataster der Steuergemeinde

Index

CPSIA information can be obtained at www.ICGtesting.com
Printed in the USA
BVOW06s1929250916

463224BV00002B/5/P

9 780615 771991